THE DISCIPLESHIP PARADIGM

BIBLICAL INTERPRETATION SERIES

Editors
R. ALAN CULPEPPER
ROLF RENDTORFF

Assistant Editor
DAVID E. ORTON

Editorial Advisory Board
JANICE CAPEL ANDERSON · MIEKE BAL
PHYLLIS A. BIRD · ERHARD BLUM · ROBERT P. CARROLL
WERNER H. KELBER · EKKEHARD STEGEMANN
ANTHONY C. THISELTON · VINCENT L. WIMBUSH · JEAN ZUMSTEIN

VOLUME 27

THE DISCIPLESHIP PARADIGM
Readers and Anonymous Characters in the Fourth Gospel

BY

DAVID R. BECK

BRILL
LEIDEN · NEW YORK · KÖLN
1997

This book is printed on acid-free paper.

Library of Congress Cataloging-in-Publication Data

Beck, David R.
  The discipleship paradigm : readers and anonymous characters in the fourth Gospel / by David R. Beck.
      p. cm. — (Biblical interpretation series, ISSN 0928-0731 ; v. 27)
  Includes bibliographical references and index.
  ISBN 9004107002 (alk. paper)
  1. Jesus Christ—Disciples—Biography—History and criticism. 2. Bible. N.T. John—Criticism, interpretation, etc. 3. Christian life—Biblical teaching. 4. Bible. N.T. John—Language, style. 5. Names in the Bible. I. Title. II. Series.
BS2440.B38   1997
226.5'066—dc21   97-19022
                                                                         CIP

Die Deutsche Bibliothek – CIP-Einheitsaufnahme

Beck, David R.:
The discipleship paradigm: readers and anonymous characters in the fourth gospel / David R. Beck. - Leiden ; New York ; Köln : Brill, 1997
  (Biblical interpretation series ; Vol. 27)
  ISBN 90-04-10700-2 Gewebe

ISSN   0928-0731
ISBN   90 04 10700 2

© *Copyright 1997 by Koninklijke Brill NV, Leiden, The Netherlands*

All rights reserved. No part of this publication may be reproduced, translated, stored in a retrieval system, or transmitted in any form or by any means, electronic, mechanical, photocopying, recording or otherwise, without prior written permission from the publisher.

Authorization to photocopy items for internal or personal use is granted by Brill provided that the appropriate fees are paid directly to The Copyright Clearance Center, 222 Rosewood Drive, Suite 910 Danvers MA 01923, USA. Fees are subject to change.

PRINTED IN THE NETHERLANDS

CONTENTS

Acknowledgements	vii
Chapter One: Introduction	1
Chapter Two: The Analysis of Character	6
Chapter Three: Textual Analysis of Fourth Gospel Characters	17
Chapter Four: Anonymity, Identity, and Identification: The Fourth Gospel Prologue and the Witness of John	35
Chapter Five: Anonymous Women and Models of Discipleship	51
Chapter Six: The Infirm, the Blind, the Dead, and the Misplaced	83
Chapter Seven: The Disciple Jesus Loved	108
Chapter Eight: Conclusion	137
Bibliography	147
Index of Greek Terms	163
Index of Names	165
Index of Subjects	171

ACKNOWLEDGMENTS

First and foremost I recognize the debt I owe to my wife, Jeannie. But for her love, support, patience, and sacrifice, neither this book nor much else that is worthwhile in my life would exist. Secondly, I express my thanks to our daughter, Melissa, for the love and joy she contributes to my life, with apologies that too many of her formative years revolved around "Daddy's dissertation."

Special thanks are due to my mentor in Johannine scholarship, professor D. Moody Smith, under whose tutelage this investigation began as a doctoral dissertation at Duke University. His gracious guidance, insightful suggestions, and ever-present encouragement were invaluable in bringing the initial phase of this study to completion.

I also wish to express my gratitude to Dr. Paige Patterson, president of Southeastern Baptist Theological Seminary, for lending his support to the second phase of this project and making available the resources to bring it to its completion. Even more, I am indebted to him for giving me the opportunity to teach the New Testament to a generation of men and women preparing for ministry.

CHAPTER 1

INTRODUCTION

Every reader of the Fourth Gospel[1] encounters a narrative populated with characters encountering Jesus. They respond to Jesus with varying degrees of faith, and some with outright rejection. They present the reader "a continuum of responses to Jesus which exemplify misunderstandings the reader may share and responses one might make to the depiction of Jesus in the Gospel."[2] How does a reader decide among the options presented by the spectrum of responses? What in the reading process works on/in the reader to produce an understanding of and response to the narrative, the characters who populate it, and Jesus who inhabits its center? The Fourth Gospel does not encourage bystanders, but participants, inviting "readers to enter into the revelatory dynamic themselves."[3] Gail O'Day has persuasively demonstrated that the locus of revelation is not found in the words of the Gospel alone, but in the reader's participation in the dynamic of the narrative itself. She analyzes how irony encourages and facilitates that participation, drawing the reader into an encounter with Jesus.

Irony alone does not account for the Gospel's participatory allure. Character portrayal is also primary in confronting readers with the discipleship claims of this text and its protagonist/hero. Characters remind readers of real people, even themselves, and readers may identify with characters whose narrative portrayal parallels their own life experiences as do other characterization elements. One particular element of character portrayal is uniquely prominent in the Fourth Gospel, the anonymity of its most significant characters.

The absence of a name can enhance a reader's potential for identifying with a character in a narrative. The lack of a name removes the nomination barrier that distinguishes the character from other characters and from the reader. The inducement to identify with a character occurs when anonymity combines with other elements of characterization, including a progressive unveiling of the character which is both positive and consis-

---

[1] Throughout this study, the Fourth Gospel will be the exclusive reference used for this narrative, except in direct quotes from other sources. The purpose of this is to be faithful to the anonymity of the author and guarantor of the tradition, be they the same individual or not.
[2] R. Alan Culpepper, *Anatomy of the Fourth Gospel: A Study in Literary Design*, Foundations and Facets: New Testament (Philadelphia: Fortress Press, 1983), 104.
[3] Gail R. O'Day, *Revelation in the Fourth Gospel: Narrative Mode and Theological Claim* (Philadelphia: Fortress, 1986), 95.

tent. The Fourth Gospel combines these characterization elements and establishes a paradigm of discipleship which consists of responding appropriately to the character's encounter with Jesus. This paradigm is first established with the mother of Jesus—unnamed in this narrative—and continues in the narrative portrayal of Jesus' encounter with certain significant anonymous characters. I will argue that named characters, including some who are portrayed favorably, are not offered as models for reader emulation for varied reasons.

Anonymous characters are not unique to any narrative, but usually the absence of a name indicates unimportance. Unlike the Synoptics, some Fourth Gospel anonymous characters invert this tendency, occupy more textual space, and demonstrate narrative significance by their faith response to Jesus' word, a response of witness to the efficacy of his word. Among these anonymous characters are Jesus' mother, the Samaritan woman, the royal official in chapter 4, the infirm man in 5, the blind man in 9, and in spite of the textual problems raised by the pericope, the woman caught in adultery. This study focuses on the final text of the Fourth Gospel, but takes into account the text as familiar to the majority of its real readers. This includes a decision to examine and analyze the role of the pericope of the adulterous woman in 7:53-8:11. Although its original placement in this narrative is so uncertain that its inclusion requires justification, for most readers, the episode is an integral part of their reading of the Fourth Gospel, and its jarring discordance has a certain effect on their experience of the Fourth Gospel.

After the man born blind in chapter 9, the only significant anonymous character to appear in the text is the disciple Jesus loved.[4] His anonymity facilitates reader participation in the discipleship paradigm he models. The anonymous characters who precede him draw the reader into subjective participation in the narrative, predisposing readers to identify with the disciple Jesus loved and participate in his discipleship paradigm.

Previous understandings of characters and characterization have not adequately accounted for the effect of names and namelessness on readers. Prior to my reading of the Fourth Gospel, I will examine theories of characterization for their treatment of naming, anonymity, and the role of characterization to enlist reader participation in narratives. Attention will be given to reader identification with literary characters and correlating factors in that identification.

My reading of the Fourth Gospel will account for the phenomenon of significant anonymous characters that distinguish this narrative from

---

[4] The disciple Jesus loved will be designated by a dependent clause throughout this study to prevent distorting his designation into a title or name.

contemporaneous literature including Hebrew narrative, the Synoptic Gospels, and Greek novels. If the characterization of anonymous characters is paralleled in other earlier or contemporaneous narratives, the Fourth Gospel could merely be following literary convention, lessening the special significance of anonymous characters in the Gospel. But the portrayal of certain unnamed characters in the Fourth Gospel is demonstrably different from those in contemporaneous narratives. The significance of the function of the anonymous characters within the Fourth Gospel must be sought in that narrative itself. The investigation of anonymous characters in the Gospel will focus on the combination of varied elements of their portrayal that encourage reader identification with them, anonymity being primary among them. First, however, it is necessary to establish the criteria for classifying Fourth Gospel characters in terms of their narrative role and significance.

I will focus on the reading experience, particularly the effect of character portrayal, in establishing the discipleship paradigm in the Fourth Gospel. There will be no attempt to recover a prescribed reader encoded in the text, nor will a search be conducted for an "ideal" reader possessing all necessary knowledge for a textually mandated interpretation. I remain unconvinced that an encoded reader or an ideal reader construct exists in any text; I believe, rather, that it is birthed and given substance in the mind of its "discoverer"—who is actually its creator. Instead, attention will be given both to textual clues, particularly elements of character portrayal, and to the role of readers' background information and knowledge in understanding and identifying with characters in the Fourth Gospel.

John Darr has termed this necessary background information extratextual repertoire or extratext. He defines it to include: "(1) language; (2) social norms and cultural scripts; (3) classical or canonical literature; (4) literary conventions (e.g. genres, type scenes, standard plots, stock characters) and reading rules (e.g. how to categorize, rank, and process various kinds of textual data); and (5) commonly-known historical and geographical facts."[5] This concept is related to what others have called "unstated context," "repertoire," and "interpretive communities."[6] All are terms designating the store of knowledge, facts, ideas, and concepts of acceptability within a society, group, or institution. Every reader comes

---

[5] John A. Darr, *On Character Building: The Reader and the Rhetoric of Characterization in Luke-Acts*, Literary Currents in Biblical Interpretation (Louisville: Westminster/John Knox Press, 1992), 22.

[6] E. D. Hirsch, Jr., *Cultural Literacy: What Every American Needs to Know*, (New York: Vantage Books, 1988), 2; Wolfgang Iser, *The Act of Reading: A Theory of Aesthetic Response* (Baltimore: John Hopkins University Press, 1978), 68-73; Stanley Fish, *Is There a Text in This Class? The Authority of Interpretive Communities* (Cambridge: Harvard University Press, 1980), 303-355.

with extratext included, but no two readers' extratexts are identical. For this reason, all readers need to acknowledge their interpretations as *a* reading, not *the* reading of a text. For ancient texts like the Gospels, the extratext of its first readers would be radically different from that of twentieth century readers. Readers of the same era likewise will have different extratexts from one another due to a variety of experiences. These differences include cultural distinctives, educational background, familiarity with first century Jewish culture, and the interpretive communities in which the reader participates (e.g., New Testament Scholarship, religious communities where the Gospel is a sacred text, or both). I will indicate where previous interpretations of Fourth Gospel characters have depended on readers' extratexts for their readings, consciously or not. I will attempt to remain fully cognizant of my own extratext, aware that in the final analysis, my reading is just that, firmly rooted in my own social location.[7]

The Social Location of the Reader

The concept of social location and its hermeneutical influence on every reader has been most thoroughly advocated by Fernando F. Segovia. In several publications Segovia has rightly argued that termed the social location of the reader is a necessary consideration prerequisite to any reading of any narrative.[8] All readers, Biblical scholars included, must recognize that the only reading they are capable of experiencing or recording is the one shaped and molded by their own experience and training. I am incapable of reading as a naive first-time reader, a member of another gender or nationality, or one uninvolved with the claims this narrative presents. My reading is necessarily colored by my participation in a community of faith which has long held this narrative as a sacred text. Furthermore, I am commissioned by that community to proclaim the kerygma contained in this text. I am among the privileged elite of the world, spending my entire life within the borders of one of its wealthiest nations. I have never known war, poverty, or persecution. I also read as one trained within the interpretive community of Biblical scholarship, which places me in the role I would term reader/critic, a particular type of

---

[7] The reader's ideological stance influenced by sociocultural origins and context. Fernando F. Segovia, "The Journey(s) of the Word of God," *Semeia* 53 (1991): 25.

[8] Ibid.; and more recently in "And They Began to Speak in Other Tongues': Competing Modes of Discourse in Contemporary Biblical Criticism," in *Reading from this Place*. Vol. 1, *Social Location and Biblical Interpretation in the United States*, ed. Fernando F. Segovia and Mary Ann Tolbert, Minneapolis: Fortress Press, 1994. Fernando F. Segovia and Mary Ann Tolbert (Minneapolis: Fortress Press, 1994), 1-32.

reader. Robert M. Fowler has defined this role as follows: "(1) to affirm the enduring power of the Bible in my culture and in my own life and yet (2) to remain open enough to dare to ask any question and to risk any critical judgment."[9] I would add (3) to attempt to remain sensitive to other readings produced and even necessitated by persons whose social locations differ from my own.

The Fourth Gospel establishes a paradigm of appropriate response to Jesus through the portrayal of characters who meet and respond to Jesus. Those who respond appropriately by witnessing to the power of Jesus' word are anonymous. The positive elements of their characterization and parallels between their experiences and readers' experiences encourages readers to identify with them. The potential for identification is enhanced by their anonymity which increases their indeterminacy. After looking at various understandings of characters that have been offered, and contrasting anonymous characters in the Fourth Gospel with those in contemporaneous literature, I will propose a reading that will explore the Fourth Gospel's characters' responses to Jesus, identify the paradigm of appropriate response, investigate which characters fit the paradigm and which do not, see how readers are challenged to model the responses of the characters fitting the paradigm—culminating with the disciple Jesus loved—and examine how anonymity can facilitate reader identification with characters responding appropriately to Jesus.

---

[9] Robert M. Fowler, *Let the Reader Understand: Reader-Response Criticism and the Gospel of Mark* (Minneapolis: Fortress Press, 1991), 31.

CHAPTER 2

THE ANALYSIS OF CHARACTER

As is true for all narratives, Fourth Gospel characters are not human beings but they resemble human beings, and are most often discussed in terms of human psychological reality such as motivation, beliefs, knowledge, and emotions. How can readers determine which characters are "significant," or even which representations of persons can rightfully be termed "characters"? How are readers' understanding of Fourth Gospel characters influenced by their familiarity with them from other sources or their assessment of the historicity of the narrative and its characters? Finally, how does ideology effect the majority of Fourth Gospel readers who participate in an interpretive community that venerates this narrative as a sacred text?

Among literary theorists there is little agreement concerning the narrative role of character. Although narratives are written by people, about people, and for people, "no one has yet succeeded in constructing a complete and coherent theory of character."[1] Several problems contribute to this void. These include the difficulty of determining the lines of demarcation between "human beings" and "characters," establishing criteria for classifying characters, measuring the influence of reality on readers understandings of characters, and discerning the influence of ideological view on readers' interpretations of characters.[2] My reading of the Fourth Gospel assumes a strong correlation between characters encountered and real persons, consistent with the narrative's self-claims. Without imposing a twentieth century concept of historical reliability, I read accepting the narrative's self-portrayal as a first-hand account of real events by an eye-witness whose testimony is true (20:30, 21:24).

Two different perspectives on the analysis of characters have dominated recent discussions of narrative theory, influencing those readers who would adapt narrative approaches to biblical studies. An older theory of characterization still frequently used to analyze biblical narrative is traceable to E. M. Forster, who distinguished between essential characters and those only contributing to overall effect. The essential characters

---

[1] Mieke Bal, *Narratology: The Introduction of the Theory of Narrative*, trans. Christine van Boheemen (Toronto: University of Toronto Press, 1985), 80.
[2] Ibid, 80-82.

portrayed with complex personalities he designated "round." Lesser characters lacking full development he termed "flat."[3]

In examining characters, Forster and those adopting his categories discuss "flat" characters with descriptions of their technical function, but describe the psychological essence of "round" characters.[4] This traditional approach assesses characters by the degree of psychological complexity they "possess," making them more or less believable as representatives of human beings.[5] Among biblical scholars this approach to characterization is found in the poetics of biblical narrative of Adele Berlin and Alan Culpepper.

Culpepper defines the success of a work in terms of "whether its characters are convincing, in some general sense 'life-like', and interesting."[6] After discussing Forster's "flat" and "round" character distinctions, Culpepper analyzes the characters of the Fourth Gospel for fullness of development and their function as "types" of responses to Jesus available to the reader. Adele Berlin discusses the same flat and round distinctions popularized by Forster identifying three categories of characters: the full-fledged character, the type, and the agent. She illustrates each from the characterization of women surrounding David in the narratives of Samuel and Kings.[7]

A different view of characterization prevails in structuralist theory, rooted in the work of A. J. Greimas. As understood by structuralists, character (a term usually replaced by "actants" or other designation to avoid misinterpreting it as a representation of human beings) is a narrative function that cannot be understood by comparison to human beings. These plot functionaries are abstractions filling one of six potential functions in a narrative: sender, receiver, object, subject, helper, and opponent.[8] Plot is primary in structuaralist analyses of narrative, and "character" is replaced with relations of opposition and correlation.[9] This is the understanding of character Robert Funk adopts in his biblical poetics. He replaces the term character with "participant," discussed exclusively in terms of the figure's textual function in the syntax of the narra-

---

[3] E. M. Forster, *Aspects of the Novel* (New York: Harcourt, Brace and World, 1927) 73, 81.
[4] Aleid Fokkema, *Postmodern Characterization: A Study of Characterization in British and American Fiction*, Postmodern Studies 4 (Amsterdam-Atlanta: Rodopi, 1991), 23.
[5] Ibid., 28.
[6] R. Alan Culpepper, *Anatomy of the Fourth Gospel: A Study in Literary Design*, Foundations and Facets: New Testament (Philadelphia: Fortress Press, 1983), 101.
[7] Adele Berlin, *Poetics and Interpretation of Biblical Narrative*, Bible and Literature Series, no. 9 (Sheffield: The Almond Press, 1983), 23-32.
[8] A. J. Greimas, *Sémantique structurale: récherche de méthode* (Paris: Librairie Larousse, 1966), 176-80.
[9] Fokkema, 31.

tive segment where it is located and its role in the grammar of the narrative.[10]

Dissatisfied with the limitations of these polarities, a third approach to the understanding of character in literature is provided by the semiotic model proposed by Aleid Fokkema. Her model goes beyond characters as mere representation of human beings without focusing exclusively on narratological function. Characters are understood as signs, consisting of both a signified and a signifier, with a presence in a text. Following the semiotic theory of Umberto Eco, Fokkema perceives that these signs are generated by "codes" or "conventions."[11] The reader constructs the sign of a character from literary conventions, and also constructs conventions from the world beyond the text. The construction of a character by a reader draws upon the conventions and codes both inscribed in the text and from the world beyond the text.[12]

The first and more traditional of the three approaches analyzes characters as representations of human beings, to the extent of questioning their motives and other non-narrated aspects of their "lives." The second method of character analysis, the structuralist approach, understands characters as literary functionaries, not representing actual human beings but part of the narrative structure of a work. The final option, the semiotic approach is more reader-oriented and views characters as a construction of the reading process. Each attempts to analyze characters in terms of their function for readers, but none considers how characterization entices readers into fuller participation in the narrative.

An interpretive model for understanding characterization has been designed by John Darr that recognizes the interdependence of plot and character without subordinating either to the other. It acknowledges that readers "build" characters and that through the process readers are "being positioned and maneuvered—indeed shaped—by the rhetoric of the text."[13] The approach is based largely on the reader-oriented theory of Wolfgang Iser. The reader's response to a narrative is elicited by the "indeterminacies and gaps" within the text.[14] The model focuses on both textually based information and what readers provide in their extratexts. This understand of character analysis and the reading process informs the reading of the Fourth Gospel below.

---

[10] Robert W. Funk, *The Poetics of Biblical Narrative*, Foundations & Facets, Literary Facets (Sonoma, California: Polebridge Press, 1988), 64, 166.
[11] Umberto Eco, *A Theory of Semiotics* (Bloomington, Indiana: Indiana University Press, 1976), 37-38.
[12] Fokkema, 43-48.
[13] Darr, 59.
[14] Iser, 172-75.

Some information in the Fourth Gospel is textually determined, such as the name of "the man sent from God" in 1:6. He is "John" and no other. An indeterminacy is information not provided by the text (i.e. the name of the disciple Jesus loved). The gap that is created by an indeterminacy may be filled from the reader's extratext. My reading will resist this urge in part, permitting one category of indeterminacy, anonymity, to remain unfilled, focusing on its effect on reader participation in the narrative.

Readers' empathy is evoked through many elements, but especially through character portrayal.[15] Each character representation is necessarily incomplete, requiring reader supplementation of indeterminacies to fill gaps. The more active the reader's role, the greater the reader's identification with the character is likely to be.[16] The indeterminacy presented by anonymity can intensify reader potential for identification with that character in some narratives, when present in combination with other positive characterization elements.

The Fourth Gospel is one narrative where anonymity facilitates readers' identification with characters. This has been overlooked in analyses of its characters focusing primarily on character types or characters' roles as plot functionaries. This study will demonstrate that the responses of unnamed characters, culminating with the disciple Jesus loved, are offered by the Gospel as the model of appropriate response to Jesus.

The anonymous characters in the Fourth Gospel are atypical of most biblical narrative. The anonymous characters readers commonly encounter in narratives are unnamed because of their unimportance. This is true in most biblical narratives as well. Unlike Hebrew narrative, however, anonymity in the Fourth Gospel is not an indication of textual insignificance.[17] Synoptic anonymous characters also lack significance. Unparalleled in the Synoptics, however, are the significant anonymous Fourth Gospel characters, like the Samaritan woman in chapter 4 and the man born blind in chapter 9, who enter into lengthy dialogue with Jesus and are granted considerable textual space. Also unparalleled in the Synoptics are anonymous characters readers might expect to be named: Jesus' mother and the disciple Jesus loved.

In the next chapter a textual analysis of the Fourth Gospel narrative will establish criteria for classifying characters according to their impor-

---

[15] Hans Kreitler and Shulamith Kreitler, *The Psychology of the Arts* (Durham: Duke University Press, 1972), 272.

[16] László Halász, "Self Relevant Reading in Literary Understanding," chap. 11 in *Reader Response to Literature: The Empirical Dimension*, ed. Elaine F. Nardocchio, Approaches to Semiotics 108, (New York: Mouton de Gruyter, 1992), 230.

[17] Jeffrey Lloyd Staley, "Stumbling in the Dark, Reaching for the Light: Reading Character in John 5 and 9," *Semeia* 53 (1991), 71.

tance. Characters with significance will be defined as those given meaningful textual space, whose encounters with Jesus produce a faith response. This is in contrast to named characters such as Nicodemus, who appears as an interlocutor whose query prompts a lengthy discourse from Jesus and whose textual absence during that discourse goes unexplained. Significant Fourth Gospel characters who are nameless include Jesus' mother in 2:1-5 and 19:25-27, the Samaritan woman in 4:4-42, the royal official in 4:46-53, the lame man in 5:2-16, and the blind man in 9:1-41. Despite the pericope's textual problems, the woman caught in adultery in 7:53-8:11 also fits this pattern. After the pericope of the blind man, the narrative focuses on the anonymous disciple loved by Jesus. The established scholarly practice of capitalizing his designation has subverted his anonymity by creating a name from it. I will attempt to retain—indeed, highlight—his anonymity by referring to him with his identifying phrase rather than a title. Scholarly consensus recognizes the disciple Jesus loved as the Fourth Gospel paradigm of true discipleship; this study will examine how his anonymity is one element inviting readers to identify with and participate in that paradigm.

Nomination, Anonymity, and Narrative

The name of a character in a narrative has a greater significance than merely to collect all the data the text previously provided into a neatly bound and labeled package. Naming a character is an act of distinction that sets that character apart from the surrounding narrative environment, other characters, and the reader.[18] The previous traits, actions, feelings, and conversations of the character are gathered and contained in the proper name. According to this realist or essentialist understanding of nomination, the name is the unchanging identifying mark of a character that collects the attributes and characteristics the text reveals. For some plot-oriented narrative forms, where character functions are subordinated to the plot, this view is accurate.[19] In other narratives, proper names have an existential or historical use where the name is a culmination that the character achieves through the narrative.[20] One indicator of this existential use can be the initial absence of a proper name when the reader first encounters the character.

---

[18] Thomas Docherty, *Reading (Absent) Character: Towards A Theory of Characterization in Fiction* (Oxford: Clarendon Press, 1983), 43.
[19] Ibid., 49.
[20] Ibid., 56.

Names can also function subversively, thwarting reader expectations through non-conventional nomination. This practice has been analyzed in the novels of Raymond Queneau. He uses several names for one character, names characters of one gender with names usually reserved for the other, and uses names for non-human figures without explicitly identifying them as such. Queneau's use of names destabilizes characters in the text and creates "the uncertainty of a character's ontological status."[21] The uncertainty is reinforced by the disclaimer at the beginning of *Le Dimanche de la vie* that reverses the expected: "Les personages de ce roman étant réels, toute ressemblance avec des individus imaginaires serait fortuité."[22] Since the unconventional play of names in Queneau subverts reader expectations, what effect does the absence of a character's name create, and is it consistent in every instance of narrative anonymity?

Attention was drawn to the subversive function of namelessness in the Fourth Gospel by Staley in his work on the victimization of the implied reader in the Fourth Gospel. He noted that one example of reader victimization is the sudden and unexpected appearance of the anonymous disciple in chapter 13, whose lack of specific designation overturns the reader's superior understanding.[23] Not all anonymous Fourth Gospel characters function in this way. As is the case in most narrative portrayals of anonymous characters, some Fourth Gospel characters are anonymous to mark their *insignificance*.

A character's anonymity can signal the reader about the unimportance of a character who remains unobtrusively in the background of the narrative stage or passes across the stage for a moment, only to disappear for good. Another possible use of anonymity is to indicate that a name is unnecessary for the reader's perception of a character. An example of this type of unnamed character in the Fourth Gospel occurs in 2:9 at the wedding in Cana. Two anonymous characters confront the reader, the steward and the bridegroom. Neither has significant textual space nor narrative function. Their designations (steward, bridegroom) explain their actions through their roles; the scarcity of textual information concerning them does not provoke reader dissatisfaction due to the brevity of their appearances. The lack of a name can also divert the reader's attention from the unnamed character to the named character in whose presence the unnamed character is seen. This is one possible explanation for unnamed characters present with Jesus, such as the Samaritan woman in chapter 4

---

[21] Mary Campbell-Sposito, "Onomastics as a Defamiliarizing Device in Raymond Queneau's Novels," *French Review* 5 (1988): 732.

[22] Raymond Queneau, *Le Dimanche de la vie* (Paris: Gallimard, 1952).

[23] Jeffrey Lloyd Staley, *The Print's First Kiss: A Rhetorical Investigation of the Implied Reader in the Fourth Gospel*, SBL Dissertation Series 82 (Atlanta: Scholar's Press, 1988), 108-9.

or the blind man of chapter 9. I will demonstrate below, however, that though anonymity does function in this way for these two figures, that does not provide a sufficient interpretation of the significance of these characters or the textual absence of their names. All of the above understandings of anonymity, though partially correct, fail to consider how anonymity may further a reader's identification with a character.

Thomas Docherty identifies three functions of names in the reading process. The first is to indicate authority, the second is to provide a locus for gathering traits and qualities, and the last is to provide readers with a point of view from which to observe the narrative world.[24] These functions can only be present when names are used consistently in a narrative. When names are not used consistently, or are lacking entirely, the tendency is towards the decentralization of the self, not just for characters but for readers as well.[25] A result of this decentralization can be the shift on the part of the reader from sympathy for a character that maintains the reader's separateness from the character, to empathy where the reader is "quite literally involved in and positioned within another's subjectivity," namely that of the character.[26]

When names are absent, the reader has an option for the freedom of subjectivity, whereby the reader "impersonates many positions, and informs his or her subjectivity by losing identity as a namable self."[27] When anonymity is consistently combined with indications of the character's narrative significance and positive portrayal, the identity distinction of the name is erased, creating a gap readers are invited to fill with their own identity. Identifying with the character may provide readers entry into the narrative world, confronting them with the circumstances and situations of the character in the text. As a narrative produced within the context of a community of believers that makes no secret of its propagandizing intent, the Fourth Gospel uses anonymous characters to involve readers in its narrative world and to shape their responses. They are confronted with Jesus through the characters' textual encounters with him, and they are challenged at the level of their own response to their narrative encounter with Jesus.

---

[24] Docherty, 74.
[25] Ibid., 80.
[26] Ibid., 83.
[27] Ibid., 86.

Identification with Characters and Identity Formation

How readers identify with characters is not subject to empirical observation and would differ among readers, but some possibilities for understanding this process have been suggested. A psychoanalytical model of reading as an act of identity formation has been offered by Norman Holland. He views reading as a process whereby readers' identities re-create themselves. Three modalities are at work in the reading process. First, readers interpret the experience in ways consistent with their characteristic responses to the world so that their adaptations are matched. Next, readers extract from the work fantasies correlating to their movement towards gratification. The content of the fantasy readers locate in the text is actually the expression of their own drives. Readers re-create the text on the basis of their own identity theme. In the final modality, readers' identities are re-created from the literary work "to synthesize the experience and make it part of the mind's continuing effort to balance the pressures of the drive for gratification, the restraints of conscience and reality, and one's inner need to avoid emotional and cognitive dissonance."[28] Even if the Fourth Gospel was originally heard at a public reading, as was indeed probably the case, these three modalities of identity re-formation could still operate for an original "hearer" or historical readers, including modern readers.

The reading model Holland offers views identity transformation through the reading process as a re-formulation of the text to re-create the reader's pre-existing self identity, but he believes the reader's identity may remain unaltered by the text.[29] It has been objected that a self identity unaltered by the reading process contradicts Holland's assertion that the reading process can significantly alter the variations of an individual's identity theme. It is argued that these variations on a reader's identity theme actually constitute a re-formation of self on the part of the reader.[30] Following the analyst/patient model of psychoanalysis, some critics have asserted that projective identification is always also introjective, leading to alteration and re-formation of the self. This is accomplished through reader identification with literary characters or persona,[31] a process that I would claim may be facilitated by anonymity.

---

[28] Norman Holland, "Unity Identity Text Self," in *Reader-Response Criticism: From Formalism to Post-Structuralism*, ed. Jane P. Thompkins (Baltimore: John Hopkins University Press, 1980), 126.
[29] Holland, 118-20.
[30] Marshall W. Alcorn and Mark Bracher, "Literature, Psychoanalysis and the Re-Formation of the Self: A New Direction for Reader-Response Theory," *Publications of the Modern Language Association of America* 100 (1985): 343.
[31] Ibid, 350.

The phenomenon of reader identification with characters in narratives has been investigated using both children and adult subjects. A 1984 study tested second-, fourth-, and sixth-graders to determine whether reader identification with characters increases in proportion to perceived similarity between the character and the reader. As expected, the sophistication of the character identification process increased with the age of the children. The second-graders related perceived similarity directly to story liking, while among fourth-graders the influence of perceived similarity on story liking is indirect, channeled through the process of character identification. By sixth grade another step is added between character identification and story liking, "empathic identification," whereby readers step into the character's role.[32]

A later study tested the hypothesis that adult subjects would identify more with story characters with a gender role orientation similar to their own. Stories were written with male and female characters who behaved in either a stereotypically masculine or feminine manner, though not necessarily corresponding to the character's gender. Subjects were given two commonly used gender role questionnaires to determine their gender role orientation, which does not necessarily correlate with a person's actual gender. Gender role orientation is not defined by biological gender, but is the culturally conditioned phenomenon whereby certain behavior is stereotyped as either masculine or feminine. The questionnaires are based on the dominant American culture where "males are taught to be assertive, competitive, and goal oriented, and females are taught to be sensitive, caring and gentle." They measured a person's gender role orientation as androgynous, masculine, feminine, or undifferentiated; disregarding biological gender.[33]

The stories were not suspenseful but character sketches emphasizing motives and feelings. The study demonstrated, as expected, that a reader more readily identifies with a character displaying a similar gender role orientation to the reader's own. However, an unexpected finding of the study was that actual gender similarity between reader and character had little correlation with character identification.[34] These studies do not prove the effect of character portrayal on readers of the Fourth Gospel, or any text. They do, however, suggest elements of characterization that may facilitate some readers' identification with characters. One implication for the Fourth Gospel is to suggest at least the possibility for reader

---

[32] Paul E. Jose and William F. Brewer, "Development of Story Liking: Character Identification, Suspense and Resolution," *Developmental Psychology* 20 (1984): 919.

[33] Paul E. Jose, "The Role of Gender and Gender Role Similarity in Reader's Identification with Story Characters," *Sex Roles* 21 (1989): 699.

[34] Ibid., 710.

identification with any anonymous character with whom the reader's experience correlates, regardless of biological gender correlation. This process may be hindered by other extratextual barriers (i.e. cultural, experiential, etc.) to reader identification with opposite gender characters. For any reader able to overcome gender barriers, the potential exists for participation in the discipleship paradigm presented by the disciple Jesus loved, even without gender correlation.

Readers' identification with characters is aided by the readers' desire to make such an identification with a character encountered. Some narratives, by the nature of the status they are accorded within a given interpretive community, are approached by readers with this desire already present, shaping their expectations of the reading experience. In an analysis of romance novel readers, Janice Radway interviewed sixteen women and discovered that "all of the women I spoke to, regardless of their taste in narratives, admitted they want to identify with the heroine."[35] This identification is desired for the tension, anticipation, and excitement the reader experiences as she explores all the possible ramifications of the heroine's textual encounter with the hero.

The Fourth Gospel is accorded an elevated status within the interpretive community where it is encountered by the majority of its readers who are not members of a scholarly interpretive community, either literary or biblical. The influence of interpretive communities has been explored by Stanley Fish. He argues that we interpret texts "through interpretive strategies that are finally not our own, but have their source in a publicly available system of intelligibility."[36] The systems are rooted in the interpretive communities where they function. Participants in these communities share certain conventions and norms which make interpretation possible and intelligible. The core of agreement by which some interpretations are deemed acceptable while others are rejected is not inherent within the text but within the community producing the interpretations, and is always in flux.[37]

The interpretive community through which the majority of readers are first introduced to the Fourth Gospel is a community of people who believe the claims of this narrative, venerating it as a sacred text that together with other sacred texts forms the basis for their beliefs. Even if these non-technical readers are not active participants in that community, most are introduced to this narrative for the first time, first hear portions of its text, and are initially enticed to read it for themselves through their association with that community or one of its adherents. These readers'

---

[35] Janice A. Radway, *Reading the Romance: Women Patriarchy, and Popular Literature* (Chapel Hill: University of North Carolina Press, 1984), 64.
[36] Fish, 332.
[37] Ibid., 342.

expectations are shaped to identify with the characters in the Fourth Gospel and to encounter through their reading the one whose identity is at issue throughout the narrative and whose encounter with each textual character produces crisis.

Previous attempts to understand characters and characterization have failed to consider the effect of names and namelessness on readers or the process of reader identification with characters. The effect of anonymity to facilitate identification with characters varies according to the presence of other characterization elements. When these other elements create a positive portrayal, anonymity can facilitate reader identification with characters. In the Fourth Gospel the combination of characterization elements give a positive portrayal of anonymous characters, and these present the paradigm of discipleship in which the reader is urged to participate.

CHAPTER 3

TEXTUAL ANALYSIS OF FOURTH GOSPEL CHARACTERS

Although most narratives include unnamed characters, the Fourth Gospel is unique among contemporaneous narratives in the textual prominence and narrative significance of some of its anonymous characters. The uniqueness is both demonstrable and significant to an understanding of their narrative function. If anonymous characters with meaningful textual space in the Gospel parallel those in contemporaneous Greek novels, then they may be explained as conformity to Greek literary convention. If they parallel Hebrew narratives, then they may be conforming to other sacred narratives portraying holy men venerated by the community of faith adherents. If they parallel the Synoptics then they may be explained as adherence to the source materials or oral tradition. If, however, the Fourth Gospel is unique in its portrayal of anonymous characters with greater textual prominence, then the significance must be sought in the Gospel itself.

The contrast between anonymous Fourth Gospel characters and those in contemporaneous narratives will be evinced through examining unnamed characters in ancient Greek novels from the first two centuries after Christ, Hebrew Scriptures, and the Synoptic Gospels. We will compare the textual space and narrative significance of certain Fourth Gospel anonymous characters to anonymous characters in the other narratives. It is necessary to establish criteria by which to determine the significance of anonymous characters by examining the appearance of each character in the Fourth Gospel, charting the textual length of each appearance, frequency of appearances, name or other identifying phrase, and the response of each character to their encounter with Jesus. This will indicate the differentiation between named and unnamed Fourth Gospel characters and between significant and unimportant anonymous characters.

Anonymity in the Ancient Greek Novel

Besides the Elijah/Elisha and Samuel/Kings/Chronicles narratives that were probably familiar to the Fourth Gospel's community, there are Greek novels contemporary with the production of the Fourth Gospel. It is not suggested that any of the evangelists knew these ancient novels/romances, but the texts do represent examples of Greek narratives produced during the same era as the Gospels. Examining them will broaden our base for comparing the portrayal of anonymous characters in contemporaneous narratives. What Mary Ann Tolbert says of the Second Gospel compared to the same novels could be applied to the entire Gospel genre:

Its mixing together of historiographer form and dramatic force; its synthesizing of earlier genres such as biography, memorabilia of a sage, aretalogy, and apocalypse; its stylistic techniques of episodic plot, beginning with a minimal introduction, central turning point, and final recognition scene; and most of all its fairly crude, repetitious, and conventionalized narrative display striking stylistic similarities to the popular Greek ancient novel.[1] It will be seen that the stylistic parallels do not include the function of the significant anonymous Fourth Gospel characters.

There are five complete extant ancient Greek novels in addition to numerous fragments of other examples of this genre. Of the five extant novels, four are dated prior to the third century. The fifth, Heliodorus' *An Ephesian Tale*, is dated third to late fourth century A.D. In addition to its late dating, this narrative is atypical of the genre in other ways. It is modeled after Homer, is more than twice the length of the others, and its literary composition is "incomparably more complicated" than the other representatives of this genre.[2] These characteristics also make it less closely parallel to the Gospels. Due to this and its late dating, it will be excluded from our comparison. Our consideration of Greek narratives from the first two centuries of our era will include Chariton's *Chaereas and Callirhoe* (mid-first century A.D.), Xenophon's *An Ephesian Tale* (mid-second century A.D.), Longus' *Daphnis and Chloe* (200 A.D.), and Achilles Tatius' *Leucippe and Clitophon* (late second century A.D.). We will also examine a narrative from the same era but of a different genre, a portion of a speech of Dio Chrysostom, *The Hunters of Euboea* (late first century A.D.).[3]

No anonymous characters in these texts have the narrative significance of certain anonymous Fourth Gospel characters. Chariton uses various nameless characters appearing briefly in the text. These are plot functionaries whose designations are sufficient to their purposes within the narrative. Among these are Callirhoe's nurse, a messenger sent by Chaereas, and several of the tomb robbers mentioned individually but unnamed, all

---

[1] Mary Ann Tolbert, *Sowing the Gospel: Mark's World in Literary-Historical Perspective* (Minneapolis: Fortress, 1989), 65.

[2] Tomas Hägg, *The Novel in Antiquity* (Berkeley: University of California Press, 1983), 54.

[3] B. P. Reardon, ed., *Collected Ancient Novels* (Berkeley: University of California Press, 1989), 5. Precise dating is impossible; for a more detailed discussion see Hägg, 5-42.

of these appearing in Book 1.[4] In Book 3 we read a conversation between an anonymous crewman and an unnamed helmsman at the discovery of Chaereas' funeral ship.[5] As the narrative nears its climax, Chaereas and Polycharmus are delivered from the suspicions of the Egyptians by the opportune presence of a Greek who could serve as their translator.[6] Nowhere in this narrative do we find an anonymous character who has a significant relationship or even dialogue with either of the protagonists or other prominent character.

Xenophon's *An Ephesian Tale* includes Habrocomes' aged unnamed tutor who drowns himself rather than face separation from his former pupil. The reader is given brief glimpses of a barbarian servant of Manto, an old man to whom Leucon and Rhode were sold, and the villainous father of the youth Hyperanthes, all of whom are unnamed.[7] Two anonymous characters are referenced in the text several times. The first is the ruler of Egypt, sometimes designated administrator or "governor".[8] The second is the brothel keeper to whom Anthia was sold in Tarentum, also designated as her master and her "owner in Tarentum".[9] There is no dialogue between these characters and the protagonists, nor any significant relationship. Their narrative role is fully defined by their designations, the "ruler of Egypt" sitting in judgment on Habrocomes and the "brothel master" and "owner" of Anthia. Longus also portrays anonymous characters whose appearances in the narrative are fleeting. Nameless men admire and comment on Chloe's beauty; anonymous women praise and, in one case, even kiss Daphnis. Later an unnamed local farmer steals a rope from the Methymnaean's boat.[10]

Another type of unnamed character in the narratives of both Longus and Tatius is the mythical character. An example is the elusive boy transformed into a bird in the tale Philetas tells.[11] Similar are Tatius' mythical hospitable shepherd of Tyre introduced to wine by Dionysus, the fisherman who accidentally discovers purple dye, and the animal handler in the elephant digression.[12] All are examples of anonymous characters not actually present in the primary narrative, but appearing in narratives related by characters within the primary narrative, parallel to the parables of Jesus in the Synoptics.

---

[4] Chariton *Chaereas and Callirhoe*, 1.1, 4, 9-10.
[5] Ibid., 3.3.
[6] Ibid., 1.2.
[7] Xenophon *An Ephesian Tale*, 1.14, 2.5, 10, 3.2.
[8] Ibid., 4.1-5.3.
[9] Ibid., 5.5-9.
[10] Longus *Daphnis and Chloe*, 2.13.
[11] Ibid., 2.4-6.
[12] Achilles Tatius *Clitophon et Leucippe* 2.2, 2.11, 4.4.

20   CHAPTER THREE

Tatius also provides many examples of insignificant anonymous characters appearing briefly and identified by their plot function, including Clitophon's step-mother, the pilot and a muscular young man on the first boat carrying Clitophon and Leucippe, the pilot and a sailor on the second boat they hired, and the jailer of Clitophon.[13] One unnamed character who appears repeatedly is the official functionary of Artemis first seen in 7:13 and present consistently through 8:15. His significance is limited to his role as intermediary of Artemis, advocate of the foreign maiden seeking sanctuary and redress, accuser of the one who violates the temple sanctuary, keeper of the pan-pipes, and defender of justice. His role is not a subservient role of loyalty to the protagonists but a superior one that assists in their deliverance.

Anonymity plays a different role in Dio Chrysostom's seventh discourse, *The Hunters of Euboea*, where none of the characters are named except Sotades.[14] The Euboean discourse consists of a narrative within a narrative. The first narrative is Dio Chrysostom's account of his shipwreck and meeting of the hunter whose hospitality includes an invitation to his daughter's wedding. Appearing in this narrative are fishermen, the hunter, his wife, brother-in-law, sister, sons, daughter, niece and nephews; all unnamed.[15]

The second narrative, placed early in the primary narrative, is the hunter's account of his only adult visit to the city, responding to a man seeking money, evidently a revenue official. The hunter tells how his case before the magistrates was settled favorably through the testimony of someone he had previously befriended after rescuing him from shipwreck. Upon recalling the incident and recognizing the man, the hunter calls out to him, "Hello, Sotades!" This is the only name recorded in the oration. Again, the function of anonymous characters is unlike the Fourth Gospel and the effect on the reader is different. The most obvious distinction is the absence of a named protagonist who the anonymous characters encounter.

A partial explanation for the prevalence of anonymity among the characters in Dio's narrative is its genre. The *Hunters of Euboea* is an example of epideictic oratory, the ceremonial oratory of praise and display. Everything, including character portrayal, is directed towards illustrating a moral point. The superiority of the simple pastoral life of the poor is contrasted to the luxury and vice of the urban wealthy.[16] The re-

---

[13] Ibid., 1.3, 3.3-4, 3.9, 6.14.
[14] Dio Chrysostom *The Hunters of Euboea*, 59.
[15] Ibid., 65-76.
[16] D. A. Russell, "Ethos in Oratory and Rhetoric," in *Characterization and Individuality in Greek Literature*, ed. Christopher Pelling (Oxford: Clarendon Press, 1990), 207-9.

mainder of the discourse is a lengthy exhortation which in a heavy-handed manner attempts to reinforce the moral point already dealt with convincingly by the narrative alone.[17]

The difference between the function and significance of anonymous characters in ancient Greek novels and the Gospels is also partially a matter of genre distinction. These novels share a focus on romantic love, usually coupled with travel, adventure, and violence; all designed to satisfy a growing appetite for entertainment. According to some scholars, the genre emerged at a time when the small city-states had been replaced by large empires and individuals were less intensely concerned with political matters and more focused on personal experiences. "The novel is a reflection of their personal experience, as the older forms of tragedy and Old Comedy had been a reflection of their civic experience."[18]

It has been proposed that these ancient novels had their origins in the mystery cults and that their meaning was only fully intelligible to initiates of these cults.[19] This theory of origins has been effectively refuted and is no longer dominant,[20] but the role of religion in these narratives is undeniable. The theme of separated lovers ultimately reunited has striking parallels with the myth of Isis and Osiris.[21] The protagonists cry out to the deities, bemoaning the lot fate has cast them. The practitioners and officials of the mystery cults are presented favorably.

Despite the religious overtones present in the ancient novels, they differ significantly from the narrative structure of the Gospels. Their plots of necessity are dual, following the journeys and misadventures of both protagonists, the hero and the heroine. In the Gospels the only plot line is that of Jesus.[22] Unlike the Gospels, none of the Greek novels examined presents a religious figure as a person for the reader to identify with and/or emulate, therefore anonymity never functions to facilitate identification. Anonymous characters in ancient Greek novels do not parallel the significant Fourth Gospel anonymous characters, indicating that they do not simply reproduce a literary convention of Greek novelistic narrative.

---

[17] Dio Chyrsostom, 7.81-152.
[18] Reardon, 7.
[19] Reinhold Merkelbach, *Roman und Mysterium in der Antike* (Munich: C. H. Beck, 1962).
[20] Hägg, 101.
[21] Merkelbach.
[22] Mary Ann Tolbert, "The Gospel in Greco-Roman Culture," in *The Book and the Text: The Bible and Literary Theory*, ed. Regina Schwartz (Oxford: Basil Blackwell, 1990), 266.

Anonymity in Hebrew Narrative

The members of the community producing the Fourth Gospel were familiar with the religious narratives of Hebrew Scriptures from their Jewish heritage or adopted them as Gentile converts to Christianity. Anonymous characters are also extant in these narratives, but their narrative function is unlike that of the Fourth Gospel. Minor characters in Hebrew Scriptures remain embedded in the background as to go practically unnoticed, even when they could provide the raw materials for fascinating narratives. It has been suggested by Uriel Simon that their elliptical quality is "a formal expression of the subordination of the minor to the chief character."[23] They further the plot, focus the reader's attention on the hero, lend greater meaning and depth to the narrative by illuminating either the situation or the main character, and are a means for the moral evaluation of the protagonist. Simon's analysis makes no distinction between named and unnamed minor characters, which is not unreasonable since they function identically in most cases.

A recent study by Adele Reinhartz examining significant anonymous characters in the Books of Samuel argues that anonymity creates distance between the reader and the unnamed character, directing the reader's attention to the main character.[24] It is suggested that their anonymity expresses a negative value judgment. For some it expresses their subservience to the protagonist, while for others it focuses attention on their narrative function (e.g. as mediators between named characters) rather than on their own personalities. Reinhartz's discussion focuses on three anonymous women, the medium of Endor (1 Sam. 28:4-25), the wise women of Tekoa (2 Sam: 14:2-20), and Abel Bethmaacah (2 Sam. 20:16-20) and argues that they are autonomous functionaries whose designations are not personal traits but professional offices. The anonymity of the characters directs the focus on their professions, hence their narrative function in relation to the protagonists.[25] These three women do not parallel the function of significant Fourth Gospel anonymous characters, whose designations do not denote professions, and whose personal traits are much in evidence in their portrayal.

For the narrative of Judges, Mieke Bal has offered an understanding of the anonymity of three victims of violence as a power issue, specifically the subordination of three anonymous women to the male-domination of

---

[23] Uriel Simon, "Minor Characters in Biblical Narrative," *Journal for the Study of the Old Testament* 46 (1990): 13.

[24] Adele Reinhartz, "Anonymity and Character in the Books of Samuel," *Semeia* 63 (1993), 132.

[25] Ibid., 132-7.

men. These women include Jepthah's daughter who is sacrificed to fulfill a bargain with Yahweh (Judges 11:34-39), a concubine sacrificed to the lustful appetites of drunken men and the cowardice of her master (Judges 19:22-29), and Samson's wife immolated to revenge Samson's rampage (Judges 15:1-6). To level the playing field Bal begins her analysis by giving these women textually appropriate names, not to embellish the text but for "the emancipation of the reader—and the characters—from it."[26] Her need to name these victims illustrates their divergence from several Fourth Gospels anonymous characters. The narrative portrayal of female characters in the Gospel is not one of subordination. Some of the strongest, most positively portrayed characters in the Fourth Gospel are women.

In another portion of Hebrew narrative, the Genesis account of Abraham, anonymous characters include Pharaoh (12:14), Lot's wife (19:15,26), sons-in-law (19:14) and daughters (19:15-16, 30-38), and Abraham's oldest servant who sought a wife for Isaac (24:2-66). None of these characters is noble, nor are they in any way elevated by the narrative as models to emulate. Joseph's narrative includes anonymous characters: the man finding Joseph wandering and looking for his brothers (37:15-17), Judah's wife the daughter of Shua (considered by the RSV translators to be the proper name Bath-shua 38:2-5), Potipher's wife (39:7-19), the chief jailer (39:21-3), Pharaoh's cup bearer (40:1-23, 41:9-13), Pharaoh's chief baker (40:1-22), Pharaoh (41-50), and Joseph's steward (43:16-24, 44:1-10). None parallels the space nor significance of some Fourth Gospel anonymous characters.

The narratives of Samuel in 1 Samuel include the following anonymous characters: the priest's servant (2:13-17), the man of God prophesying against the house of Eli (2:27-36), the Benjamite who brought the news of the death of Eli's sons (4:12-17), and Phinehas' wife (4:19-22). None of these is given significant textual space, and they are identified by their narrative roles, appropriate for the brevity and purpose of their appearances. The narratives of Saul, David, and Solomon also reveal similar anonymous characters with little significance. None of these anonymous characters in Hebrew Scriptures parallels the narrative significance or functional prominence accorded to the significant anonymous Fourth Gospel characters. Instead, they parallel the textually insignificant anonymous Fourth Gospel characters (to be discussed below) whose minimal identification is sufficient for their narrative roles and adequate for reader satisfaction. They therefore furnish no clue for understanding

---

[26] Mieke Bal, "Dealing/With/Women: Daughters in the Book of Judges," in *The Book and the Text: The Bible and Literary Theory*, ed. Regina Schwartz (Oxford: Basil Blackwell, 1990), 19.

how anonymity functions for the unnamed characters who are accorded significant space in their encounters with Jesus in the Fourth Gospel.

The Elijah/Elisha cycle of 1 Kings 17-2 Kings 13 has many aspects closely paralleling the Gospels. Both focus on the exploits of a man of God whose life is an example of obedience and service. Both narrate an itinerant ministry, a gathering of disciples, miraculous healings, the multiplication of food, and the raising of the dead. Both portray confrontations with leaders the reader would expect to be faithful to Yahweh, but are not. Miraculous occurrences mark the end of the ministry of both Elijah and Elisha that parallel the death, resurrection, and ascension of Jesus.[27] The striking parallels between the Fourth Gospel and the Elijah/Elisha cycle might raise expectations of a parallel narrative function for significant anonymous characters. The analysis below will show that both have anonymous characters which have greater textual prominence than the anonymous characters of Hebrew narrative above, but they also differ from those in the Fourth Gospel.

Neither the Phoenician widow whose hospitality was rewarded with the unending supply of flour and oil nor her son whom Elijah raised from the dead is named (1 Kings 17:9-24). A literary analysis of this passage leads to a recognition of the textual placement of this anonymous woman in juxtaposition with the named Phoenician woman, Jezebel. Both outlive their husbands. Only in these two narratives and in the similar account in Elisha's ministry (2 Kings 4:10) does the word for "roofchamber," עליה, appear in the Books of Kings. Like the widow, Jezebel's son dies, but whereas Elijah miraculously reverses the widow's filial loss by raising her son, he prophesies death for the son of Jezebel (2 Kings 1:16). The widow's confession, partial in 1 Kings 17:12 but complete in 1 Kings 17:24, stands in contrast to Jezebel's oath of destruction on the prophet of Yahweh (1 Kings 19:2). The anonymous Phoenician widow stands in the narrative as a positive counterpart to the named Phoenician Queen Jezebel, whose desire to murder the prophet of Yahweh results in her own destruction.[28] The widow's portrayal is positive, but unlike the charactersm who encounter Jesus in the Fourth Gospel, her encounter with the protagonist is unrepeatable because the text makes no claims of his continuing availability to readers. The three other anonymous characters in the narrative of Elijah—Elijah's servant (1 Kings 18:43) and two anonymous men from among the sons of the prophets (1 Kings 20:35-7)—do not share this textual prominence or narrative significance.

---

[27] Raymond Brown, "Jesus and Elijah," *Perspectives* 12 (1971): 85-104.

[28] K. A. D. Smelik, "The Literary Function of 1 Kings 17.8-24," in *Pentateuchal and Deuteronomistic Studies: Papers Read at the XIIth IOSOT Congress Leuven 1989* (Leuven: Leuven University Press, 1990), 242-43.

Elisha miraculously multiplies oil for an anonymous widow of one of his followers (2 Kings 4:1-7). Immediately after this, the text records the hospitality of the anonymous Shunammite woman whose prominence is indicated both adjectivally and by her presence throughout 28 verses. Her husband and son are unnamed as well, but lack her textual prominence. Burke O. Long has demonstrated that in this narrative a conflict exists between protocol and a determination motivated by desperate need. The protocol, culturally mandated and reinforced by narrative presentation, is seen in the distance and subservience of the woman. She provides a furnished room on the roof, apart from the comings and goings of her family. Although most of Elisha's dialogue is about this woman, he does not address her even when she is present. The final scene of her narrative finds her prostrate at the prophet's feet.

Throughout the text, however, the widow violates protocol in a way that enhances her individuation and forces the prophet to do her bidding. She requisitions the prophet's private quarters for her son's death chamber (4:21). She refuses to have her problem mediated through a go-between (2 Kings 4:26-27, 29-30). She grabs Elisha's feet, normally a submissive gesture but here functioning to force him to do her will, to accept the consequences of this devastating reversal of his promise of a son. She is elevated by her superior knowledge of events, in contrast to the prophet's unusual ignorance. In spite of her final prostration before Elisha, this woman possesses superior knowledge, forces the prophet's hand, and manipulates his power, resulting in the fulfillment of her desire.[29] Although she does not closely parallel any Fourth Gospel character, her greater narrative significance and potential for individuation sets her apart from most other anonymous characters in Hebrew Scriptures. She is like the hemorrhaging woman (Mark 8:43-48 and parallels) or the Syro-Phonecian (Mark 7:25-30; Matthew 15:21-28), neither of whom would be denied.

The text of the Elijah/Elisha narrative cycle mentions several other brief appearances by unnamed persons: the man who comes from Baal-shalishah with twenty loaves of barley bread (2 Kings 4:42), Naaman's wife and her Israelite slave girl (2 Kings 5:2-3), Elisha's servant following the banishment of Gehazi (2 Kings 6:15), the woman who complains about her neighbor who backs out of the agreement to feed on each of their sons during a famine (2 Kings 6:26-9), and the royal officer trampled in accordance with Elisha's prophesy. Later in 2 Kings the reader briefly encounters a watchman, a horseman, and a second horseman Joram sends as messengers (2 Kings 9:17-20). None of these unnamed

---

[29] Burke O. Long, "The Shunammite Woman: In the Shadow of the Prophet?," *Bible Review* 7 (1991): 14-17.

characters has either the textual space or narrative depth to entice the reader's involvement with the narrative as does the hospitable widow of Zarephath and the Shunammite woman.

Anonymity in Synoptic Narrative

The Fourth Gospel shares its genre with the Synoptics. Each portrays the life, ministry, and passion of Jesus as one who performed miracles, healed the sick, and taught about God. In all the Gospels Jesus is portrayed as the anticipated Jewish Messiah. The Fourth Gospel also relates many episodes and characters in common with the Synoptics. Nonetheless, the distinctiveness of the Fourth Gospel is obvious when contrasted with the "same eyes" perspective of the Synoptics, as has been documented from the days of the earliest Christian communities. Clement of Alexandria's oft-quoted statement of these differences bears testimony to their jarring quality even to the first hearer/readers who heard/read these narratives over against each other. He stated that the fourth evangelist, aware "that the outward (or bodily) facts had been set forth in the Gospels, urged by his disciples, and divinely moved by the Spirit, composed a spiritual Gospel."[30]

The distinctiveness is further illustrated by statistical analysis. Less than 18% of the Fourth Gospel narrative is paralleled in the Synoptics.[31] A simple comparison of all verses in each chapter reveals that of 868 verses in this gospel, only 153 have Synoptic parallels, or 17.6%. Of the 153 verses paralleled, 90, or 58.8%, are found in the passion narrative (chaps. 12-20). Excluding the passion narrative, only 63 out of 550 verses, or 11.5% have Synoptic parallels. When Fourth Gospel episodes are parallel, there is virtually no verbatim agreement. The presentation of Jesus' ministry differs both chronologically and geographically in the Fourth Gospel. The miracles of Jesus have different vocabulary (σημεῖα versus δυνάμεις), function, and content. The only Synoptic miracle paralleled unquestionably in the Fourth Gospel is the miraculous feeding in chapter 6 (John 6:1-15; Matt. 14:13-20, Mark 6:32-44, Luke 9:10b-17). It is possible that the healing of the royal official's son in chapter 4 is also paralleled, but enough differences are present to make the parallel uncertain (John 4:46b-54; Matt. 8:5-13, Luke 7:1-10). The Fourth Gospel narrates no demon exorcisms or leper cleansings and its σημεῖα generally produce lengthy dialogues focusing on Jesus' identity.

---

[30] Eusebius *Ecclesiastical History* 6.14.7.
[31] Bruno de Solages, *Jean et les Synoptiques* (Leiden: E. J. Brill, 1979), 22.

The teaching of Jesus is different in the Fourth Gospel. Missing are the Synoptic aphorisms and parables, replaced by lengthy discourses. Instead of the Synoptic emphasis on God's kingdom, in the Fourth Gospel Jesus teaches Christology. Finally, typical Synoptic vocabulary (e.g. βασιλεία) is replaced with vocabulary rarely found in the other Gospels (e.g. ἀγαπάω, ἀλήθεια, and γινώσκω).[32]

These distinctions partially account for the different function of anonymity in the Fourth Gospel, as a comparison of anonymous characters in each Gospel confirms. One type of Synoptic anonymity occurs with characters in parables such as Luke's compassionate Samaritan or the father and his wayward sons. These are not characters present in the narrative the evangelists relate, but in narratives Jesus relates within the evangelists' narratives, like the characters in Dio Chrysostom's story within a story. None of these appears in the Fourth Gospel because Jesus tells no parables. Most anonymous Synoptic characters appear in Jesus' exorcisms and healings. Since these actions are not paralleled in the Fourth Gospel, there are no parallels with these characters. Anonymous Synoptic characters tend to appear very briefly and without dialogue with Jesus. Table 1 lists each of these anonymous Synoptic characters along with the length of their textual appearance. The only anonymous Synoptic charac-

Table 1: Anonymous Synoptic Characters

designation	Mark	Matthew	Luke
demoniac in synagogue	1:23-36		4:33-35
Peter's mother-in-law	1:30-31	8:14-15	4:38-39
a leper	1:40-45	8:1-4	5:12-14
a paralytic	2:3-12	9:2-7	5:18-25
man with withered hand	3:1-5	12:10-13	6:6-10
Centurion in Capernaum[33]		8:5-13	7:2-10
widow and son at Nain			7:12-15
scribe(Matt)/man(Luke)		8:18	9:57
another (disciple)		8:21-22	9:59-60
another			9:61-62
Gerasene demoniac	5:2-20	8:28-33	8:27-39

---

[32] These differences are discussed at some length in D. Moody Smith *John Among the Gospels: The Relationship in Twentieth-Century Research* (Minneapolis: Fortress Press, 1992), 2-6.

[33] Possibly paralleled in the Fourth Gospel as βασιλικός (4:46-53).

Table 1: Anonymous Synoptic Characters (cont.)

ruler[34]		9:18	
woman with hemorrhage	5:25-34	9:20-22	8:43-48
Jairus' daughter	5:39-43	9:24-25	8:52-55
blind man[35]			18:35-43
dumb demoniac		9:32f; 12:22f	11:14
Herodias' daughter	6:22-28	14:6-11	
Syrophoenician woman	7:25-30	15:22-28	
deaf mute	7:32-35		
blind man at Bethsaida	8:22-26		
father of epileptic	9:17-24	17:14-16	9:38-42
epileptic son	9:20-27	17:28	9:42
child in their midst	9:36	18:2	9:47
rich man/ruler	10:17-22	19:16-22	18:18-23
scribe/lawyer	12:28-34	22:35-36	10:25-28
Pharisee dinner host			11:37-38
woman infirm 18 years			13:11-13
man with dropsy			14:2-4
thankful leper			17:15-19
Zebedee's sons mother		20:21	
poor widow	12:42		21:2
woman anointing Jesus[36]	14:3	26:7	7:37-50
one who drew sword[37]	14:47	26:51	22:50
high priest's slave[38]	14:47	26:51	22:50
naked youth	14:51-52		
maid	14:66-67	26:69	22:56
maid/another	14:69	26:71	22:58
still another[39]			22:59
one of the criminals			23:39
the other			23:40-42
Centurian	25:39	27:54	23:47

[34] Jairus in Mark and Luke.
[35] Two blind men in Matthean doublet (9:27-31/20:29-43); named Bartimaeus in Mark 10:46-52.
[36] paralleled in the Fourth Gospel, but named there.
[37] paralleled in the Fourth Gospel, but named there.
[38] paralleled in the Fourth Gospel, but named there
[39] In the Fourth Gospel, a kinsman of the man whose ear was cur off.

ters prior to the passion narrative not found in healings or exorcisms are the following: the three who make excuses to Jesus (scribe/man, another, another) in Matthew 8 and Luke 9; Herodias' daughter (Mark 6; Matthew 14); the child in their midst (Mark 9:36 and parallels); the rich man/ruler (Mark 10 and parallels); the scribe/lawyer (Mark 12 and parallels); the Pharisee dinner host (Luke 11:37-8); the mother of the sons of Zebedee (Matthew 20:21); and the poor widow (Mark 12:42; Luke 21:2). None of these engage in significant dialogue with Jesus nor are their appearances extended.

Most anonymous Synoptic characters in the passion narrative are paralleled in the Fourth Gospel, but several who are anonymous in the Synoptics are named in the Fourth Gospel. The naked youth who fled, the criminals as individual characters, and the Centurion are not present in the Fourth Gospel. The "someone else" who questions Peter becomes a servant related to the man whose ear was cut off. The woman who anointed Jesus is identified as Mary, sister of Martha and Lazarus (12:3); the one who cut off the ear is identified as Peter (18:10); and the one who lost his ear is identified as Malchus (18:10).

Also paralleled in the Fourth Gospel is the Centurion of Capernaum whose servant/slave is sick (Lu 7:1-10, Matt 8:5-13), but he is identified in John 4:46 as a βασιλικός whose son is ill. The similarities are not exact and make it difficult to know whether we are dealing with a genuine parallel or not. In contrast to these anonymous Synoptic characters, several named characters are given significant textual prominence in the Synoptics. These include Mary, John the Baptist, Peter, James, and John. Extended dialogue or interaction between Jesus and another character in the Synoptics usually involves named characters (e.g. Zacchaeus, Levi/Matthew, Pilate). The analysis of the Fourth Gospel below will reveal the opposite tendency.

Individual Characters In The Fourth Gospel

An analysis of the individual Fourth Gospel characters will establish criteria for determining narrative significance and illustrate the contrast between named and unnamed characters. Table 2 lists all of the individual named characters present in the text. The named characters who are given more than a brief passing mention in the text are John (the Baptist), Peter, Nicodemus, Judas, Mary, Martha, Pilate, Mary Magdelene, and Thomas. Of these, John (never referenced as "the Baptist" in the Fourth Gospel), Peter, Nicodemus, Mary of Bethany, Martha, Mary Magdelene, and Thomas are all given some degree of favorable treatment in the text. Since I will argue that anonymity is used in this narrative to encourage

Table 2: Individual Fourth Gospel Characters (named)

John (the Baptist)	1:6-8, 15, 19-36; 3:23-36
Andrew	1:35-42; 6:8-9; 12:23
Peter	1:41-42; 6:68-69; 13:6-9, 24, 36-37; 18:10-11, 15-18, 25-27; 20:2-10; 21:2-22
Phillip	1:43-46; 6:5-7; 12:21-22; 13:8-9
Nathanael	1:45-49; 21:2
Nicodemus	3:1-9; 7:50-52; 19:39-41
Judas	6:71; 12:4-6; 13:2, 26-30; 18:2-5
Lazarus	11:1-44; 12:1-2
Mary	11:1-35; 12:1-3
Martha	11:1-40
Thomas	11:16; 14:5; 20:24-29; 21:2
Annas	18:13-24
Malchus	18:10
Pilate	18:29-19:22, 38.
Barabbas	18:40
Mary (Jesus' aunt)	19:25
Mary Magdalene	19:25; 20:1-2, 11-18.
Joseph of Arimathea	19:38-42

reader identification, and these characters receive varying degrees of favorable treatment, it will be necessary to examine their roles to determine why they are named, discouraging readers from identifying with them. In the Fourth Gospel each named character whose textual presentation is favorable and who is given significant textual space and thereby might be considered an appropriate model for reader identification is disqualified from this role, as will be seen below. Each is positioned for the reader in contrast to another character who is anonymous. Table 3 lists those significant anonymous characters appearing in the text of the Fourth Gospel.

Table 4 is a comparison of tables 2 and 3 illustrating the juxtapositioning of named characters with the corresponding anonymous characters. Included are only those named and anonymous characters with significant textual space who converse with Jesus, serving as more than simple plot functionaries or minor role players. Table 4 demonstrates that it is only Peter and the disciple Jesus loved who appear in the text with much frequency, and all of Peter's appearances coincide with the textual presence of an anonymous disciple, most often specified as the disciple Jesus loved, except for 6:68-69. Nicodemus is contrasted to the nameless woman of Samaria in his first and most extended appearance, and his final appearance, often used by those who argue he is counted among Jesus' followers,[40] is immediately preceded by the claim of the faithfulness of the eyewitness whose testimony is recorded in this Gospel, the disciple Jesus loved. Mary and Martha appear in a transition marking the conclusion of Jesus' public ministry and the beginning of his passion. Their roles in the seventh and final σημεῖον of Jesus places them in contrast to participants in the sixth σημεῖον, particularly the blind man.

Table 3: Individual Fourth Gospel Characters (anonymous)

mother of Jesus	2:1-5, 12; 19:25-27
steward	2:9-10
bridegroom	2:9
a Jew	3:25
woman of Samaria	4:7-27, 39-42
royal official	4:46-53
man ill for 38 years	5:5-15
lad with loaves and fish	6:9
adulterous woman	8:3-11
blind man	9:1-38
disciple Jesus loved	13:23-25; 19:26-27, 35; 20:2-10; 21:7, 20-24
another disciple	18:15
maid who kept the door	18:17
one of the officers	18:22
one of the servants	18:26

Table 4: Juxtapositioning of Named and Anonymous Characters

location	named characters	anonymous characters
chap. 1	John, Peter	
chap. 2		Jesus' mother
chap. 3	Nicodemus, John	
chap. 4		Samaritan woman, βασιλικός

---

[40] Raymond Brown, *The Community of the Beloved Disciple* (New York: Paulist Press, 1979), 72n. 128.

Table 4: Juxtapositioning of Named and Anonymous Characters (cont.)

chap. 5		lame man
chap. 6	Peter, Judas,	
chap. 7	Nicodemus	
chap. 8		adulterous woman
chap. 9		blind man
chap. 10		
chap. 11	Mary of Bethany, Martha, Thomas	
chap. 12	Martha, Mary of Bethany, Judas	
chap. 13	Judas, Peter	disciple Jesus loved
chaps 14-17		
chaps 18	Judas, Peter, Pilate	another disciple
chap. 19	Pilate Mary Magdalene Nicodemus	Jesus' mother disciple Jesus loved
chap. 20	Mary Magdalene Peter Mary Magdalene Thomas	disciple Jesus loved
chap. 21	Peter	disciple Jesus loved

Mary Magdelene's first appearance in the narrative at the cross of Jesus juxtapositions her with the mother of Jesus and the disciple Jesus loved. Into her narrative of the discovery of the empty tomb and misidentification of Jesus is interpolated the empty tomb experience of Peter and the disciple Jesus loved. Thomas' confession, where his textual presence is the greatest and where he is presented most favorably, contrasts him with later believers who believe without seeing, not the least of whom is potentially the reader ("Blessed are those who have not seen and yet believe," 20:29). The purpose statement of this Gospel lets readers know that this is precisely the intention of the narrative, to persuade them to believe even though they are unable to physically to "see" the risen Christ, ("these are written that you might believe that Jesus is the Christ, the Son of God, and that believing you might have life in his name," 20:31). His final appearance in the list of those present by the sea in the appendix of the Fourth Gospel, chapter 21, contrasts him to the two whose story is coming to closure in the appendix of this narrative, Simon Peter and the disciple Jesus loved.

These contrasts between named and unnamed characters will be explored in greater depth below as each of the anonymous characters with narrative significance and textual space is examined. Our reading will discover why these named characters we would expect to be models for reader identification are inappropriate for that role.

Anonymous characters in the Fourth Gospel

A comparison of tables 1 and 3 indicates that there are relatively few individual anonymous characters in the Fourth Gospel. Only fifteen appear, compared with forty-one in the Synoptics. Mark has twenty-five anonymous characters, Matthew twenty-six, and Luke thirty-four; each at least 60% more than the Fourth Gospel.

Several anonymous Fourth Gospel characters fit the pattern in contemporaneous narratives, having limited function and significance while appearing only briefly. They remain unobtrusively in the background, have no dialogue with Jesus, and function only to direct focus on Jesus or the σημεῖον he has worked. Their minimal designation explains their identity in terms of their narrative roles and is sufficient to satisfy readers. Among these are the steward and bridegroom discussed above, the Jew who disputes with John's disciples (3:25), the lad who provides the fish and loaves (6:9), and the three whose challenges to Peter in the courtyard facilitate his denial (18:17, 22, 26). The "anonymous disciple" with Andrew in 1:35-39 is never presented as an individual in the text. The presence of "another disciple" in 18:15-16 will be considered along with the textual presentations of the disciple Jesus loved.

The seven remaining Fourth Gospel anonymous characters receive a greater amount of textual space and a major narrative function unparalleled in contemporaneous literature. Their positive and consistent portrayal combines with their anonymity to facilitate the reader's entry into and involvement with the narrative world. Through that involvement the reader faces the challenge of Jesus' identity and is prodded to respond in faith through identification with the paradigm of discipleship presented, most completely by the disciple Jesus loved. We will now closely examine the narratives of these anonymous characters, contrasting them to the named characters with whom they are juxtaposed, and explore how anonymity entices reader participation and facilitates identification with each of the anonymous character.

CHAPTER 4

ANONYMITY, IDENTITY, AND IDENTIFICATION: THE FOURTH GOSPEL PROLOGUE AND THE WITNESS OF JOHN

The prologue is the first portion of the narrative the reader encounters, thereby establishing the readers familiarity with the themes and the characters to be encountered in this text. It includes the first naming act in the Fourth Gospel, naming the λόγος "Jesus Christ" (1:17). The initial foray into the Gospel prepares readers for future encounters with characters and establishes readers' expectations concerning the focus of the Gospel. The prologue installs Jesus' identity and origins as the primary issue, and the rest of chapter 1 prepares readers to assess characters according to their response to Jesus.

Traditional interpretations of the prologue have searched for the origin of the λόγος concept. Suggestions for its background have included the late Jewish sophia/wisdom parallels, the Hellenistic-Gnostic redeemer myth, the Hebrew concept of דבר, the λόγος doctrines of Heraclitus and the Stoics, the Aramaic concept מימר, and an understanding of the λόγος breaking the divine silence against the background of Jewish longing for a new prophet.[1] The assumption of a pre-Christian origin lying behind the concept of λόγος in the Fourth Gospel prologue has not met with universal acceptance among scholars. Recently Ed Miller has argued against all attempts to locate the origin of the Johannine λόγος in any external sources. He rejects each of the above theories on the grounds of their number and diversity, the problems of dating the proposed sources, accessibility of the sources to the evangelist, the striking differences that accompany the λόγος parallels in the external sources, and the "incompatibility of these theories with the character of the Fourth Gospel."[2] Miller believes that in the prologue, λόγος is a full-blown christological title, for which the prologue of the first Johannine Epistle was "a kind of rough draft."[3] Another scholar who rejects the necessity of a pre-Christian source behind this prologue is Thomas Brodie. He thinks it unnecessary to resort to the "unworkable hypothesis of a half-hidden hymn." Instead he accounts for the "interweaving of soaring poetry with

---

[1] For an overview see Raymond Brown, *The Gospel According to John (i-xii)*, The Anchor Bible (Garden City, New York: Doubleday & Company, Inc., 1966), 519-24.
[2] Ed. L. Miller, "The Johannine Origins of the Johannine Logos," *Journal of Biblical Literature* 112, (1993): 449-50.
[3] Ibid., 453-4.

simple prose" on the basis of the utilization of the form of the language to express one of the ideas central to the prologue: "the descent of the (soaring, poetic) Word into the (prosaic) reality of human life."[4]

The origin of the λόγος *concept*, however, is not the issue in the Gospel, but the origin of the λόγος *himself*. Several recent studies of the Fourth Gospel have chosen to examine the prologue in terms of its relationship to the rest of the narrative, regardless of what, if any, sources lie behind the prologue. Having earlier noted the concentric chiastic pattern of the surface structure,[5] R. Alan Culpepper's literary critical analysis *Anatomy of the Fourth Gospel*, analyzes the prologue in terms of its symbolism and the role that those symbols play throughout the Gospel. He notes that "the prologue links λόγος, life, and light so powerfully that the cluster dominates the symbolic system of the entire narrative."[6] He further acknowledges that the symbols introduced in the prologue are indicative of the conflict which is the central focus of this Gospel. "Primarily the conflict is between Jesus, who is 'from above' and those who cannot and will not recognize his identity."[7] This failure to recognize the identity of Jesus and to identify with him is at the very core of the Fourth Gospel. Therefore, it is not the reader's ability to identify "sources" behind the λόγος concept that is significant, but the prologue's impact in establishing the origin of the λόγος, setting the agenda for the reader's interaction with the rest of the Fourth Gospel narrative.

The structure of the prologue has frequently been analyzed to discover features that will determine which verses are original and which are interpolations. Recent studies whose emphases are the prologue's structure avoid this pitfall. Ignace de la Potterie focuses on the prologue's development of its concentric spirals and understands the repetitions as a deliberate artistic device.[8] This recognition of the symmetry of the prologue of the Fourth Gospel and its concentric structure is developed further by Jeffrey Lloyd Staley in his rhetorical investigation of the implied reader in the Fourth Gospel. He examines the prologue in terms of its thematic, symmetrical structure with concentric patterns. Staley understands this concentric pattern of the prologue as paradigmatic for the concentric structure he discovers throughout the rest of the Fourth Gospel narrative. That structure can be diagrammed as follows:

---

[4] Thomas Brodie, *The Gospel According to John: A Literary and Theological Commentary* (New York: Oxford University Press, 1993), 134; cf. Barrett, 150-1.

[5] R. Alan Culpepper, "The Pivot of John's Prologue," *New Testament Studies* 27 (1980): 1-31.

[6] Culpepper, *Anatomy*, 190.

[7] Ibid., 200.

[8] Ignace de la Potterie, "Structure du Prologue de Saint Jean," *New Testament Studies* 30 (1984): 359.

A) the relationship of the λόγος to God/creation/humanity (vv 1-5)
B) the witness of John (vv 6-8)
C) the journey of the φῶς to the world (vv 9-11)
****
C') the journey of the λόγος to the world (v 14)
B') the witness of John (v 15)
A') the relationship of the λόγος to humanity/re-creation/God (vv 16-18)[9]

This concentric structure he finds through the rest of the Fourth Gospel narrative consists of four ministry tours, each of which are interpolated between journeys of Jesus, both physical and metaphorical. This concentric structure gives a feel of closure to each journey, but this sense of closure is only illusory as the reader soon discovers. Furthermore this structure is constantly focusing the reader back to previous scenes which s/he is forced to reevaluate.[10] The prologue sets the stage for both the structure and the significance of the rest of the Fourth Gospel narrative. Others have understood the structure on the basis of an Hebraic structure of synthetic parallelism.[11] If this parallelism is the basic structure present in the Fourth Gospel prologue, it too would provide for the restatement of previously stated symbols and themes, as with Staley's concentric understanding of the structure, and would cause the reader's focus to return to previous scenes to reevaluate her/his understanding of them.

Mark Stibbe's literary interpretation sees a three-fold prologue function: interactional, intratextual, and intertextual. Interactionally it creates a relationship between narrative and reader; intertextually it hints at literary traditions beyond itself (including wisdom traditions, the narratives of Moses, and the first book of beginnings, Genesis); and intratextually it introduces the protagonist, the plot, important Fourth Gospel themes, and rhetorical strategies the narrative will employ. These include chiasmus, concentric spirals, inclusio (ending a passage where it began, forming a compositional ring), dualism, irony, multivalence (multiple levels of meaning), and stair-step progression (beginning component parts by repeating the end of the preceding part).[12]

---

[9] Staley, *Print's First Kiss*, 59.
[10] Ibid., 70.
[11] Michael Theobald, *Die Fleischwerdung Des Logos: Studien zum Verhältnis des Johannesprologs zum Corpus des Evangeliums und zu 1 Joh* (Münster: Aschendorff, 1988), 140-1.
[12] Mark W. G. Stibbe, *John*, Readings, A New Biblical Commentary (Sheffield: JSOT Press, 1993), 22-30.

Another literary analysis, this by Frank Kermode, alleges that the literary critic can avoid many questions often occupying critical discussions of the prologue. Among these are source critical issues, attempts to distinguish original verses from interpolations, and subtle theological distinctions between the verses comprising the prologue and the rest of the Gospel. Instead, according to Kermode, the literary critic should "assume a real and intelligible relation between the prologue and the narrative it introduces," a position termed "postcritical" rather than "precritical."[13] The prologue can be read as a "threshold" poem with the key words ἦν and ἐγένετο (was and became), "common words used in an uncommon way."[14] "Was" is used in an eternal sense, crossing the threshold into what is "becoming." Being surrenders to becoming in the incarnation, Word becomes flesh. This emphasis focuses on the issue of the origins and identity of Jesus—the crux of the Fourth Gospel, first brought to the reader's attention in the prologue.

Fernando Segovia analyzes the plot of the Fourth Gospel as an example of ancient biography, a genre characterized by journeys or travel accounts such as those noted by Staley as a common motif. He designates the plot as the journeys of the Word of God. In this schema the prologue fits the pattern of ancient biography by providing a narrative of Jesus' origins.[15] His literary analysis focuses on Jesus' origins, the recognition of his identity, and the response to that recognition.

Werner Kelber reads the prologue to narrate three beginnings, that of the λόγος, that of John, and that of Jesus' earthly ministry.[16] These three distinct beginnings express the Fourth Gospel's concerns for origins and focus upon identity claims and characters' responses to those claims. The Gospel begins with a concern for origin and identity, and designates the unnamable presence of God as λόγος. The reader is informed that the privilege of being God's child awaits those who believe in the name of

---

[13] Frank Kermode, "John," in *The Literary Guide to the Bible*, ed. Robert Alter and Frank Kermode (Cambridge: The Belknap Press of Harvard University Press), 441. Other recent assessments of the narrative relationship of the prologue to the rest of the gospel include John Painter, *The Quest for the Messiah: The History, Literature and Theology of the Johannine Community* (Edinbourough: T & T Clark, 1991), 21: "a God's-eye view which places the reader in a position of advantage over the characters in the story"; Adele Reinhartz, *The Word in the World: The Cosmological Tale in the Fourth Gospel*, Society of Biblical Literature Monograph Series, no. 45 (Atlanta: Scholars' Press, 1992), 16: "The prologue provides the reader with a precis of the cosmological tale"; and Norman R. Peterson, *The Gospel of John and the Sociology of Light: Language and Characterization in the Fourth Gospel*, (Valley Forge, PA: Trinity Press International, 1993), 44: "the prologue is the interpretive key to this episode, as it is to the whole of John's narrative."

[14] Kermode, 445.

[15] Fernando F. Segovia, "The Journey(s) of the Word of God: a Reading of the Plot of the Fourth Gospel," *Semeia* 53 (1991), 35-36.

[16] Werner H. Kelber, "The Birth of a Beginning: John 1:1-18," *Semeia* 52 (1990): 132.

the λόγος, a name as yet unrevealed. The question of origins is present at the outset and continues to be the focal point for the debate surrounding Jesus, and the question of origins is at the same time the question of Jesus' identity.[17] The crisis of recognizing Jesus' identity and responding appropriately recurs throughout the Gospel.

This theologically weighty language of "beginnings" immediately informs the reader of the origin of the λόγος as one with no beginning, only being; alerting the reader to the special relationship of the λόγος to God. The first four verses use three different tenses indicating three stages of the existence of the λόγος. The imperfect of the verb of being, ἦν (vv. 1-2), reveals a unity of God and the λόγος that exists before time, having no beginning point; the aorist ἐγένετο (v. 3ab) reflects the past role of the λόγος in God's creative act, and the perfect γέγονεν (v. 3c) indicates the continuing relevance of creation for both narrative and reader.[18]

The prologue focuses reader attention on beginnings, particularly the divine origin and identity of Jesus. In these few verses the reader encounters the origination of the narrative, the origin of Jesus, the origin of the witness concerning him, and the origin of the conflict surrounding him. By their knowledge of both Jesus' heavenly origins and the reality of his rejection by some, readers are prepared to assess characters ahead in the text according to their recognition, reception, and response to Jesus.

Another function of the prologue is to introduce readers to the import of names and their absence. The reader is informed of the cruciallity of receiving Jesus/believing in his name (v. 12). The reader confronts the dilemma of belief in a name the text has not revealed. Is the reader, for example, to understand λόγος as a name? Does the narrative assume an extratextual knowledge of his name? Indeed the name is soon revealed (v. 17), but only as one who conveys grace and truth. Nowhere is he explicitly identified as the λόγος, who was God, the true light, who became flesh. Although most readers' extratexts can provide the missing connection without difficulty, the problem of identity and naming is now established and will remain throughout the reading experience. The prologue's naming the λόγος "Jesus Christ" significantly effects readers' understandings of Jesus' origin and identity, impacts their views of characters

---

[17] Andreas Detwiler, "Le prologue johannique (Jean 1,1-18)," in *La communauté johannique et son histoire: La trajectoire de l'évangile de Jean aux deux premiers siècles*, ed. Jean-Daniel Kaestli, Jean-Michel Poffet, et Jean Zumstein (Geneva: Labor et Fides, 1990), 220.

[18] Francis J. Moloney, *Belief in the Word: Reading the Fourth Gospel: John 1-4* (Minneapolis: Fortress Press, 1993), 31-32.

on the basis of the character's ability to grasp Jesus' identity, and creates awareness of the elusiveness of names.

The Witness of John

The first character introduced is John,[19] portrayed totally positive, yet not offered as a model for reader identification. His inappropriateness for reader emulation arises from his unique and unrepeatable role as a contemporaneous witness to Jesus. His presentation differs significantly from his Synoptic portrayal; in the Fourth Gospel, his task is not preparation for Jesus' coming but witness to the λόγος who is already dominating the narrative when John appears (1:6). Prior to John's first recorded presence (1:19), Jesus is identified as the λόγος become flesh. John's "becoming" is contrasted with the eternal "being" of the λόγος; his ministry is therefore "not so much the precursor of Jesus as a witness contemporaneous with Jesus."[20]

The appearance of John is the reader's first encounter with an historical character. His introduction anchors the supra-historical presence of the λόγος firmly in human history, in which the reader is a participant. The seemingly discordant introduction of John in vv.6-8 prepares the reader for the entry of the λόγος into the Fourth Gospel's narrated history in vv. 9-14.[21] The subtle "coming into the world" (v. 9) is developed until the jarring moment when the reader encounters the graphic statement that the λόγος became σάρξ (v. 14) and pitched his tent along side us.

John is immediately named in his first reference, yet his identity is elusive, revealed through negation. When first encountered, he is the one sent from God to bear witness to the light, but is not himself the light (1:7-8). His reappearance leads to a direct identity query from "the Jews"[22] (appearing here for the first time), "Who are you?" (1:19). John's answer to this straightforward question is significant to the reader's response to identity issues in the Gospel. An emphatic tripartite formula, "He confessed, he did not deny, but confessed," (1:20) introduces a

---

[19] John is never designated the Baptist in the Fourth Gospel. He is the only character named John in the Gospel and will be referred to simply as John throughout this study.

[20] M. J. J. Menken, "The Quotation from Isaiah 40,3 in John 1,23," *Biblica* 66:2 (1985): 203.

[21] Moloney, 35.

[22] The significance of the Fourth Gospel's reservation of this term to designate Jesus' opponents is beyond the scope of this study of individual characters. For a detailed discussion see Culpepper, *Anatomy*, 125-32.

"confession" that is not a confession, but a denial.[23] Instead of revealing his own identity, John denies that he is the Christ. Yet this is a confession of his identity as a subordinate of Jesus, with whom John is not to be confused. He confesses not only that he is not the Christ, but also that he is not Elijah or the prophet. The attention given to John's portrayal as witness to Jesus indicates the essential nature of witness in this narrative for comprehending the origin and identity of Jesus,[24] and installs "witness" as an element of appropriate response to Jesus' identity. The emphasis on John's role as a witness to Jesus offsets John's narrative priority, his appearance preceding Jesus' entry into the text.

Subsequent references to John confirm his identity in terms of who he is not. In chapter 3 he restates "I am not the Christ" and announces the time has arrived for him to fade out of the picture (vv.28-30). Each additional reference to John reinforces his subordination to Jesus. Jesus made more disciples (4:1), has a greater testimony (5:36), and through his words and actions proved the veracity of John's testimony of Jesus' superiority (10:41). John's appearances provide the reader/critic with fodder for speculation about intended readers and the Sitz im Leben of this narrative;[25] they also enhance Jesus' superiority, confirm his origins, and increase reader understanding of his identity by corroborating John's initial testimony.

Kermode notes that the body of the narrative is linked to the preceding hymn by the language of being and becoming and the distinction between these concepts.[26] "The one coming after me has become before me, because before me he was" (1:30, Kermode's translation). The positivity of being expressed in the λόγος is contrasted with the negativity of the world, that which becomes, as reflected in the person of John. "It is what he is not that links him to the poem."[27]

John's continued dialogue with his interlocutors contributes to their difficulty in establishing his identity. They repeat the direct question "Who are you?," and he responds with descriptions of function, not a name. He is the voice (1:23), the one baptizing only with water (1:26),

---

[23] Marinus de Jonge, "John the Baptist and Elijah in the Fourth Gospel," in *The Conversation Continues: Studies in Paul and John in Honor of J. Louis Martyn*, ed Robert T. Fortna and Beverly Gaventa (Nashville: Abingdon, 1990), 302.

[24] Francis X. D'Sa, "The Language of God and the God of Language: The Relation Between God, Human Beings, the World and Language in Saint John," in *God in Language*, ed. Robert P. Scharlemann and Gilbert E. M. Ogutu (New York: Paragon House Publishers, 1987), 40.

[25] For a discussion of adherents of John the Baptist among the intended readers of this gospel and its possible use as a missionary tractate directed towards them see Brown, *Gospel*, lxvii-lxx.

[26] Kermode, 447.

[27] Ibid., 446.

and the unworthy one (1:27). On each of two successive days John begins his words with the same powerful witness, "Behold, the Lamb of God!" (1:29,36). He identifies himself as the one who failed to recognize Jesus (1:31), but witnessed the Spirit's descent (1:32). John's identity is meaningful only in terms of his relationship to the one he confesses not to be. His primary identity is the subordinate μαρτύριαν of the λόγος/φῶς/χριστός."[28] The corroborative testimony of the three primary witnesses to the identity of Jesus in the Gospel: John (chapters 1-3), the Holy Spirit (chapters 14 and 16), and the Father (chapters 5-8, 10, 12, 15, 17); appear together in 1:29-34.[29] Just as John chronologically preceded Jesus, his witness precedes that of the other two. The primacy of witness for understanding Jesus' identity and responding appropriately to him is confirmed.

The first recorded speech in the Fourth Gospel is John's testimony. His words and language parallel the words and language of Jesus and the narrator. Examples include the negative counterpart of Jesus' "I am" (ἐγω; οὐκ εἰμι;) in 1:20, admission of ignorance of Jesus' origin ("among you stands one whom you do not know" in 1:26 and "I did not know him" in 1:31),[30] and the references to familiar themes including Jesus' sin-atoning death, his pre-existence, and the role of the Spirit.[31] Narratively, John speaks first and at some length. In Jesus' first words (1:38), he adopts the previously recorded language of the narrator and John.[32] This makes John's subordination to Jesus even more remarkable. It is self-chosen, willingly undertaken by one whose self-understanding is unwavering, as is his obedience to the voice of God. Even though he appears and speaks prior to Jesus, he rejoices in the role of "friend of the bridegroom" (3:29). His relationship with Jesus is characterized by "complete inner agreement."[33] He rejoices in the elevation of one he recognizes as superior at the expense of his own status. John's responses to

---

[28] Rudolf Bultmann, *The Gospel of John: A Commentary*, trans. G. R. Beasley-Murray, R. W. N. Hoare, and J. K. Riches (Philadelphia: Westminster Press, 1971), 84-97.

[29] J. Daryl Charles, "'Will the Court Please Call in the Prime Witness?': John 1:29-34 and the 'Witness'-Motif," *Trinity Journal*, n.s., 10 (1989): 71.

[30] Rudolf Schnackenburg, *The Gospel According to Saint John, Volume One: Introduction and Commentary on Chapters 1-4*, trans. Kevin Smith (New York: Crossroads, 1990), 294.

[31] Brown, *Gospel*, 58.

[32] Sjef van Tilborg, *Imaginative Love in John*, Biblical Interpretation Series, vol. 2 (Leiden: E.J. Brill, 1993), 61.

[33] Ibid., 77.

his inquisitors lead the reader back to the prologue, the narrative of Jesus' superior origins.[34]

John's negative self-identification and his failure to recognize Jesus without special revelation reveal the difficulty of establishing identity in this narrative. This includes the identity of characters encountering Jesus, the character's recognition of Jesus' identity, and readers' recognition of Jesus' identity and identification with him. Characters are not permitted to gaze upon Jesus from afar, but are brought through their encounters into a close and direct confrontation with him. They are "asked to become the hero," and the ones who fit the paradigm of appropriate response facilitate readers in identifying with the hero as well. The Fourth Gospel invites reader identification with Jesus "by examining the responses of the secondary characters, experiencing their dilemma and recognizing it as their own."[35] This invitation to "become the hero" is reinforced when Jesus prays "that they may be one, even as we are one" (17:12). The readers discover themselves specifically referenced when Jesus expands his prayer to include "those who believe in me through their word, that they may all be one," even as Jesus and his Father are one (17:20-21). He tells them he will be "in" them through the Spirit (14:17) and they will be "in him" and he "in" them even as he is "in" his Father (14:18). The "oneness" of Jesus, the Father, and his disciples expressed in the farewell discourses confirms the narrative goal of reader identification with Jesus by becoming one with him.

Jesus' Initial Encounters with Individual Characters

With v. 29 the narrative becomes episodic with a succession of "next day" references (vv. 29, 35, and 43) followed by the "on the third day" reference that begins the second chapter. Readers have offered widely varied interpretations of the significance of these "day" references,[36] usu-

---

[34] Peterson, 25; contra Staley, who believes John "appears as a weak and faltering witness," and is "tongue-tied, shackled by the priests and Levites incessant questioning," *Print's First Kiss*, 77.

[35] Diana Culbertson, *The Poetics of Revelation: Recognition and the Narrative Tradition*, Studies in American Biblical Hermeneutics 4 (Macon, GA: Mercer University Press, 1989), 178-79.

[36] These include days of a new creation, Thomas Barrosse, "The Seven Days of the New Creation in Saint John's Gospel," *Catholic Biblical Quarterly* 21 (1959): 507-16; a holy week, Marie-Emile Boismard, "Les traditions johanniques concernant le Baptiste," *Revue Biblique* 70 (1963): 5-42, a week of anti-Baptist teaching, A. Geyser, "The Semeion at Cana of the Galilee," in *Studies in John Presented to Professor J. N. Sevenster on the Occasion of his Seventieth Birthday*, Novum Testamentum Supplements 24 (Leiden: E. J. Brill, 1970), 12-21; and the Rabbinic tradition of a week of preparation for the theophany

ally in the context of a symbolic "week," but any reference to a "week" requires that the arrival of the delegation inquiring into John's identity in v. 19 occur on the "first day," a purely extratextual identification.[37] Apart from any special theological significance, these references frame the remainder of the first chapter into a series of snapshot portrayals of several characters' first encounter with Jesus.

Many Fourth Gospel readers have noted its designs to decisively impact them; the Gospel calls the reader to decision. Its story is told by one who correctly understands Jesus' narrative, responded positively to Jesus, and seeks to persuade the reader to do the same. It was not written to entertain its readers, but to change their lives.[38] These scholars have not, however, shown how characters function in the Fourth Gospel to call readers to decision. The prologue and the account of John's witness precedes Jesus' encounters with characters, raising the question of Jesus' identity and thus framing all ensuing encounters within that question. After introducing Jesus' origins as the λόγος and presenting the reader with the initial character encounters, the text offers an eclectic gathering of initial "followers" of Jesus, who first encounter Jesus through varied means.

The first individual characters to appear after John are two of his disciples, introduced immediately after the first "next day" designation (1:35-42). They are distinguished from the collective group of characters preceding them: "priests and Levites from Jerusalem" (1:19), "sent from the Pharisees" (1:24). Furthermore, their pairing is disrupted by the identification of one as Andrew, leaving the other silent and anonymous, inviting exegetical speculation, and subtly enticing the reader. This anonymous character stands early in the narrative as an indicator that others followed Jesus besides the well-known and outspoken, and opens to readers the possibility for them to be numbered among Jesus' followers. Thomas Brodie notes that prior to the identification of Andrew in v. 40, "it is not a picture of particular disciples, but rather of discipleship as such. No names are used. It could be a picture of anybody or everybody."[39]

The appearance of these unidentified followers of Jesus early in the Gospel invites readers to include themselves among his followers. This

---

at Sinai, J. Potin, *La fête juive de la Pentecôte*, Lectio Divina 65, Vol 1, (Paris: Editions du Cerf, 1971): 314-17.

[37] Ernst Haenchen, *A Commentary on the Gospel of John Chapters 1-6*, ed. Ulrich Busse, trans. Robert W. Funk (Philadelphia: Fortress Press, 1984), 152.

[38] Moloney, 12; Reinhartz, *Word in the World*, 29; and Culbertson, 186.

[39] Thomas Brodie, *The Gospel According to John: A Literary and Theological Commentary* (New York: Oxford University Press, 1993), 161.

invitation is reiterated by another Fourth Gospel distinctive; the marked preference for "disciple" to designate followers of Jesus. It appears seventy-eight times, more than any other Gospel,[40] compared to only four occurrences of "the twelve." Also absent is the designation "apostle," except for 13:16 where it is found in an aphorism not directly referring to any particular followers of Jesus. The choice of "disciple" over "the twelve" or "apostle" to designate Jesus' followers is appropriate their role in this Gospel as representatives with whom readers may identify since "disciple" is more inclusive and readily includes readers.[41] The act of following (ἀκολουθοῦντας) includes the concept of discipleship. According to Kevin Quast's analysis, of its nineteen occurrences in the Fourth Gospel, only one is unquestionably literal (11:31), while at least eight require a figurative understanding (1:43, 8:12, 10:4, 5, 27, 12:26, 21:19, 22).[42] This establishes at least a strong presumption that the verb is to be understood symbolically in all but one of its appearances. Four of its occurrences appear in the initial "call sequence" (1:37, 38, 40, 43), and ten are on the lips of Jesus, including the eight that Quast believes require a figurative understanding. On the two other occasions when Jesus speaks of "following" he is in dialogue with Peter concerning Peter's inability to follow Jesus to his death (13:36, 2x and 37). Eight occurrences of "following" involve Peter: five times in dialogue with Jesus, once in a literal description of Peter following Jesus after his arrest (18:15), once following the disciple Jesus loved to the tomb (20:6), and once observing this disciple following Jesus and Peter (21:20). The only time Quast believes this verb is meant literally is when the mourners follow Mary to Lazarus' tomb (11:31).

The first appearances of "following" and the designation "disciple" coincide with the introduction of the two disciples in 1:35, and works rhetorically to influence readers' responses to the Fourth Gospel. These two respond to John's witness by following Jesus, already established as the focus of this narrative. They do not respond because of a direct encounter with Jesus, but as a result of the witness of another. They respond to the witness of John who himself responded to the witness of the Father and the Spirit. Andrew is the witness to whom Philip responds, and Philip in turn witnesses to Nathanael. This is in contrast to the Synoptics, where

---

[40] Fernando, F. Segovia, "Peace I leave with you; My Peace I Give unto You: Discipleship in the Fourth Gospel," in *Discipleship in the New Testament*, ed. with an introduction Fernando F. Segovia (Philadelphia: Fortress, 1985), 95n.6.

[41] Culpepper, *Anatomy*, 115.

[42] Kevin Quast, *Peter and the Beloved Disciple: Figures for a Community in Crisis*, Journal for the Study of the New Testament Supplement Series 32 (Sheffield: JSOT Press, 1989), 28.

a direct encounter with Jesus prompts discipleship. The presence of what Staley characterizes as a "two-tiered call to discipleship," establishes a model of response based upon the secondary experience of another. This encourages readers to respond to the Gospel's characters and identify with their life-changing responses prompted by the characters' encounters with Jesus.[43]

The anonymous disciple in 1:35-40 has from ancient times been the focus of readers' attempts to fill the indeterminacy of his identity with the identity of someone familiar. He has often been identified as the disciple Jesus loved, traditionally understood as John, son of Zebedee. An alternative suggestion has been to identify him with Philip. More recently he has been identified with the disciple Jesus loved, understood as someone other than John, the son of Zebedee.[44] The uncertainty surrounding his identity indicates the extent to which the narrative resists its readers' urge to identify and name anonymous characters. The identity of this disciple is indeterminable, and to identify him as the disciple Jesus loved is unlikely precisely because of the lack of the identifying clause ὃν ἠγάπα ὁ' Ἰησοῦς. Brown's explanation that he is not so identified because "he achieved his identity in a christological context,"[45] is not convincing. Brown's explanation requires that Jesus' love for the disciple was earned through a growing understanding of Jesus' identity, but no such growth nor progressive faith is indicated for the disciple Jesus loved, who appears suddenly during Jesus' final visit to Jerusalem in chapter 13.

The primacy given to the person of Jesus causes the first public words of Jesus in each Gospel to have particular import for shaping the reader's understanding of Jesus' identity.[46] These include Jesus' call to repent in Mark 1:14-15, his concern for the fulfillment of righteousness in Matthew 3:15, and his proclamation of the acceptable year of the Lord and the presence of God's Spirit on him to preach the gospel to the poor in Luke 4:18-19. In the Fourth Gospel Jesus' first public utterance is "What do you seek?" (1:38). It is a question put to those who would follow Jesus, including the reader. What are you after? What do you hope to gain by following me? Who do you understand me to be that you would follow after me? What are your life's goals and how do you expect to attain them?[47] As Jesus questions these two initial followers concerning expec-

---

[43] Staley, *Print's First Kiss*, 80-81.
[44] For an extended discussion of the traditional and alternative identifications of this disciple see Frans Nierynck, "The Anonymous Disciple in John 1," *Ephemerides Theologicae Lovanionses* 66:1 (1990), 5-37.
[45] Brown, *Community*, 33.
[46] Robert H. Smith, "'Seeking Jesus' in the Gospel of John," *Currents in Theology and Mission* 15 (1988), 51.
[47] Ibid., 53; cf. Culbertson, 160; Schnackenburg, 308; Bultmann, 100; Brown, 78.

tations they have yet to formulate and understandings they have not yet reached, the Gospel prepares readers to allow their expectations for discipleship and their understandings of Jesus to be shaped, challenged, and remolded by their narrative encounters with Jesus.

In 1:35-42 the reader encounters a series of verbs denoting movement: standing, walking, followed, turned, come and see, came and saw, stayed, followed, found, brought. This series of movements, in Brodie's words, "converge on one place—the place where Jesus abides." No geographic references are present to concretize the place of Jesus' abode. The verb μένω has already appeared twice (1:32-33) in the Gospel, both times referring not to a geographical location but to the Spirit's presence remaining/abiding upon Jesus. The reader is thus led to conclude that "regardless of where Jesus abode physically, his primary abode was spiritual,"[48] enabling any reader to encounter him without chronological or geographical hindrances.

The silence of Peter (named successively Simon Peter, Simon, Simon son of John, Cephas, and Peter in the space of only three verses) coupled with Jesus' recognition of him without introduction, provides the reader with a narrative hint that the initiative for following Jesus (i.e. discipleship) is not the disciples' but Jesus'.[49] This suggestion that Jesus is the initiator is reinforced when he gives Simon a new name, thereby providing the reader a prolepsis,[50] creating reader expectation and speculation concerning future events to be related that will make sense of this renaming. Quast has observed that for all the speculative interpretations of Peter's renaming offered by exegetes through the centuries, all are extratextual; unlike Matthew, the Fourth Gospel "leaves the final interpretation unsaid."[51]

Jesus' initiative in gathering disciples is further indicated by the declaration that Jesus "found" Philip (v. 43). Characters' difficulty in fully comprehending Jesus' identity and accepting his initiative is displayed when Philip claims to have been the "finder" rather than the "find" (v. 45).[52] This helps create reader anticipation of the potential for misunderstanding and misidentification as characters respond to meeting Jesus.

---

[48] Brodie, 158-159.
[49] Moloney, 68.
[50] Prolepses are textual references to future events not yet narrated, Gérard Genette, *Narrative Discourses: An Essay in Method*, trans. Jane E. Lewin (Ithica, NY: Cornell University Press, 1980), 68-77. For discussions of the use of prolepses in the Fourth Gospel see Culpepper, *Anatomy*, 61-68 and Adele Reinhartz, "Jesus as Prophet: Predictive Prolepses in the Fourth Gospel," *Journal for the Study of the New Testament* 36 (1989), 3-16.
[51] Quast, 39.
[52] Moloney, 70.

Jesus' meeting and dialogue with Nathanael is the most extended of the "snapshot" encounters which conclude the first chapter. For an informed reader/critic, much significant symbolism connects his encounter with the messianic hopes of ancient Israel. These include Old Testament allusions to Genesis and Zechariah and the use of the fig tree image for Israel. The first to bear the name Israel, Jacob (Gen 32:28), was noted for his guile (Gen 27:35) and witnessed angels ascending and descending a ladder (Gen 28:12). The fig tree under which Nathanael is found (1:48) alludes to Zech 3:10, "a man will call his neighbor under a vine and under a fig tree." Fig tree imagery is also found in 1 Kgs 4:25, Mic 4:4, and 1 Macc 14:11-12. The Old Testament imagery portrays Jesus as the fulfillment of messianic hope and Nathanael as a representative figure for Israel.[53]

Nathanael's skepticism concerning Jesus' origins concerns, according to Culbertson, "not only and specifically a village in Galilee, but the world and the flesh in which Jesus is rooted—the very obscurity in which he is discovered." The obscurity of origins is reinforced at Cana where the steward has no idea where the additional wine has come from (2:9), by Nicodemus' total inability to comprehend the concept of born ἄνωθεν (again/from above, 3:3-9), and by the blind man's incredulity at the Pharisees' ignorance of Jesus' origins (9:30).[54] The reader does not share this ignorance; any obscurity concerning Jesus' origins was eliminated by the declarations of the prologue. It does, however, signal that Jesus' identity and origins are hidden from other characters.

Would real readers many times removed from the Gospel's production, without the background knowledge of an informed reader/critic, recognize the Old Testament allusions? Almost certainly not, yet for any reader the narrative produces expectation and anticipation for what follows through the sheer variety of the characters Jesus has brought to him, who seek him out, or who are sought by him. The lack of particular information in a reader's extratext would not prevent the recognition of the variety of characters, means, and motivations among the narrated encounters with Jesus. For the reader, this allows for the possibility of a real encounter with Jesus through the Gospel, unhindered by time and distance or inability to duplicate a particular character's exact experience.

Sjef van Tilborg has assessed the formation of this band of followers according to their outward expansion from the initial juxtapositioning of Jesus and John. Jesus appears narratively in proximity to John, but not

---

[53] For a recent explication of this symbolism see Craig R. Koester, "Messianic Exegesis and the Call of Nathanael," *Journal for the Study of the New Testament* 39 (1990), 23-34.

[54] Culbertson, 165.

subordinate to him. Then two members of John's group transfer their allegiance to Jesus. This group then expands along the lines of family relations (Simon, the brother of Andrew, is brought next to Jesus). The next expansion includes one whom Jesus finds, probably not a disciple of John. The next addition to the growing number is one who needs convincing.[55] One of the first persons to become a follower of Jesus is renamed for no apparent reason, while another remains unidentified by name, family ties, ethnic or economic background. Another has a name probably indicating a representative of Hellenistic followers of Jesus, a role the text reinforces in 12:20-21 when Philip is chosen by Hellenists as their intermediary with Jesus. The final member of this group of four is introduced against a background of symbols for Israel, yet is found nowhere else in the New Testament except for a brief post-resurrection mention in 21:2 as a member of the group including the sons of Zebedee—the only reference to them in the Gospel.[56]

Not only is the readers' potential for inclusion among Jesus' followers assisted by the sheer variety of these first characters gathered as disciples, there is a generic quality about their portrayal. This is most fully expressed in the lingering anonymity of one of the first to become a follower of Jesus. The first chapter of the Gospel opens up possibilities for each reader's own encounter with Jesus, in and through the encounters of the Gospel characters. The primary role of witness in identifying with Jesus is indicated. Each encounter with Jesus is unique, however, warning the reader against the expectation of an exact blueprint match, while building potential for reader identification with these and other characters and ultimately, through them, with Jesus.

The purpose of the Fourth Gospel is far from hidden. Even the most obtuse reader, experiencing the prologue, would understand that the primary issue is Jesus' identity and appropriate response to him. The narrative does not leave this awareness to chance, declaring the narrative's primary persuasive purpose and the object of that persuasion: "that you might believe that Jesus is the Christ and believing you may have life in his name" (20:31).[57] The plot of the Fourth Gospel, repeated anew in each episodic encounter between Jesus and various characters, "is a matter of how Jesus' identity comes to be recognized...will Nicodemus, the Samaritan woman, or the lame man recognize Jesus and thereby receive

---

[55] Tilborg, 113-116.
[56] Brodie, 167.
[57] Martin Warner, "The Fourth Gospel's Art of Rational Persuasion," in *The Bible as Rhetoric: Studies in Biblical Persuasion and Credibility*, ed. Martin Warner, 153-77, Warwick Studies in Philosophy and Literature (London: Routledge, 1990), 153.

eternal life?"[58] What is expected of characters is also available to readers through identification with them, an identification dependent upon elements of their characterization.

An objection could be raised to the expectation that first-time readers would have the advantage of knowledge of the purpose statement in 20:30-31. But it is not necessary to posit a first-time reader in an interpretation of the reader's experience of the Gospel. Unlike many literary genres, "the gospels are intended by their implied authors to be read and re-read many times." In the final pages "the reader is given information at the end of the gospel which prompts a re-evaluation of the entire gospel."[59]

---

[58] Culpepper, *Anatomy*, 88.
[59] Reinhartz, *Word*, 12.

CHAPTER FIVE

ANONYMOUS WOMEN AND MODELS OF DISCIPLESHIP

Literary Frames

The Fourth Gospel's depiction of Jesus is not so much a portrait but a panoramic montage of overlapping images whose borders are indistinct. Though the borders of the individual sketches are admittedly blurred, when viewed through the eyes of a reader, "frames" can be detected focusing attention upon segments within the whole. The locations of the frames are not fixed; as the reader's focus shifts, one frame may become clear while another fades. Depending on a reader's extratext, recognition of particular frames will vary. For ancient texts like the Fourth Gospel, the extratext of its first readers would be radically different from that of a twentieth century reader. Modern readers also have different extratexts from one another. Factors creating this diversity include cultural distinctives, educational background, familiarity with first century Jewish culture, and the interpretive communities in which the reader is a participant (e.g., New Testament Scholarship, religious communities where the Fourth Gospel is a sacred text, or both).

Any reader may note the frame created by the double reference to Cana in the wine transformation in chapter 2 and the healing of the official's son in chapter 4. However, without either a critical or Jewish background, the "double frame" provided by the wedding in chapter 2, John as bridegroom in chapter 3, and the Old Testament betrothal type-scene at the well enacted between Jesus and the woman at Samaria may go unnoticed. This will alter, but not invalidate, a particular reader's experience and the meaning it produces.

In the Fourth Gospel several episodes are linked together by framing, a literary technique where an event, appearance of a character, or a geographic detail reminds the reader of an earlier appearance of the same event, person, or detail. An example of this is John's reappearance in 3:25-36, reminiscent of his statements in 1:19-34. The similarity of his appearances frames the material which comes between for the reader, in this instance the first sign in Cana of Galilee, the incident in the temple, and the encounter with Nicodemus. Another example of this phenomenon is Jesus going up to Jerusalem for the Passover in 2:13 and again for another festival in 5:1. These two Jerusalem journeys form boundaries around the temple disruption, the encounter with Nicodemus, John's reappearance, the meeting with the woman in Samaria and the healing of the official's[1] son.

There are many other examples of details that could frame episodes for the reader. The two appearances of the mother of Jesus at Cana and at the cross, first foreshadowing, then witnessing the fulfillment of his hour of glorification; the replacement of the real or supposed benefits of water with the efficacy of Jesus' word at the Cana wedding, Jacob's well, and the pool of Bethzatha; and the death and resurrection of Lazarus and Jesus' own death and resurrection are but a few of the possibilities. With adequate scrutiny a reader could formulate an almost indefinite number of examples of events framed by similar details. It is certain most readers will not notice all or even most of these boundaries, and no two readers will experience identical frames in reading the Fourth Gospel. As Adele Reinhartz has noted, "The length of the gospel, the number of characters, its theological complexity and other factors all create the possibility that one or another of the patterns, strands, or other points will be missed, even by an attentive reader."[2] To compensate for this probability, each of the episodic encounters between Jesus and various characters are self-contained and communicate the primary themes of the Gospel.[3] This does not invalidate the process by which literary frames focus attention on episodes gathered during reading. This study will frequently refer to details that remind the reader of previous episodes or anticipate narratively future events. In utilizing "framing" to interpret a narrative, it is necessary to be cautious concerning assumptions of the universality of a particular reading or its objective presence within the text.

From Cana to Cana: Women Disciples in the Fourth Gospel

One example of framing often noted by readers, and considered by many to mark one of the natural divisions within the Fourth Gospel, is provided by the two references to a "σημεῖον" in Cana (2:1-11 and 4:46-53), which are linked both "by localization and enumeration."[4] The wine

---

[1] Greek βασιλικός. Since it is impossible to determine with certainty the exact nature of this man's position (see below), we will retain the ambiguity of his designation by retaining the Greek or translating it with the neutral term "official."

[2] Adele Reinhartz, "Great Expectations: A Reader-Oriented Approach to Johannine Christology and Eschatology," *Journal of Literature and Theology* 3 (1989): 71.

[3] Kermode, "John," 451; cf. C. H. Dodd, *The Interpretation of the Fourth Gospel* (Cambridge: Cambridge University Press, 1968), 384.

[4] Schnackenburg, I. 464. On this section as a major division in the narrative see Brown, *John* I. cxxxviii-cxliv; Dodd, *Interpretation*, 289-90, 297; Francis J. Moloney, "From Cana to Cana (John 2:1-4:54) and the Fourth Evangelist's Concept of Correct (and

transformation and the healing of the son of the βασιλικός are connected for the reader and border a series of episodes where various characters encounter Jesus and respond to his word.[5] Within this frame, both the first and the textually most prominent of the people are women. Despite their status in the era of the Gospel's production and their lack of prominence in contemporaneous literature, Turid Seim accurately characterizes women in the Fourth Gospel: "There is no need to light a lamp and sweep the house and seek diligently in every nook and cranny to find the women in the Gospel of John."[6] Women come to the fore as paradigms of discipleship, modeling what it means to correctly understand Jesus' identity, enter into right relationship with him, and respond appropriately to his words. On many occasions women fare better than men in their understanding of and response to Jesus.[7] They have an existence independent of men that is quite extraordinary for literature of this era.[8] Their independence gives them evocative power that enables and enhances reader identification, especially for readers whose extratext includes a sense of disenfranchisement due to their gender or other factors.

Not every reader has agreed with dividing the narrative at 2:1 and 4:54. Some see a closer connection between 1:19-51 and 2:1-11, basing their decision upon the repetition of the theme of ἡμέρα.[9] Another alternative divides the narrative based on the journeys of Jesus, identifying the first unit after the prologue as 1:19-3:36.[10] The variety of proposed divisions illustrates the extent of the reader's influence on reading, and the importance of extratext in what each reader discovers "in the text."

Incorrect) Faith," in *Studia Biblica* 1978: II Papers on the Gospels, ed. E. A. Livingstone, Journal for the Study of the New Testament Supplement Series, no. 2 (Sheffield: JSOT Press, 1980), 187-89.

[5] Moloney, "Cana," 191.

[6] Turid Karlsen Seim, "Roles of Women in the Gospel of John," in *Aspects on the Johannine Literature: Papers Presented at a Conference of Scandinavian New Testament Exegetes at Uppsala, June 16-19, 1986*, ed. Lars Hartman and Birger Olsson, Coniectanea biblica, New Testament 18 (Uppsala: Almquist and Wiksell International, 1987), 57.

[7] Elizabeth Moltmann, *The Women Around Jesus*, trans. John Bowden (New York: Crossroad, 1987), 3; Fiorenza, 333; John Rena, Women in the Gospel of John," Église et Théologie 17 (1986): 145; Jane Kopas, "Critic's Corner: Jesus and Women: John's Gospel," *Theology Today* 41 (1984): 205.

[8] Tilborg, 171.

[9] see above chap. 4, note 26.

[10] Matthew Rissi, "Der Aufbau des vierten Evangeliums," *New Testament Studies* 29 (1983): 52; Staley, "Print's," 58-62.

The Mother of Jesus: A New Relationship

Immediately after Jesus promised the disciples they would see greater things than a supernatural awareness of Nathanael's repose (1:50), the reader encounters two tangible demonstrations of Jesus' identity and mission. A wedding is announced on "τῇ ἡμέρᾳ τῇ τρίτῃ (2:1). Many readers are reluctant to make much of this, admitting only that it "may be John's faint foreshadowing of the resurrection."[11] For readers whose communities revere the Jesus tradition, the "third day" associated with Jesus necessarily reminds them of the resurrection. This is supported by a close reading that reveals only here and in 2:19, where it is explicitly identified as a resurrection reference (2:22), is the number three used to refer to a period of days.[12]

The wedding begins with the first reference to Jesus' mother in the Fourth Gospel. Her role in this episode has been interpreted in vastly different ways, running the gamut from being numbered among those who "despite their good intentions, misunderstand Jesus," and "a representative of unbelief,"[13] to her portrayal as one who forces Jesus' hand by assuming command, advancing herself to center-stage so that "nobody, and most of all Jesus himself, can withdraw from her influence."[14]

Between these two extreme readings, an intriguing interpretation is offered by Turid Karlsen Seim, for whom Jesus' mother represents "a Johannine version of the familia Dei through which a new pneumatic birth/rebirth takes the place of a family relationship defined by the flesh...the mother must give way to the Father."[15] Her reading recognizes the crucial role of Jesus' relationship to his mother and links the passage with the immediate narrative context. The prologue informed the reader of Jesus' origins and his special relationship to God as his Father (1:14). Readers' understanding of Jesus as the one sent from God his Father is facilitated by the textual absence of a biological father. This absence "is opposed by the presence of an imaginary father...textually omnipresent. The absence of the one creates the space for the presence of the other."[16]

---

[11] Peter F. Ellis, *The Genius of John: A Composition-Critical Commentary on the Fourth Gospel* (Collegeville, Minn.: Liturgical Press, 1984), 41.

[12] Brodie, 131.

[13] Raymond Brown E., Karl P. Donfried, Joseph A. Fitzmyer, and John Reumann, eds., *Mary in the New Testament: A Collaborative Assessment by Protestant and Roman Catholic Scholars* (Philadelphia: Fortress, 1978; New York: Paulist, 1978), 193; Matthew Rissi, "Die Hochzeit in Kana (Joh 2, 1-11)," in *Oikonomia: Oscar Cullman gewidmet*, ed. F. Christ, 76-92, (Hamburg: Reich, 1967), 88.

[14] Tilborg, 243.

[15] Seim, 62.

[16] Tilborg, 32.

After a partial guest list is given, the story turns to a catering *faux pas*; the wine gives out, and Jesus' mother informs him. Many have speculated about her state of mind, motives, and expectations.[17] The ambiguity of her motives and expectations require extratextual supplementation. The ambiguity is retained in Brown's cautious reading: "Mary does seem to expect some action or answer on Jesus' part. The exact nature of that expectation is not clear from the narrative, and none of the many guesses by the commentators is convincing."[18] More suggestive for its effect on readers is the undermining of the filial relationship between Jesus and his mother.

The explicit identification of Jesus' mother by this most poignant of human relationships, followed by Jesus' failure to acknowledge her as "Mother," is revealing. It signals the reader that there is more to this mother/son relationship that needs clarification. Instead of mother, Jesus addresses her as γύναι. This is not necessarily the harsh "woman" it becomes in English translation, but is better captured by the polite, but formal "Madam." This is Jesus' normal address for women in the Gospels, and will be used by him with the Samaritan, the adulterous woman, and Mary of Magdala (4:21, 8:10, 20:13). It is not any harshness inherent in this address that is startling, but rather its addressee, Jesus' mother. "Mother," with all of the intimacy and warmth implied therein, is precisely what Jesus does not call her. As an address by a son for his mother, γύναι is unique, having no Jewish or Greco-Roman parallels.[19] It "distances Jesus from his biological mother and rejects any claims she might have on him because of her family relationship to him."[20] Simultaneously, by associating her with others whom Jesus addresses in like manner, it places her on equal footing with the Samaritan woman and Mary of Magdala, both of whom have been identified by some readers as "apostolic witnesses and exemplary disciples."[21]

The meaning of Jesus' rebuke of his mother's expectations is almost as difficult to determine as the precise knowledge of the content of her expectations. Interpretations of the Semitic idiom τί ἐμοὶ καὶ σοί range from the allegorizing of D'Sa who paraphrases the dialogue:

---

[17] e.g. Edward J Kilmartin, "The Mother of Jesus was there: The Significance of Mary in Jn 2, 3-5 and Jn 19, 25-27," *Sciences Ecclesiastiques* 15 (1963): 215, who speaks of "certainty" in assessing Mary's psychological state.

[18] Brown, *John*, I, 102.

[19] Brown, Donfried, et al., 188.

[20] Ibid.

[21] Elizabeth Schüssler Fiorenza, *In Memory of Her: A Feminist Theological Reconstruction of Christian Origins* (New York: Crossroads, 1983), 327. On the validity of this identification, see discussion of each below.

Mother: 'They do not have the Spirit.'
Son: 'This is really no concern of ours. For when the Spirit will be given out is determined only by the Father';

to the brief assessment by Haenchen that "Jesus gruffly refuses."[22] The ambiguity of the phrase is indicated by Birger Olsson who states that its meaning depends "on context and intonation...always dominated by strong tensions...then marks a protest, a serious objection."[23] Schnackenburg's examination of its parallels in Old Testament and Jewish literature as well as Greek and Hellenistic writings lead to his conclusion that it never means "What concern is that of yours and mine," a common interpretation.[24] It actually denotes a distance and distinction between the addressee and the speaker. This is supported by its appearance on the lips of demons in all five of its Synoptic parallels (Mt 8:29, Mk 5:7, Lu 8:28, Mk 1:24, Lu 4:34).[25] In each, its purpose is to delineate the identity of the demons from Jesus and to challenge Jesus' association with Satan's work. Regardless of any harshness possibly inherent in this idiom, the Synoptic parallels reinforce the surprising coolness and distance suggested by γύναι. The interchange challenges a casual reading and creates a tension in readers regarding their response to the narrative.[26]

Jesus provides the clue to the meaning of his words when he adds "οὔπω ἥκει ἡ ὥρα μου" (My hour has not yet come, 2:4). The initial reference here to Jesus' "hour" remains unexplained. Readers may provide the meaning extratextually, or its explanation could be still lie ahead in the narrative;[27] both are possible. Readers familiar with the kerygma of the Christian faith through their participation in communities of believers, either ancient or modern, would have as a part of their extratext familiarity with the phrase "my hour," referring to Jesus' crucifixion and its soteriological significance. A reader unaware of the kerygma would be alerted for textual clues to its meaning. According to Moloney, this strange reference to Jesus' mother's position "'outside' a mysterious 'hour' that is part of some unknowable union between the Father and the Son,"[28] creates reader expectation that more explanation is forthcoming and increases sensitivity to its presence when it appears. It places "the

---

[22] D'Sa, 52; Haenchen, 176.
[23] Birger Olsson, *Structure and Meaning in the Fourth Gospel: A Text-Linguistic Analysis of John 2:1-11 and 4:1-42*, Coniectanea biblica, New Testament 6 (Lund, Sweden: CWK Gleerup, 1974), 38.
[24] Schnackenburg, I. 328.
[25] Arthur H. Maynard, "ΤΙ ΕΜΟΙ ΚΑΙ ΣΟΙ," *New Testament Studies* 31 (1985): 582.
[26] Reinhartz, "Great Expectations," 66.
[27] Culpepper, *Anatomy*, 222.
[28] Moloney, *Belief*, 81.

whole narrative under the shadow of a 'not yet'," leaving the reader unsatisfied and looking ahead.[29]

Jesus will repeat the reference by the well in Samaria (4:21, 23), speaking of a time of revolutionary worship, and again near a pool called Bethzatha outside Jerusalem after the Sabbath healing of the infirm man (5:25, 28). In both instances the time is narratively nearer as Jesus adds the phrase, "καὶ νῦν ἐστίν" (4:23, 5:25). The animosity towards Jesus becomes more animated, but attempts to take him by force are thwarted, not through any act of intervention, but because "his hour had not yet come" (7:30, 8:20), revealing God's sovereignty regarding his hour.[30] It is only in 12:23, in the passion narrative, that it is stated that Jesus' hour has come. All remaining references to Jesus' hour confirm that in his passion his hour has arrived (12:27, 13:1, 16:32, 17:1).

Whether readers already possesses an understanding of Jesus' hour or arrive at one it through their reading experience, Jesus clearly makes the "not yet" status of "his hour" the basis for his response distancing him from his mother and calling into question the significance of their biological relationship.[31] Jesus' rebuke signals the need for his mother to redefine her understanding of his identity, as do readers who share his mother's misconceptions. A newly revealed hierarchy is in place defining his role exclusively in terms of his Father's sovereignty, with no place for human familial obligation.[32]

Even more surprising than Jesus' address/rebuke is his mother's response to it. She responds in a paradigmatic manner which will be repeated among significant anonymous characters, and lacking or deficient in the response of many named characters. She not only accepts his revelation of his unique identity and the reevaluation of her relationship to him it implies, she bears witness to the efficacy of his words and challenges others to heed what he says (2:5). Her response is not verbal affirmation or confession; verbal responses alone are usually evaluated negatively by the Fourth Gospel for their lack of understanding. Instead she herself accepts his word, and believes its power, prior to and without benefit of any "sign," and bears witness of it to someone else. The pattern will be repeated in the portrayal of the Samaritan woman, the βασιλικός, the infirm man at Bethzatha, the blind man, and in a special way in the disciple Jesus loved.

---

[29] Ibid., 88-89.
[30] Schnackenburg, I. 330.
[31] Brodie, 174; Tilborg, 5; Maynard, 585.
[32] Marianne Meye Thompson, *The Humanity of Jesus in the Fourth Gospel* (Philadelphia: Fortress, 1988), 74; Brown, *John*, I. 109; Bultmann, *John*, 117.

Jesus' mother's response is not a complete comprehension of Jesus' meaning or his soteriological role and significance, as D'Sa and others would have it.[33] Nor is it the power-move some have claimed, forcing Jesus' hand, giving him no choice but to perform an act he does not want to do.[34] Her response is one of faith and witness, even without full comprehension. Its wonder lies in what immediately precedes it in 2:4, Jesus' jarring address/rebuke. While his answer is surprising, the prologue's revelation of Jesus' identity and origins combined with readers' extratextual knowledge of the Jesus tradition cause "surprising" behavior/words from Jesus to be, if not expected, at least "appropriate." His mother, on the other hand, is not privy to this information, and her positive reaction and failure to challenge Jesus concerning his enigmatic words (something neither Nicodemus nor the Samaritan woman are hesitant to do), demonstrates an amazing sense of appropriate response to Jesus, coming prior to the revelation his "hour" will provide. Her response leaves to him the option to act, and the nature of any action is fully in Jesus' control. Her directions to the servants "do not anticipate Jesus' action, since the conditional and generalized relative clause does not oblige Jesus to speak and does not determine what he may say."[35] If we are correct in our assessment that Jesus' address/rebuke was an indication that only his Father and he would determine when and how he would reveal himself, his mother appears both to receive and to accept that message.

The actual sign itself is not narrated, and is "discovered" by one who has no indication of anything out of the ordinary occurring (other than holding back the "good" wine, 2:9). Instead, the reader's attention focuses on the source of the water and the abundance and quality of the product. The symbolism contained in the miraculous transformation of the water into wine and the details surrounding it have been discussed at length.[36] The most frequently noted symbolism is that of Messianic significance, eschatological wine, Wisdom, and the eucharist. Brodie suggests that within the wedding context, the wine transformation symbolizes "the ultimate togetherness of Jesus with his Father...and suggests intimate two-way communication."[37] Michael Edwards looks to the sign's proximity to Peter's re-naming and suggests that "by placing the trans-

---

[33] D'Sa, 52; cf. Joseph A. Grassi, "The Role of Jesus' Mother in John's Gospel," *Catholic Biblical Quarterly* 48 (1986): 78.
[34] Stibbe, 45; Tilborg, 6.
[35] Schnackenburg, I. 331.
[36] For a concise summary see Schnackenburg, I. 337-40.
[37] Brodie, 173.

formation of the water so soon after the transformation of a name, John is perhaps imitating the role of language itself in creation."[38]

The above symbolism may help readers produce meaning from the narrative, depending upon their familiarity with the Old Testament and Jewish messianic narratives, mythological wine legends, or other components of various symbolic interpretations as a part of the content of their extratext. Readers would also need to connect certain details, such as wine and the eucharist or the intimacy of a marriage and the wedding setting of this sign at Cana, with or without the help of an interpreter.

While most of these symbolic elements are not textually obvious, one symbolic element is underscored in the narrative itself. It is found in the comment that these water containers had a specific purpose, "for the Jewish rites of purification" (2:6). While it is certainly possible to overlook this comment as an unnecessary detail, a reader who takes note of it will find its significance confirmed by incidents to follow in the narrative. Immediately after Jesus transforms the water reserved for "Jewish purification rites" into wine, he strides into the temple, the central symbol of the Jewish faith, and at the very least disrupts business as usual. He then proceeds to make shocking predictions of its destruction (2:13-19). In the pericope immediately following the temple disruption, Jesus is approached at night by one who embodies everything the temple represents. Jesus thoroughly confuses him by telling him of the need for a new birth from above (3:3). Within this environment, and conscious of the replacement nature of the wine transformation, one symbolic understanding of the first Cana sign is the replacement of the old, embodied in cultic Judaism, with the new, embodied in Jesus.[39]

The episode at the Cana wedding closes with a statement identifying the act as Jesus' first σημεῖον, and declaring that it revealed Jesus' glory and produced belief in his disciples (2:11). "σημεῖον" used to describe a miraculous occurrence is not unique; in fact, the LXX uses it (e.g. Exodus 4:8).[40] Surprise at its use here is due to readers' extratextual awareness of the Synoptic miracle tradition and its designation of Jesus' miracles as δυνάμεις. Even for a reader unaware of this Synoptic designation, the choice of σημεῖον to designate the wine transformation shifts readers'

---

[38] Michael Edwards, "The World Could not Contain the Books," in *The Bible as Rhetoric: Studies in Biblical Persuasion and Credibility*, Warwick Studies in Philosophy and Literature, ed. Martin Warner (London: Routledge, 1990), 189.

[39] C. K. Barrett, *The Gospel According to John: An Introduction with Commentary and Notes on the Greek Text*, 2d ed. (Philadelphia: Westminster, 1978), 192; Schnackenburg, 339.

[40] Barrett, 75-78.

focus from Jesus' action to its meaning.[41] The reference to Jesus' δόξα indicates that his action is a manifestation of his glory, echoing its previous appearance in the prologue, but it leaves the reader puzzling over exactly how the wine transformation revealed Jesus' glory, and to whom. The wedding participants and guests are in the dark concerning Jesus' role in the production of the wine. Only his mother, disciples, and the servants appear to know that Jesus has any association with the wine.

The belief engendered in Jesus' disciples, however, is merely stated, not detailed. The reader is satisfied for the moment, but will soon be offered a corrective to a completely positive evaluation of their belief. After the temple disruption, the reader learns that their belief in his word was only a post-resurrection occurrence (2:22). Furthermore, "many believed (ἐπίστευσαν) in his name when they saw the σημεῖα which he did; but Jesus did not trust (οὐκ ἐπίστευεν) himself to them" (2:23-24). In Brodie's words "πιστεύω" is the heartbeat of the gospel, and the negating of that verb—for the first time in the gospel, and by Jesus!—means that in some sense the heart has missed a beat."[42] A belief based on "seeing signs" is cause for suspicion; its untrustworthiness is revealed by Jesus' wariness. Yet the sign is precisely the basis for his disciples' belief after the Cana wine transformation, requiring a reevaluation of the disciples' response.

What has been established concerning an appropriate response to Jesus? If the belief of Jesus' disciples is less than exemplary, as is soon revealed, the responses of other characters are more positively portrayed. The response of Jesus' mother is not denigrated, though her initial request may have been. Without any "sign" or stated reason for her belief, other than Jesus' words themselves, "she has communicated her trust in the word of Jesus through this command to the servants...She bases her confidence in an unshakable trust that Jesus' word will be efficacious."[43] The transformation of the water into wine is not through any physical manipulation of the water by Jesus, but through the servants' acceptance of Jesus' word.[44] Just as the prologue and the narrative beginning emphasizes the witness of John and the role of his witness in leading others to encounter Jesus, the embodiment of the λόγος (see chapter 3 above); so also the sign at Cana is accomplished through Jesus' mother's witness to the to the efficacy of Jesus' words. This pattern will be repeated throughout the narrative when unnamed characters encounter Jesus. The implicit

---

[41] Barnabas Lindars, *The Gospel of John*, New Century Bible Commentary (Grand Rapids, Mich.: Eerdmans, 1972), 132.
[42] Brodie, 192.
[43] Moloney, *Belief*, 83-84.
[44] Brodie, 173.

warning against needing to see to believe (2:23-25) is reinforced by its position within the frame of the two Cana miracles, both of which occur off the narrative stage, revealed by unknowing witnesses without any knowledge of Jesus' participation in what has occurred.[45]

Jesus' mother heeds the words of Jesus, and she is able to accept correction of her understanding of his identity and her relationship to him. She accepts and believes in his ability prior to any "sign" or demonstration of what he can or will do. She responds by witnessing to others the need to obey his word, while putting no restrictions on its content or consequences. This pattern of committing to Jesus' word then witnessing to others concerning it, first experienced in Jesus' mother, "provides a model response to Jesus which may be understood as an expression of authentic faith."[46]

The unusual and unexpected address of Jesus for his mother, the accompanying rebuke, the failure to narrate the actual transformation, and the continuing ignorance of the source of the wine by its recipients; all heighten awareness of the act's significance, yet leave the reader puzzling over its meaning. The commonly recognized use of the historic present tense, especially in narrative speaking (λέγει 2:3, 4, 5, 7, 8, 10) "lifts the spoken word out of the past and makes it a speech-event for the reader."[47] These signals of the significance of this σημεῖον and the historic present tense draw the reader into participation in the narrative world.[48]

How is the reader enabled to enter into the events and dialogue to fully participate in them? Many discordant elements present themselves, initially grabbing readers' attention. These include the ambiguity of identity created by the anonymity of Jesus' mother, particularly if her name is familiar to readers, who would then expect its occurrence in her narrative. When the expectation of its presence is strong enough, her name may be "read" even when absent. This occurs whenever a reader refers to "Mary's" presence in the Fourth Gospel, and by readers who make reference to her name, such as Kermode's assertion that she exemplifies the Evangelist's preference "to deal with named persons."[49] Kermode's questionable assertion ignores both the prominence and the anonymity of the Samaritan woman (chapter 4), the blind man (chapter 9), and the disciple Jesus loved (chapters 13-21). Readers' ability to accept the anonymity of Jesus' mother prepare them to enter and participate in her encounter with

---

[45] Staley, 86.
[46] Moloney, *Belief*, 92.
[47] Stibbe, 47.
[48] Culpepper, 31.
[49] Kermode, "John," 11.

Jesus, accessing her openness to a new understanding of Jesus, her response of faith, and her role as witness.

If it is assumed that most of the first readers of the Gospel were familiar with the kerygma of the earliest Christian communities, would the mother of Jesus have been an unknown figure? If she was not, then they, as well as later readers, would know her identification as Mary of Nazareth. If this information was part of their extratext, then her anonymity would be all the more striking. It is interesting that some readers have not only ignored her anonymity, but, in effect, denied it. Bultmann states that "she must be mentioned explicitly by name, because of the role she will presently have to play."[50] Her presence is specified, her relationship to Jesus is noted, but "by name" is precisely how she is not designated. As the first unnamed character to have an extended textual presence and dialogue with Jesus, how does her characterization effect the reader? The absence of the excluding function of names removes one potential barrier to reader identification with her, enabling readers to make her response to Jesus their own. Since names not only identify, but exclude as well,[51] when readers identify Jesus' mother by name, supplying the name "Mary of Nazareth" from their extratext, full reader identification is thwarted. However, once the reader notes her anonymity, and her familial relationship to Jesus is altered, then readers can more easily identify with her, especially if their life experiences closely parallel hers. Most parents eventually need to reconfigure their understanding of their relationship with adult children who can no longer be expected to act merely because of parental request. The parallels between their experience and the challenge faced by Jesus' mother can provide them an entry point into the narrative.

Although Jesus' mother disappears from the scene somewhat abruptly, she will make another appearance, at the cross (19:25-27) with the disciple Jesus loved that will be examined in chapter 7 below. It is important to note that Jesus' challenge to his mother's understanding of their relationship is connected to the "not yet" status of his "hour" and that her next appearance is in the midst of that hour and its climax on the cross. "Jesus' mother has, and apparently can have, no role until that time...She has nothing more to do with him until his hour has come."[52]

---

[50] Bultmann, *John*, 115.
[51] William W. Watty, "The Significance of Anonymity in the Fourth Gospel," *The Expository Times* 90 (1979): 212.
[52] Culpepper, *Anatomy*, 133.

Nicodemus: Out of the Dark?

Turning to Nicodemus, the next character with significant textual space, there is a marked contrast between his lack of response and the positive responses of the two anonymous women on either side of his textual location. An interesting juxtapositioning of Jesus' mother and Nicodemus occurs in the Gospel, illustrated in Table 5. In 6:42 Jesus' mother is referenced but not present (the only mention of her in the Fourth Gospel outside of chapters 2 and 19) in the midst of a dispute over Jesus' origins. The Jews refute his statements about his origins as one from above, sent from his Father, by identifying him as one of them, whose mother and father (named) are known to them. The reader knows that their identification of his origins and lineage is faulty and needs reconfiguring, just as his mother has already done.

Table 5: Juxtaposition of Nicodemus and Jesus' Mother

Jesus' Mother		Nicodemus	
wedding at Cana	2:1-11	by night	3:1-12
referenced (not present) during dispute over Jesus' origin	6:42	present during dispute over Jesus' origins	7:45-52
at the cross	19:25-27	at the cross	19:38-42

Nicodemus' appearance in chapter 7 is also in the midst of a dispute concerning Jesus' identity and origins. At the very least, alerted to the significance of anonymous and named characters and the contrast between them, readers noticing the proximity of these references to Jesus' mother and Nicodemus, will focus on the differences between them in their contrasting responses to Jesus.

The primary question concerning the characterization of Nicodemus in the Fourth Gospel is how the reader should evaluate him. Does he remain a negative example of the unbelieving Jews or does his understanding of and commitment to Jesus develop to the point of his portrayal in chapter 19 as a valid model of discipleship? Readers are divided on this issue. Brown views Nicodemus as a positive paradigm of discipleship and states that Nicodemus represents those "among the Jewish leaders who hesitatingly came to believe in Jesus."[53] Bolder still are Moloney's assessment that "Nicodemus will make his own journey into faith (and into the Jo-

---

[53] Brown *John*, I. 129.

hannine community)," and Gibbons who compares Nicodemus to Lazarus as "each is brought from darkness to light." Gibbons further refers to Nicodemus' "final success" and says that in the end he "came forward in faith."[54] A very different assessment is offered by those who preclude the possibility of Nicodemus as a positive paradigm of discipleship. Culpepper states "he remains, therefore, 'one of them'...he remains outside," and Rensberger, who characterizes Nicodemus' appearance at the cross as "more likely an act of unbelief," declaring that the text shows him having "nothing to do with Jesus except with his corpse...Nicodemus does not expect a resurrection anymore than he expects a second birth."[55]

Either option is possible, but each requires the Fourth Gospel to be supplemented from the reader's extratext. The characterization of Nicodemus in his three appearances is ambiguous, demonstrated by the certainty with which interpreters have been able to argue their diametrically opposed positions. Indeed, some readers attempt to straddle the fence of ambiguity, accepting the indeterminacy concerning Nicodemus' ultimate fate. Margaret Pamment has characterized him as "the only individual character who fails to make a decision," uncondemned but uncommitted.[56] Jouette M. Bassler investigates the "mixed signals" readers find in the Gospel's characterization of Nicodemus, who "appears in the narrative often enough to evoke curiosity, but not, it seems, often enough to satisfy it."[57] The ambiguity of Nicodemus' portrayal results from many textual features, including the perspectives from which the reader can view and evaluate Nicodemus. Among these are "his point of origin (the 'Jews,' Pharisees, night) and his present location (coming to Jesus, confessing him as teacher sent from God, defending him, attending to his burial rites)."[58]

---

[54] Moloney, *Belief*, 120; Debbie Gibbons, "Nicodemus: Character Development, Irony and Repetition in the Fourth Gospel," *in Proceedings: Eastern Great Lakes and Midwest Biblical Societies* 11 (1991): 119, 120, 123; also see Beasley-Murray, 359; Brodie, 559; Lindars, 592; Schnackenburg, III. 296-7; Sandra M. Schneiders, "Born Anew," *Theology Today* 44:2 (1987): 194-6.

[55] Culpepper, *Anatomy*, 136; David Rensberger, *Johannine Faith and Liberating Community* (Philadelphia: Westminster, 1988), 40; see also Raymond F. Collins, "Representative Figures in the Fourth Gospel," *The Downside Review* 94 (1976): 36; J. Louis Martyn, *History and Theology in the Fourth Gospel*, rev. ed. (Nashville: Abingdon, 1979), 86-9; Wayne Meeks, "The Man from Heaven in Johannine Sectarianism," Journal of Biblical Literature 91 (1972): 113-55; Dennis D. Sylva, "Nicodemus and His Spices," *New Testament Studies* 34 (1988):148-51.

[56] Margaret Pamment, "Focus in the Fourth Gospel," *The Expository Times* 97.3 (1985): 73.

[57] Jouette M. Bassler, "Mixed Signals: Nicodemus in the Fourth Gospel," *Journal of Biblical Literature* 108 (1989): 635.

[58] Ibid., 643.

Nicodemus is introduced immediately following the first caution concerning a belief based on signs (2:23). That warning comes on the heels of Jesus' challenge to the old and obsolete understandings of long established Jewish traditions in the Cana wine transformation's explicit reference to Jewish purification (2:6) and the temple disruption (2:31-22). Nicodemus arrives on the scene in chapter 3 and is immediately identified as a representative of those very traditions, both "ἐκ τῶν Φαρισαίων" and "ἄρχων τῶν Ἰουδαίων" (3:1), "a specimen upper-class Jew."[59] Dodd says it is almost as if the Gospel warns the reader, "Here comes one of them now, those whom Jesus knows better than to trust."[60]

Two details claiming readers' attention in Nicodemus' first appearance is the nocturnal nature of his visit and his preconceived evaluation of Jesus' identity (3:2). The choice of the cover of night for his visit to Jesus is often viewed as an indication of Nicodemus' fear and as a symbol of the darkness of ignorance evil men prefer (3:19-20), the very darkness Jesus came as the light to pierce and dispel (2:5).[61] An alternative reading offered by Bultmann suggests the practice of nighttime study and debate was lauded by the Rabbis; thus, his arrival at night is "more likely...intended to show his great zeal."[62] The ambiguity is better retained by Bassler: "If it is true that Nicodemus came by night, it is equally true that he came to Jesus."[63]

The second detail for scrutiny is Nicodemus' evaluation of Jesus in his initial address. He demonstrates respect and some recognition, aware that Jesus' origins are divine and acknowledging him as a διδάσκαλος from God.[64] Jesus will apply the same recognition as "teacher" to Nicodemus in 3:10, but there some readers have detected a hint that Nicodemus feels confident he is on an equal footing with Jesus, as "one teacher to another."[65] A reading of Nicodemus' intention to engage in theological discussion on an equal footing with a fellow teacher, however, requires extratextual supplementation. Explicit are his position within established Judaism and the temporal setting of his encounter with Jesus. His motivation for coming, information he sought, or questions he came prepared

---

[59] Frank Kermode, "New Ways with Bible Stories," in *Parable and Story in Judaism and Christianity*, ed. Clemons Thoma and Michael Whschogrod (New York: Paulist, 1989), 130.
[60] Dodd, *Interpretation*, 303; Barrett, 206; John W. Pryor, *John: Evangelist of the Covenant People: The Narrative and Themes of the Fourth Gospel* (Downers Grove, Illinois: InterVarsity Press, 1992), 18.
[61] Brown, *John*, I. 130.
[62] Bultmann, *John*, 145.
[63] Bassler, 638.
[64] Ibid., 637.
[65] Brodie, 196; Rensberger, 39.

to ask are indeterminate.[66] Before Nicodemus can move beyond polite address and the understanding of Jesus it implies, he is challenged by Jesus to a new understanding of the kingdom of God. Jesus takes the initiative, establishes the ground rules, and undercuts any sense of equality or priority that might be suggested by Nicodemus' initial query.[67]

The Nicodemus dialogue/monologue contains echoes of the prologue. Birth is the subject of both 3:3-8 and 1:12-13.[68] The theme of witness occurs here in verses 11-12, echoing the witness of John (1:6-8). Jesus' heavenly origins are echoed in 3:13; the theme of life (1:4) reappears in 3:15-16; the opposition of light and darkness first narrated in 1:4-5 is restated in 3:19-21. Nicodemus responds to Jesus' teachings with incredulity and dwindling speech, apparently unable to understand and believe what Jesus is saying.[69] His contributions to the dialogue lessen until, in the end, Jesus delivers a monologue to unidentified addressees, and Nicodemus disappears from the narrative, at least for the moment. He is never portrayed leaving nor reacting to Jesus' words after Jesus' final address to him in verse 10. His verbal output in verse two amounts to 24 words, in verse four this reduces to 18, and with his final contribution in verse nine he produces only four words, demonstrating to the reader a deflation of his conversational importance and personal evaluation.[70]

Nicodemus' words are progressively less an answer and more a confession of misunderstanding. His answer in 3:4 picks up the thread of Jesus' statement, advancing the conversation with his query of possibility and his attempt to prove Jesus' declaration ludicrous, but his final words in 3:9 merely express confusion, indicating that, according to Meeks, "the first and primary message of this dialogue is thus simply that Jesus is incomprehensible to Nicodemus."[71] Reversing the downward spiral of Nicodemus' words, Jesus' responses to Nicodemus become progressively longer (3:3, 3:5-8, 3:10-21). The increasing length of Jesus' words gains the narrative advantage over Nicodemus' increasingly shorter utterances.[72]

The reader is directly addressed in Jesus' dialogue/monologue with Nicodemus. Even if readers do not sense their inclusion in Nicodemus' use of plural verb forms (i.e. "we know," 3:2), the plural forms indicate that Nicodemus represents to others besides himself an example of possi-

---

[66] Barrett, 202.
[67] Cottrell, F. P, "The Nicodemus Conversation: A Fresh Appraisal," *The Expository Times* 96 (1985): 239.
[68] Peterson, 44.
[69] Meeks, 149; Moloney, *Belief*, 115-6; Culpepper, *Anatomy*, 136.
[70] Cotterell, 240.
[71] Meeks, 148.
[72] Brodie, 195.

ble response to Jesus. Jesus also uses the plural form of address (3:7, 11-12), thereby directly addressing readers.[73] Nicodemus' indecision appears to stem from his inability/unwillingness to make any response to Jesus. Two response options are presented by this dialogue, acceptance or rejection of a new birth from above; Nicodemus opts out of choosing between them. They are established by the contrast between "Jesus with his extraordinary word about a rebirth from above" (3:3), and "Nicodemus with his 'commonsense' reply" (3:4).[74] Jesus' monologue, drawing on themes from the prologue, places the options in distinctly antipathetic terms. There are clear polarities of destruction/eternal life (3:16), condemnation/salvation (3:17), belief/unbelief (3:18), light/darkness (3:19-21). The narrative "challenges the reader to recognize that a decision must be made...one cannot be indifferent."[75] According to the paradigm established by Jesus' mother at Cana, Nicodemus' response to Jesus here is not merely inadequate, it is non-existent. He fails to indicate any acceptance, or even comprehension of Jesus' word. He never makes an active faith response to Jesus, or even a verbal confession. He does not witness to anyone concerning what he has seen and heard from Jesus. His is not a wrong response, but a non-response.

By the conclusion of Jesus' monologue, Nicodemus' initial involvement seems insignificant. His disappearance is real, but not permanent, as he reappears twice in the Gospel. Readers who argue for a positive portrayal of Nicodemus as a model of discipleship[76] base their claim on the progression they perceive in the second and final appearances of Nicodemus. While acknowledging his failure in chapter 3, they point out that "Nicodemus keeps coming back, back to Jesus as well as back into the narrative."[77] Bassler's recognition of Nicodemus' ambiguity refutes that assessment. Nicodemus does keep reappearing, each occurrence signaling the need to withhold final judgment until all the evidence is in, but what Nicodemus *never* does is return *to Jesus*.

Although Jesus is not present with Nicodemus and the rest of the Jewish leadership in chapter 7, he is the central focus of their concerns, and once more the portrayal of Nicodemus is ambiguous. He does not "champion Jesus,"[78] and while he does speak against an improper and illegal plot against Jesus, his "defense" is more accurately a concern for

---

[73] Moloney, *Belief*, 115; Haenchen, 201.
[74] Moloney, *Belief*, 114.
[75] Ibid., 119.
[76] See note 58 above.
[77] Bassler, 638.
[78] Contra Haenchen, II. 18.

the legality of the proceedings."[79] His reference to "our law" (7:51), from the Fourth Gospel's perspective would seem to place him among the Pharisaic proponents of the law.[80] The identification of Nicodemus as "one of them" (7:50) has been read with two different antecedents. Is he one of the "authorities and Pharisees" or one of the crowd they consider "cursed?"[81] On the basis of his designation "teacher of Israel" at his earlier nocturnal appearance, one might believe the former. On the other hand, a positive evaluation of Nicodemus in chapter 7 is suggested by the reaction of his fellow Pharisees to the technical point of law he raises; they seem to "read it as pro-Christian."[82] His allegiance remains an open question, especially in light of his failure to seize the opportunity presented to openly declare his belief in, and response to, Jesus. Stibbe appears correct that "the reader is certainly meant to view Nicodemus as 'the best of a bad lot'."[83]

The assertion above that Nicodemus never comes back to Jesus could be challenged on the basis of his final appearance in chapter 19. Something of a positive progression on Nicodemus' part can be read in this final appearance. Whereas before he came at night and passed on the opportunity to declare allegiance to Jesus, he now responds openly with a public act of devotion. Nonetheless, ambiguity remains despite his acting openly; there is no expression of faith and Jesus is not present, only his lifeless body remains.[84] Stibbe considers this "a burial fit for the king of kings,"[85] but weighing down Jesus' body with 'one hundred pounds' of embalming spices clearly indicates that he does not understand Jesus' death.[86] Does Nicodemus come back to Jesus? The "Word become flesh" first introduced in the prologue is narratively present until 19:30 when Jesus declares "$\tau\epsilon\tau\acute{\epsilon}\lambda\epsilon\sigma\tau\alpha\iota$" and surrenders his spirit." He physically reappears in the text at 20:14, but during the interval between his "hour" on the cross (19:30) and his reappearance in chapter 20, Jesus' body does not suffice for his presence. His own words support this in 16:7 when he states his going is to his disciples' advantage, and in 20:17 when he rebukes Mary of Magdala for clinging to him.

---

[79] Bassler, 640.
[80] Rensberger, 39.
[81] Marla J. Selvidge, "Nicodemus and the Woman with Five Husbands," in *Proceedings, Eastern Great Lakes Biblical Society* 2, ed. P. Sigal. (1982): 69.
[82] Kermode, "New Ways," 131.
[83] Stibbe, 94.
[84] Sarah J. Tanzer, "Salvation is of the Jews: Secret Christians in the Gospel of John," in *The Future of Early Christianity: Essays in Honor of Helmut Koester*, ed. Birger A. Pearson (Minneapolis: Fortress, 1991), 292.
[85] Stibbe, 197
[86] Meeks, 149.

The argument that Nicodemus is a positive model of discipleship must assume that he changes his allegiance from the Pharisees in chapter 3 to his explicit identification as a disciple, albeit a secret one, in chapter 19. As evidence for this claim, his speech is said to be replaced by action: from the relative verbosity of chapter 3, through the single cautious utterance of chapter 7, to the action of burial in chapter 19. It is further argued that he has moved from darkness and its surrounding secrecy into the light of a public act.[87] An opposite reading of the same "evidence" understands his silence in chapter 19 not as a positive progression to action but as part of his negative characterization. He is silent in response to Jesus (3:11-21), the taunting of the Pharisees (7:52), and in the presence of Joseph of Arimethea request for Jesus' body from the authorities.[88]

How can we evaluate Nicodemus as a model of response to Jesus' witness to his identity? Nicodemus' final allegiance is an unresolved indeterminacy in the Fourth Gospel. His first and most extensive textual appearance is framed by the two scenes disclosing John's faithful witness (1:19-34 and 3:25-36). His three appearances are juxtaposed with the two appearances of Jesus' mother and the single reference to her. Her first episode established the criteria for a paradigmatic response to Jesus' identity. It requires an acceptance of and belief in the efficacy of his word, and a faith response of bearing witness to the power of his word to others; Nicodemus fails on both counts. Appropriately his name stands as a barrier to reader identification with the response model he offers.

A reading that accepts Nicodemus' ambiguous characterization will not pass final judgment on his response to Jesus. He stands in the text as a potential disciple who has progressed toward, but has not yet arrived at an appropriate response to Jesus. Bassler is right that "what is needed to bring closure to Nicodemus is a final, definite encounter with Jesus, but none is recorded in the text."[89] Instead the narrative challenges readers to go beyond Nicodemus in responding to Jesus.[90] His characterization leaves open the potential for him to choose discipleship, but that is not the model presented as paradigmatic; in the end his indecision is a decision not to commit.

Interpolated between Jesus' encounter with Nicodemus and his encounter with the woman of Samaria is the witness of John (3:25-36). John's witness is a recognition of his own identity, who he is not, and an acceptance of the identity of the one from above. The bridegroom im-

---

[87] Gibbons, 117-8.
[88] Mary Margaret Pazdan, "Nicodemus and the Samaritan Woman: Contrasting Models of Discipleship," *Biblical Theology Bulletin* 17 (1987): 147.
[89] Bassler, 643.
[90] Tanzer, 294.

agery (3:29) recalls the paradigmatic response of Jesus' mother to Jesus' word at the wedding in Cana. The one narratively portrayed as the witness to the Word, now himself "demonstrates openness to the word of Jesus, even though it means he must disappear."[91] John's positive response reflects back on Nicodemus and ahead to the woman of Samaria, without being offered as a model for reader identification. John's unique and unrepeatable contemporaneous witness to Jesus is not accessible for reader participation.

An Anonymous Woman of Samaria

The episode of Jesus' encounter with the Samaritan woman has received a great deal of attention. Recent substantial monographs devoted exclusively to the interpretation of this episode, or offering lengthy analyses of it, include those by Birger Olsson, Gail O'Day, Hendrikus Boers, Teresa Okure, and J. Eugene Botha.[92] Olsson's study includes the Cana wedding episode with Jesus' mother and approaches these narratives linguistically. Somewhat related in method is Botha's stylistic analysis using speech act theory. O'Day focuses on the presence of irony and its revelatory function in the Fourth Gospel narrative. Boers analyzes the structure of the episode using Greimas' semiotic theory. Okure examines the episode within the context of Jesus' mission. None focuses primarily on the characterization of the Samaritan woman. O'Day's study is the most helpful to the reading offered here because of her attention to how the Gospel affects readers' understanding of Jesus' claims through facilitating their participation in the narrative.

The episode begins on a discordant note, influencing reader expectation concerning the subsequent encounter and dialogue with the Samaritan woman. Prior to chapter 4, readers can be confident of their understanding of Jesus, including the report of Jesus' baptizing activity in 3:22. This self-assurance is undermined by 4:2 where the earlier report is denied; it wasn't Jesus who was baptizing after all. Bultmann considers this

---

[91] Moloney, *Belief*, 127.

[92] Birger Olsson, *Structure and Meaning in the Fourth Gospel: A Text-Linguistic Analysis of John 2:1-11 and 4:1-42*, Coniectanea biblica, New Testament 6, (Lund, Sweedon: CWK Gleerup, 1974); Gail R. O'Day, *Revelation in the Fourth Gospel: Narrative Mode and Theological Claim*, (Philadelphia: Fortress, 1986); Hendrikus Boers, *Neither on this Mountain nor in Jerusalem: A Study of John 4*, Society of Biblical Literature Monograph Series 35, (Atlanta: Scholars Press, 1988); Okure, Teresa. *The Johannine Approach to Mission: A Contextual Study of John 4:1-42*, Wissenschaftliche Untersuchungen zum Neuen Testament 2, Reihe 31, (Tübingen: J.C.B. Mohr, 1988); J. Eugene Botha, *Jesus and the Samaritan Woman: A Speech Act Reading of John 4:1-42*, Novum Testamentum Supplements 65 (Leiden: E.J. Brill, 1991).

to be an editorial correction, but he admits it is difficult to explain why it would be placed here instead of simply correcting 3:22.[93] Moloney sees 4:2 as a reflection of the theme of Jesus' word and identity having precedence over his work, so the narrator "decides that the reader must experience Jesus' withdrawal from a baptizing ministry."[94] Moloney's extratext converts a denial of Jesus' baptizing activity into his withdrawal from it. Brodie offers a similar reading, claiming the Gospel alerts the reader to Jesus' changing role. His baptizing role gives way to the disciples because "Jesus is exhausted, literally labored out (4:6 κεκοπιακὼς)."[95] He finds chronological support for his reading because "the encounter with the woman took place at the (death-evoking) sixth hour...it was at such an hour that Jesus was condemned to death." The assertion that follows, "such dimensions of the story are easy to miss,"[96] assumes Brodie's reading is textually bound and fails to recognize the role of his extratext in the production of his reading. Brodie errs in dismissing readings other than his own as the product of an oversight of an important detail by careless or obtuse readers.

Jeffrey Staley reads this passage as the first example of a rhetorical technique he terms "reader victimization." This occurs when readers, "set-up" through their confidence in their superior understanding of the Fourth Gospel, have the rug pulled out from underneath them by words or actions that undercut information about which they were confident. This strategy is more than a ploy to make readers feel foolish; it reminds the reader "that in spite of his high degree of knowledge, he still does not know everything. The gospel, as well as being an aesthetic whole, is a learning program."[97] The advantage of Staley's reading is its focus on the rhetorical effect of the Gospel's contradictory statements, which avoids disregarding or excising them as later editorial insertions.[98] Reader's confidence is unsettled by the corrective of 4:2, challenging prior understandings and preparing them to expect the unexpected in the characterization of Jesus in the Fourth Gospel.

Another occasion for reader puzzlement is Jesus' statement in 4:4 that he "had" to pass through Samaria. The reader asks "why?", and no explanation is immediately forthcoming. Geographically, the trip through Samaria was not necessary, though more direct and convenient. The reason behind this need will unfold throughout the episode, where it will be dis-

---

[93] Bultmann, 176n.2.
[94] Moloney, *Belief*, 136.
[95] Brodie, 220.
[96] Ibid., 221.
[97] Staley, 96-98.
[98] Bultmann, 175-6; Brown, *John*, I. 164-5; Schnackenburg, I. 422n.6.

covered that the necessity is divine.[99] The radical element in this meeting may not be obvious for readers whose extratexts lack knowledge of Jewish/Samaritan relations, but it is soon made explicit that "Jews have no dealings with Samaritans" (4:9).

Jesus waits seated by a well as the woman of Samaria approaches and the Gospel describes their meeting in the typological imagery of Hebrew narrative.[100] The scene is reminiscent of the betrothal "type-scene" frequent in Hebrew Scriptures constructed around the meeting of a man and a woman at a well (e.g. Genesis 24:10-61, 29:1-20).[101] The basic elements identified by Robert Alter are present here. A man traveling in a foreign land meets a woman at a well and is given water; the woman runs home to tell; the man is invited to stay; and the betrothal occurs. Several of these paradigmatic elements are altered in Jesus' meeting with the Samaritan woman. Most importantly, Jesus is not given water to drink, even though it is requested, and no actual betrothal is portrayed. This leads Brodie to see here "an 'unbetrothal'—the liberating of a woman who had been over-betrothed physically—and, more positively,...a betrothal of belief."[102]

Jesus' seemingly innocent request for refreshment is unthinkable, because of the distinctiveness of their respective gender, ethnic, and cultural identities. The woman's response is, according to acceptable practice, more correct than Jesus' request—it would seem that she is rebuking him.[103] Seim sees here an emphasis on her gender and cultural identity; in verses 7-9 "the juxtaposition of 'Samaritan woman' is repeated three-times, obviously stressing the double qualification alienating her from him."[104] However, a progression can be noted; after verse 9 she is designated only as "the woman,"[105] suggesting this aspect of her alienation has been overcome through her dialogue with Jesus. This feature of the narrative places her in direct opposition to Nicodemus' failure as a conversation partner with Jesus. The woman actively engages in dialogue, just as she later will engage in the mission of witnessing to Jesus' word.[106] She challenges this stranger when his behavior moves outside acceptable

---

[99] J. Eugene Botha, "Reader 'Entrapment' as Literary Device in John 4:1-42," *Neotestimentica* 24 (1990): 40; Moloney, *Belief*, 137.
[100] Botha, "Entrapment," 40.
[101] Robert Alter, *The Art of Biblical Narrative* (New York: Basic Books, 1981), 51-62; on this narrative as a betrothal type-scene see Olsson, 162-73; Joseph P. Cahill, "Narrative Art in John IV," *Religious Studies Bulletin* 2 (1982): 41-48; Staley, 177-85; Duke 101-3.
[102] Brodie, 218.
[103] Ibid., 41.
[104] Seim, 68.
[105] Cahill, 47.
[106] Boers, 87.

boundaries of social convention (4:9). She raises the issues of the religious and social barriers separating Samaritans and Jews. Her probing elicits the always crucial issue of Jesus' identity. Her dialogue participation "surpasses in skill, wit, insight, and audacity the performance of Nicodemus, the teacher of Israel."[107] These elements combine for a strong positive portrayal of the woman of Samaria, important in reader identification with a character.

The question of the woman's sinfulness has received far greater attention from some readers than the narration of it seems to warrant. Nowhere in this scene is there any textual evidence of repentance, nor is Jesus portrayed requesting it of her.[108] It is undeniable that by the standards of most cultures, five husbands is excessive, and living with a man not one's husband is usually deemed unacceptable. Readers whose extratexts include knowledge of common cultural marital standards would find her spousal history notable. Some readers have found symbolic significance in the number of husbands. Barrett offers some of the possibilities for a symbolic understanding: the five Samaritan gods with the tribal god of each numbered among these five, and the one who is not a husband representing the false worship of Israel's God; the Samaritan's acceptance of the Pentateuch alone as Scripture; or (this according to Heraclean) all material evil.[109] Again, extratextual knowledge necessary to recognize this symbolism may not be present for most readers. Furthermore, understanding the Samaritan woman's marital facts as an expression of her sinfulness ignores Jesus' lack of condemnation. Seim condemns this view because it fails to "take into account that matters of marriage and divorce were primarily men's privileges."[110] Even if this reading is only possible from a modern perspective of culpability, it is congruous with the failure of the Gospel to convey any expression of concern for her marital status on Jesus' part. Again the reader must accept the indeterminacy surrounding these issues and focus on what the narrative chooses to reveal.

The woman of Samaria demonstrates a developing understanding of Jesus' identity leading to a progression of belief, a pattern that will also occur with the blind man in chapter 9. She begins resisting Jesus' bold approach, rejecting his initial offer of 'living water' (v. 10) with skepticism (vv. 11-12). Her scorn yields to the polite address κύριε (v. 11), then she recognizes him as a προφήτης (v. 19), and finally affirms him as Messiah (v. 29).[111]

---

[107] Rena, 138; cf. Selvidge, 65; Boers, 182; Tilborg, 182; Okure, 128.
[108] Moloney, *Belief*, 148; Selvidge, 66.
[109] Barrett, 235.
[110] Seim, 68.
[111] Boers, 4; Moloney, *Belief*, 154.

74   CHAPTER FIVE

Throughout the woman's meeting and dialogue with Jesus, the reader encounters some interesting "staging" of the scene.[112] Front-stage are Jesus and the woman, while simultaneously the disciples appear backstage, arriving as she departs (vv. 27-28). Then the disciples move front-stage and the reader views the Samaritan villagers arriving back-stage.[113] All of this creates considerable movement as we repeatedly read verbs of coming and going. The stage directions for the disciples, the woman, and the villagers have all of them arriving and departing, sometimes simultaneously. The one exception to this scurrying about, on and off-stage, is Jesus. He remains center stage, as the one "who was sent" (v. 34) and will become the one who "remains" (ἔμεινεν v. 40).[114] This not only fulfills the criteria of the type-scene, it previews the Fourth Gospel's use of the theologically significant concept μένω in Jesus' farewell discourses (15:4-10).

The disciples' arrival inevitably leads readers to contrast them to Jesus, on the one hand, in their attitudes towards the woman, and to the woman, on the other, in their understanding of Jesus' identity and mission. They are shocked, not to find him talking to a Samaritan woman, or a woman of her reputation and character, but simply a woman (v. 27).[115] In this narrative the genders do not get equal billing. The text repeatedly references the woman, some form of the root γύναι occurring twelve times in verses 7-42. This compares with only five occurrences of any form of ἀνήρ, all present in verses 16-18.[116] Yet, the woman stands alone as the only member of her gender in an episode populated by males and male figures referenced but not present: Jesus, Jacob and his sons (v. 12), the disciples of Jesus, "our fathers" (v. 20), five husbands and "one who is not a husband" (16-18), and God the Father.[117] Readers may read much significance into her gender because of the multiple references to it, the woman's first words address it (v. 9). Indeed it is the only aspect of her identity Jesus' disciples note (v. 27). However, we discover that the woman's gender is not an issue for Jesus in his missionary partnership with her.

A specific textual detail receiving much attention in interpretations of this pericope is the jar the woman left behind in v. 28. This seemingly innocuous detail could be nothing more than the result of the woman's

---

[112] On the use of dramatic staging in the Fourth Gospel, see Martyn, 26-37.
[113] Stibbe, 64.
[114] Cahill, 43.
[115] Seim, 59.
[116] Stibbe, 63; cf. Olsson, 194.
[117] Tilborg, 178.

haste and the speed with which she departs.[118] Few readers, however, have been inclined to leave it at that. The reader looks for significance in this detail, precisely because it is the only one of its kind. No other physical description of the scene, the characters, the city, or even the well occurs. The water jar stands alone as the one physical detail in the midst of dialogue. It has been interpreted to represent the negation of the need for the sustenance she came to find. The quest for water is abandoned in favor of the successful quest for the water of life.[119] Others have noted here a visible demonstration of the first prerequisite of discipleship: leaving everything to follow Jesus. This would parallel the Synoptics account of the disciples leaving their nets to follow Jesus.[120]

The woman's witness in verse 29 has caused some readers to question the adequacy of her belief. She does not give witness to her conversation with Jesus about the life-giving water, the theological debate concerning true worship, or even Jesus' self-revelation. Instead she says, he "told me all that I ever did," then with an ambiguous μήτι, wonders, "Can this perhaps be the Christ?" (v. 29). The ambiguity of this particle is well illustrated by Bultmann's assertion that her statement is "expecting an affirmative answer," while Brown states "the Greek question with μήτι implies an unlikelihood," both of them citing as their evidence the same paragraph from Blass and Debrunner.[121]

Blass and Debrunner actually retain the ambiguity, citing John 4:29 as either "This must be the Messiah at last" or "Perhaps this is the Messiah."[122] Okure admits the ambiguity of the construction, but reads in the woman's narrative her "complete belief," indicated by "the progressive movement of the woman's response," the Gospel's designation of her report to the villagers as μαρτυρούσης (v.39), and the Samaritans' themselves who recognize her witness "as the initial grounds of their belief."[123] It has been argued the ambiguity is not in the woman's belief in Jesus, but deliberate in her witness to the villagers so as not to "preclude their participation by overwhelming them with unprocessible information."[124] This ability to know the woman's psyche must be processed from the reader's extratext. Whatever the woman's intent, the ambiguity of her μητι does produce the need for reflection and necessitate decision, not

---

[118] Barrett, 240; Schnackenburg, I., 443; Okure, 121.
[119] Boers, 115, 183; Botha, 163.
[120] Stibbe, 67; Selvidge, 67.
[121] Bultmann, 193n.3; Brown, *John*, I. 173.
[122] Friedrich Blass and Albert Debrunner, *A Greek Grammer of the New Testament and Other Early Christian Literature*, trans. Robert W. Funk (Chicago: University of Chicago Press, 1961), 427 (2).
[123] Okure, 169-71.
[124] Botha, 164; cf. Okure, 174.

only on the part of the villagers in the narrative, but on the part of the reader as well.[125]

How is the reader to evaluate the Samaritan woman in her narrative portrayal? Her full participation in the dialogue with Jesus contrasts her with the disappearing Nicodemus of chapter 3 and the disciples who dared not verbalize their concerns and puzzlement to Jesus (4:27). She responds to Jesus' words, not "to signs." She does not answer with verbal confession, but with an active witness to others concerning Jesus' words, the paradigm of appropriate response to Jesus as established with Jesus' mother at Cana. Her witness, moreover, provides interesting parallels to the witness of John. On her word, as on his in 1:35-37, her hearers leave her to seek after Jesus.[126] Like John, following her initial testimony, she does not speak again and is not even portrayed among the crowd who seeks him out, for like John "she has decreased, while Jesus has increased."[127] Her role has been identified as apostolic: "she calls others as Jesus called the disciples, 'come and see;'"[128] (1:39, 4:29; the wording is not identical, but similar).

Jesus' words to the disciples concerning their role in the "harvest," place this woman squarely in the heart of their mission, which is the mission of Jesus (vv. 34-38).[129] Immediately upon the return of the disciples and the departure of the woman, Jesus speaks of his mission, given him by the one who sent him (v. 34), then explains this mission in terms of harvesting. Jesus distinguishes a sower from a reaper, then speaks of those who have labored, and into whose labor the disciples will now enter (vv. 36-38). How can the reader determine the uncertain antecedents of these pronouns in this agricultural illustration? Talbert answers this in terms of the overall missionary theme of the Fourth Gospel. Jesus is God's envoy, who in turn sends the disciples as his underlaborers.[130] Brown suggests it is Jesus sowing the word in the woman; Old Testament figures; or John the Baptist.[131] Each of these suggestions ignores the context of these words. The only person who has been portrayed as a "sower" laboring for a harvest, other than Jesus himself, is the woman. In

---

[125] O'Day, 76.
[126] Pazdan, 148.
[127] Rena, 140; Rolf Walker, "Jüngerwort und Herrenwort. Zur Auslegung von Joh 4,39-42, *Zeitschrift für neutestamentliche Wissenschaft* 57 (1966): 50; Tilborg goes as far as to state that this woman "is made anonymous," 250, but this is to redefine anonymity as significance or prominence rather than nomination.
[128] Culpepper, 137; cf. Barrett, 242; Beasley-Murray, 39.
[129] Brodie, 217.
[130] Charles H. Talbert, *Reading John: A Literary and Theological Commentary on the Fourth Gospel and the Johannine Epistles*, Reading the New Testament Series, (New York: Crossroad, 1992), 117.
[131] Brown, *John*, I. 183; cf. Moloney, *Belief*, 167.

the context of her apostolic portrayal as the faithful witness of Jesus, she must be among these ἄλλοι, laboring while the disciples are absent. But now that they have returned (v. 27), the Samaritans among whom she has "labored" arrive (v. 40), and the disciples can harvest.[132] This reading does not preclude, however, also reading here a foreshadowing of the later missionary activity of the disciples and even the Fourth Gospel community.[133]

Is the reader to contrast the efficacy of the woman's words with Jesus' words? Does she only speak λαλιά in contrast to Jesus' λόγος? It has been claimed that the vocabulary here demonstrates that human words will always fall short in their witness to Jesus. The woman's λαλιά "cannot be said to parallel the Johannine use of the expression λόγος."[134] Yet, the Fourth Gospel's penchant for synonyms has been documented,[135] and the episode's vocabulary does not allow for such a dichotomy of these synonyms. In verse 39, in fact, many are said to have come to believe in him through τὸν λόγον τῆς γυναικὸς μαρτυρούσης. Furthermore, the verb form λαλοῦμεν is used of Jesus' own testimony in 3:11, and λόγος and λαλιά are interchangeable in Jesus' words in 8:31 and 8:43.[136] The emphasis on the villagers' response to Jesus' words is an affirmation of the role of witness in the Fourth Gospel, as established in the paradigm of Jesus' mother, to influence others to experience Jesus' words for themselves.[137]

The positive evaluation of the Samaritan woman is enhanced by the contrast between her response of witness with the misunderstanding of the disciples and Nicodemus. She also compares favorably to the other anonymous woman appearing thus far in the Gospel, Jesus' mother. The disciples draw attention to the woman's active participation in dialogue with Jesus (v. 27) and pale by comparison. Unlike her, they are unwilling or unable to voice their concerns. Like her, their initial comments surround physical sustenance, but unlike her, they never move beyond that concern. Reminiscent of Nicodemus, they lapse into silence while Jesus speaks of things they do not comprehend. The disciples' silence mirrors the unsuccessful dialogue of Nicodemus, whose voice trails off and finally disappears altogether, taking him with it.

---

[132] Boers, 33; Olsson, 233.
[133] Okure, 159-60.
[134] Moloney, *Belief*, 171; cf. Brown 174-5, Bultmann, who calls it a "mediatory proclamation" until Jesus' word is heard, 201.
[135] Edwin D. Freed, "Variations in the Language and Thought of John," *Zeitschrift für die neutestamentliche Wissenschaft* 55 (1964): 167-97.
[136] Okure, 171.
[137] Ibid., 173; cf. Schnackenburg, I. 456.

The reader's identification with the woman is encouraged by her positive textual portrayal and facilitated by her anonymity. Her initial introduction may strike a resonant chord with readers whose extratexts include the experience of disenfranchisement, either by gender, ethnicity, or consequential life choices—choices they may feel were beyond their control. Pazdan believes the woman's resulting marginal status "is transformed because of her deep commitment as a disciple to Jesus. She represents the invitation of Jesus to each person regardless of background."[138] The negative elements of her characterization appear early, then are left behind as the focus moves forward to Jesus' role in her present rather than her past struggles. Their fleeting narrative presence prevent them from hindering reader identification with her, even for readers who do not share these life characteristics. Combined with her anonymity are the positive portrayal of her dialogue with Jesus, her openness to grow in her understanding of him, and her response of witnessing to the efficacy of his words, all aspects of the appropriate response paradigm established by Jesus' mother at Cana.

This reader is challenged to full participation in the revelatory dialogue in which Jesus engages the woman. It does not "force the reader to decide but allows the reader to become engaged."[139] The variety of viewpoints and understandings among the characters in this narrative, the reader "victimization" concerning certain (mis)understandings the reader has arrived at, the initial ironic misunderstandings of characters about the spiritual level on which Jesus speaks, the ambiguity of words and details discussed above, the movement on and off stage contrasted with Jesus' "remaining," and the identity gap the woman's anonymity presents—all are "built in devices to ensure the attention of the readers, and of course, their participation."[140] The Fourth Gospel does not merely present the story of Jesus in a way that informs and entertains, nor can it to be ignored. Instead the narrative cajoles, entices, and requires "that the reader participates in the narrative and the revelatory experience communicated by it."[141]

The βασιλικός of Cana

One narrative remains within the boundaries of the literary frame provided by the two Cana references. The paradigm for appropriate response

---

[138] Pazdan, 148.
[139] O'Day, 91.
[140] Botha, 190.
[141] O'Day, 89.

to Jesus' words in the narrative of Jesus' mother provides the first border of the "Cana to Cana" frame. The telling of the event underscored that the elements being transformed were part of the rites of Judaism. The account was followed by Jesus' temple disruption and a nocturnal visit by one whose initial identification established him as the representative of what the stone jars and temple precinct symbolize. Nicodemus' dialogue was aborted and no progress was made, at least in his initial appearance, towards understanding and responding appropriately to Jesus' words of revelation concerning himself and his work.

Nicodemus' failed dialogue was immediately followed by a much more successful communication with Jesus. It began with even greater distance between Jesus and his anonymous dialogue partner than was initially present between Jesus and Nicodemus. But in contrast to Nicodemus' befuddlement, the Samaritan woman grows in her ability to understand until she is able to respond by carrying witness of Jesus' words to others, a witness that succeeds as the others seek out Jesus to hear his words for themselves; upon hearing, their initial belief is confirmed. No sign is required for this belief, and it comes from the traditional enemies (Samaritans) of Judaism, represented by the stone waterpots, temple, and Nicodemus.

When Jesus returns to Cana, a man comes to him identified ambiguously as a βασιλικός (4:46). The second reference to Cana recalls the σημεῖον Jesus worked there, but more importantly for the reader who remembers the warning against reading too much significance into signs (2:23-25), it recalls the response of Jesus' mother to his word and the paradigm it established. The parallels between these two narratives urge a connection be made. Besides the return to Cana, the first Cana σημεῖον is twice explicitly referenced (vv. 46, 54).[142] In both Cana episodes Jesus arrives in Galilee on a third day (2:1 4:43); both include Jesus' rebuke to the initial request made of him (2:4, 4:48); in both, third parties who are not directly involved come to believe (2:11 4:53); and on neither occasion is the miracle recorded or explained. Every σημεῖον *except these two Cana σημεῖα* leads to a discourse, and after both of the Cana episodes Jesus journeys to Jerusalem and goes up to the temple (2:13, 5:1).[143]

The identification of the βασιλικός has proven elusive, because again the Fourth Gospel presents the reader with ambiguity in a character's identification. The term has a variety of possible meanings: it could refer to a person of royal blood, a servant to a royal household, a soldier of

---

[142] Brown, *John*, I. 194.
[143] Brodie, 226.

Herodian kings or the emperor, or a royal scribe.[144] What cannot be determined is whether the βασιλικός here is Jew or Gentile. Only through the questionable assumption that this episode has a Synoptic parallel in the tradition of the Centurion's son can the reader identify with confidence that the official is a Gentile.[145] Such a reading is certainly possible for readers who know the Synoptics. I believe it is more constructive, however, to retain the ambiguity and its accompanying uncertainty. Although anonymous, a naming progression is present for the βασιλικός, just as it was for the Samaritan woman, and will be present in the narrative of the blind man in chapter 9. In verse 46 he is a "certain official," by verse 50 he is "a man," and in verse 53 his designation becomes "father."[146] Without the barrier of a name, the more generic his designation, and the easier a reader can identify with him, provided the other elements of his characterization provide the reader a positive assessment of him.

Jesus' rebuke in verse 48 appears unprovoked, in the same way that Jesus' mother's rebuke resulted from nothing a reader would normally consider wrong on her part (2:4). Here, the plural forms in Jesus' rebuke prevent it from being addressed only to the βασιλικός, the reader is also included in this address.[147] The father does not refute the rebuke or debate Jesus; he merely restates his request. According to Bultmann, this indicates "I do not ask you to give proof of your authority, I come only in my distress and ask your help for my child."[148] Jesus responds to the repeated plea with a command: "Go," depart and have your faith confirmed.

Readers are informed that the man believed Jesus' word and went as he was told. In the midst of his obedience, he meets his servants. Their presence raises reader expectation as they echo the servants in the first Cana σημεῖον, who responded to Jesus' word and were witnesses to his σημεῖον. They bring the news of the boy's healing and temporal confirmation of the efficacy of Jesus' word. In response to the report, it is stated again that the man "believed" (ἐπίστευσεν, v. 53), only this time he witnesses to his servants, identifying Jesus' words as the source of the healing; the servants themselves were witnesses to the healing power of Jesus' words.

---

[144] Uwe Wegner, *Der Hauptmann von Kafarnaum (Mt 7,28a; 8,5-10.13 par Lk 7,1-10): Ein Beitrag zur Q-Forschung*, Wissenschaftliche Untersuchungen zum Neuen Testament 2, Reihe 14. (Tübingen: J.C.B. Mohr [Paul Siebeck], 1985), 57-60.
[145] Pryor, 24.
[146] Moloney, *Belief*, 188.
[147] Barrett, 247.
[148] Bultmann, *John*, 207.

Are we to understand ἐπίστευσεν in verse 50 somehow differently than in verse 53? Bultmann calls this the movement from "the preliminary stage of faith (v. 50) to faith proper."[149] Moloney claims it is impossible for the repetition to indicate two moments of faith. He supports this linguistically by reading the ἐπίστευσεν of verse 53 "as a complexive, rather than an ingressive aorist."[150] The emphasis that the man's faith is based in the word of Jesus does not function as a criticism in the Fourth Gospel. The power of Jesus' word is precisely what the characters are encouraged to witness to others. Van Aarde is one reader who preserves the narrative ambiguity. He suggests that there is no indication "whether the one 'belief' excludes or perhaps complements the other." His faith "spreads outward and his entire household is able to share it."[151] The distinction that a reader might make between simply believing the veracity or efficacy of Jesus' word and "believing" in the sense of coming to faith in Jesus may be theologically valid, and even supported in this pericope by the absence of an object in verse 53, but it is not inherent within the two occurrences of ἐπίστευσεν in verses 50 and 53. The vocabulary is identical, and readers must supply an understanding of different degrees, or kinds, or stages of development of faith from their extratexts.

The conclusion of this episode provides an unexpected twist for any reader expecting exact parallels with the first Cana miracle. In 2:12 the various characters are gathered and moved forward in the narrative, through the series of episodes examined above. But in 4:54, the narrative looks backward instead of forward, asking readers to remember the episodes that have preceded.[152] Based on the knowledge accumulated thus far in the reading experience, readers are aware that the βασιλικός has embodied the paradigm of appropriate response to Jesus' word. He accepted the rebuke without complaint, believed in Jesus' power to heal his son, made an active faith response to Jesus' word by beginning the journey home, and then witnessed to his servants and household concerning Jesus' words and work.

How does the characterization of the man facilitate reader identification with him? His background quickly becomes incidental, as he becomes simply "the man" and "the father," designations easier to identify with than βασιλικός. His ethnicity is indeterminable; his royal household

---

[149] Bultmann, 209; see also Schnackenburg, 467-8; Haenchen, 235, 237; Dodd, *Historical Traditions*, 193; Barrett, 248.
[150] Moloney, *Belief*, 187-8.
[151] A. G. Van Aarde, "Narrative Criticism Applied to John 4:43-54," in *Text & Interpretation: New Approaches in the Criticism of the NT*, eds. P. Hartin & J. Petzer, 101-28, New Testament Tools and Studies 15 (Leiden: E. J. Brill, 1991), 124-6.
[152] Moloney, *Belief*, 189.

privileges are worthless before his son's illness. Many readers can share both the man's concern for a loved one's illness and his frustration at facing circumstances that resources or position can do nothing to alter. The man fulfills the paradigm of appropriate response when he believes in Jesus' word and witnesses to others concerning Jesus' word. His positive portrayal combined with the indeterminacies of his characterization, including his anonymity, facilitates reader entry into the narrative and identification with the man.

Although the decision to allow the two Cana σημεῖα to establish unit boundaries is somewhat arbitrary, it does bring into focus the paradigmatic responses of Jesus' mother, the Samaritan woman, and the βασιλικός. The frame also heightens the contrast between the appropriate responses and Nicodemus' ambivalent non-response, as well as the disciples' non-witness that subordinates their missionary activities to the woman's fruitful witness. In the next chapter I will examine four characters whose conditions are characterized by their lack: one lacks mobility, another sight, a third life, and the fourth a "position."

CHAPTER 6

THE INFIRM, THE BLIND, THE DEAD, AND THE MISPLACED

While accurately reflecting a possible, even probable, frame of reference for readers, the distinction between the section designated "Cana to Cana" and the rest of the Fourth Gospel must not be overdrawn. There is no major break or interruption to set apart Jesus' encounter with the βασιλικός from his encounter with the infirm man that follows. The one major textual division of the Fourth Gospel almost universally recognized separates Jesus' public ministry from his passion. The different titles used to designate the two portions by various readers reflect their different understandings of the emphases of each section. Furthermore, readers divide the two sections in different locations, but almost all place it within the context of the beginning of Jesus' final journey to Jerusalem, initiated narratively by the illness and death of Lazarus.

Some interpreters denote 11:1 as the beginning of the second part of the narrative, while most would place this break after 12:50, typified by Dodd's description of a Book of Signs that "divides itself into seven episodes, each consisting of one or more narratives of significant acts of Jesus, accompanied by one or more discourses designed to bring out the significance of the narrative."[1] Haenchen places the division at 13:30 on the basis of his understanding of chapter 13 as the conclusion of the portion he designates "Jesus and the world," preceding 13:31-17:26, which he designates "Jesus and his own."[2] Peter Ellis understands the Fourth Gospel in terms of a chiastic structure and divides the narrative at 12:12 on the basis of this structure.[3]

Many literary approaches subsequent to Culpepper's seminal contribution to narrative study of the Fourth Gospel follow the tradition that breaks the Gospel at 12:50. Culpepper does not provide a specific verse to mark the break, but recognizes that chapter 12 is pivotal for the plot of this narrative, calling it a "transitional chapter".[4] Recent studies of the Gospel focusing on Jesus' journeys (see chap. 4 n.11 above) divide the

---

[1] Dodd, *Interpretation*, 290; see also Brown, *John*, I. cxxxviii-cxliv; Bultmann, *John*, 457-461; Barrett, 11-15; Schnackenburg, III. 1; Beasley-Murray, xc-xcii.
[2] Haenchen, *John*, I. 86.
[3] Peter F. Ellis, *The Genius of John: A Composition-Critical Commentary on the Fourth Gospel*," (Collegeville, Minnesota: The Liturgical Press, 1984), 13-14, 195.
[4] Culpepper, *Anatomy*, 94; also Talbert, 64; Pryor, 54; Stibbe, 139; Brodie, 16.

narrative at 11:1, where Jesus begins his final journey leading him to Jerusalem for the last time and to his hour of glorification on the cross.[5]

Table 6: Patterns of Jesus' Public ministry

Chapter	Discourse/witness	Action/brief or group encounter	Extended encounter
chap. 1:1-14	prologue		
15-34	John's witness		
19-28		identity dispute	
35-51		disciple's call	
chap. 2:1-12			wine σημεῖα
13-25		temple disruption	
chap. 3:1-15			Nicodemus
16-21	God's love		
22-36	John's witness		
chap. 4:1-30			Samaritan woman
31-38		Jesus' disciples	
39-42		villagers	
43-54			βασιλικός
chap. 5:1-9			infirm man
10-18		identity dispute	
19-47	Jesus' witness		
chap. 6:1-15		5,000 fed	
16-21		walking on water	
22-40	bread of life		
41-71		identity dispute	
chap. 7:1-44		identity dispute	
45-52		Nicodemus	
chap. 7:53-8:11			adulteress[6]
chap. 8:12-59		identity dispute	
chap. 9:1-12			blind man
13-41		identity dispute	
chap. 10:1-18	good shepherd		
19-42		identity dispute	
chap. 11:1-44			Lazarus
45-57		plot to kill Jesus	

---

[5] Rissi, "Aufbau," 50-51; Staley, 66-68; Segovia, 44.
[6] See below for the rationale to include this textually problematic character.

Table 6 above reveal interesting patterns in Jesus' ministry that come to light when the witness/discourse episodes, Jesus' extended encounters with individual characters, brief encounters with individuals, other actions, and encounters with groups are compared. The first column represents extended episodes of Jesus' teaching, Jesus' witness concerning his identity and origins, or others' witness to Jesus' identity and origins. The second column lists episodes of activity by Jesus, including brief encounters between Jesus and individual characters and Jesus' encounters with various groups. The last column contains Jesus' extended encounters with individuals. An important phenomenon manifests itself in the analyses of individual Gospel characters, especially as they relate to division of units within Jesus' public ministry. A pattern exists in which Jesus' extended encounters with individual characters are followed by another action, brief/group encounter, or witness—most often a dispute concerning Jesus' identity. The exception to this pattern is the immediate transition from the story of the βασιλικός that concludes chapter 4 and the story of the infirm man that begins chapter 5. These are the only two encounters between Jesus and an individual narrated consecutively.

The presence of a pattern does not define a necessary structure by which the narrative must be read, nor does it assume authorial intent. The table only demonstrates how readers might add to their extratexts a pattern of structure and choose to read the narrative in its interpretive light. It could be argued that the episode with the βασιλικός brings closure to the second Cana narrative, echoing what has already been narrated.[7] Conversely, the promptness with which readers leave the βασιλικός to encounter the infirm man gives them immediacy in both the text and the reading experience, inviting contrast and comparison.[8] This assumes, of course, the text as it presently stands, *contra* numerous reconstructions offered by adherents of displacement theories during the past century, culminating with Bultmann.[9] On the contrary, the reader is limited to the extant text with any and all foibles, discordant notes or jarring disruptions. The consecutive appearances of the infirm man and the βασιλικός,

---

[7] Cahill, 47.

[8] Beasley-Murray, 66-81; Robert Kysar, *John's Story of Jesus* (Philadelphia: Fortress, 1984), 31-38; Brodie, 189-92.

[9] e.g. B. W. Bacon, "Displacement of John xiv," *Journal of Biblical Literature* 13 (1894): 64-75; Frank W. Lewis, *Disarrangements in the Fourth Gospel* (Cambridge: Cambridge University Press, 1910); Thomas Cottam, "Some Displacements in the Fourth Gospel," *Expository Times* 38 (1926): 91-92; F.R. Haore, *The Original Order and Chapters of St. John's Gospel* (London: Burns, Oats & Washbourne, 1944); Bultmann, *John*, 109-10. See discussion in Haenchen, 15545-51 which concludes "the time for displacement theories is gone...they lose their cogency when one attempts to make a legible book out of a very difficult text."

the only instance of back-to-back encounters in the Gospel, precludes a distinct division between the two men.

An Infirm Man With No Man

Although the infirm man at Bethzatha follows consecutively the βασιλικός in Cana, it is the blind man in chapter 9 whose scene most closely parallels features of the infirm man's episode, just as the two Cana σημεῖα parallel each other. These parallel features include:

the description of the man's history	(5:5; 9:1)
Jesus' initiative in the healing	(5:6; 9:6)
a "healing" pool	(5:2,7; 9:7)
healing on the Sabbath	(5:9; 9:14)
the charge of Sabbath violation	(5:10; 9:16)
the interrogation of the healed man	(5:6; 9:15)
man's ignorance of Jesus' whereabouts	(5:13; 9:12)
Jesus' finds man and invites belief	(5:14; 9:35)
relationship of sin to suffering	(5:14; 9:3)
man goes to Jews/Jews cast out	(5:15; 9:34)
Jesus doing the work of his Father/ (the one who sent him)	(5:17; 9:4)[10]

Admittedly, all the parallels are not exact. The healing efficacy of a pool is replaced (though not denied) when Jesus' heals the infirm man (5:7-8), but with the blind man, Jesus requires that the man wash in the pool (9:6-7).

The relationship of sin and suffering is denied by Jesus with the blind man (9:2-3), but apparently affirmed by Jesus with the infirm man (5:14). The final conversations of each man with the Jews are also dissimilar. The infirm man initiates the contact, seeking out the Jews to tell them of Jesus' identity, which has been seen by many readers as an act of betrayal (5:15).[11] The blind man, on the other hand, is ordered to appear before the Jews and his obedience results in his expulsion. The most significant parallel for our study, nonetheless, is not mentioned by Culpepper: their shared anonymity. An important distinction between episodes is their

---

[10] Culpepper, *Anatomy*, 139-40.

[11] J. Louis Martyn, *History and Theology in the Fourth Gospel*, Rev. ed. (Nashville: Abingdon, 1979), 71; D. Moody Smith, *John*. 2d rev. ed. Proclamation Commentaries (Philadelphia: Fortress, 1986), 41; Stibbe, 75.

length and plot function. The episode of the infirm man is much shorter, but has far greater significance for plot development.[12]

With the appearance of the infirm man at the pool, some new developments arise in the narrative. The conflict between Jesus and the Jews intensifies into active opposition. Prior to the episode, the conflict is limited to the Jew's failure to understand and their lack of trustworthiness (2:18-25). Now Jesus' activity is a springboard for open debate concerning his origins and increasing opposition, including the first report of attempts to arrest and kill him (5:10-18).[13] A new method of linking episodes begins here: Jesus' activity is tied to various Jewish feasts, all with the previously noted theme of replacement.[14]

The healing is reported in a straightforward manner, with more descriptive details than the preceding episodes of the Samaritan woman and the βασιλικός. Among them are temporal and geographical designations (at feast time, 5:1; in Jerusalem, by the Sheep Gate, 5:2), a physical description of the pool (having five porticoes, 5:2), and a description of the surrounding crowd (multitudes of invalids, blind, lame, paralyzed, 5:4).

As with the Samaritan woman, Jesus initiates the encounter with the infirm man. The man does not respond affirmatively to Jesus' question nor express a desire for the healing Jesus can bring (5:6-7). Instead he makes excuses for his prior inability to receive healing. The vocabulary of volition in Jesus' question, θέλεις, previews a theme of the discourse to follow. Jesus uses the same verb to speak of the Son giving life (v. 21), once for the Jews' willingness to rejoice momentarily in the light of John (v. 15-35) and once referring to their refusal to come to him for life (v. 40). The noun form, θέλημα, appears twice in v. 30 when Jesus speaks of his will to do the will of the one who sent him. The volition to receive what Jesus offers is thus an important theme.[15]

The question Jesus asks the infirm man has been perceived as odd by some readers.[16] The apparent strangeness of the question is not surprising to readers who remember Jesus' initial "harsh" response to his mother (2:4) and his suggestion that the βασιλικός is more interested in signs than his son's health (4:48). For readers who remember Jesus' previous surprising statements, the unnecessary question heightens reader anticipation of an impressive sign.[17]

---

[12] Staley, "Stumbling," 58.
[13] John Painter, "Text and Context in John 5," *Australian Biblical Review* 35 (1987): 28; cf. Culpepper, *Anatomy*, 91.
[14] Stibbe, 74; Ellis, 86.
[15] Brodie, 236; Staley, "Stumbling," 71n.12.
[16] Haenchen, I. 255.
[17] Staley, "Stumbling," 59.

88   CHAPTER SIX

Does the infirm man fit the paradigm previously established for appropriate response to the identity and words of Jesus? The man responds in faith to Jesus' word; he believes he is healed and thus obeys the command to pick up his pallet and walk (5:9). His "belief" in Jesus' statement is not specifically narrated as it was in the case of the βασιλικός (4:50). Rather, it is implied through his active response to Jesus' initial word, as in the parallel instance of the blind man who also indicates a preliminary belief in Jesus' word through his obedience. This is not "belief" in the sense of coming to faith in Jesus (see 4:53), but it is "belief" in the efficacy of Jesus' words (see 4:50). Again, as in previous appearances of significant anonymous characters, the man's belief did not require a sign, unless it is maintained that his own healing was physically manifested prior to his response to Jesus' command. An alternative understanding is that his obedience in picking up his mat is his "means to being healed."[18]

The paradigm is also fulfilled in the man's witness to the efficacy of Jesus' word. When queried concerning his Sabbath activity (v. 10), the man insists that he is only obeying the one who directed him to do so (v. 11). Admittedly, he cannot testify to Jesus' identity (v. 13), but this is rectified by Jesus' initiative in seeking him out and warning him of the relationship between suffering and sin (v.14). Readers familiar with the Jesus tradition, particularly the story of the blind man in chapter 9, will be puzzled by the apparent contradiction with Jesus' denial there that the man's blindness has any connection with sin (9:3). Schnackenburg suggests Jesus' "work of healing the man externally and physically is a sign pointing to the greater work of transmitting eternal life." The connection is therefore, not as unrelated as first supposed.[19] Brodie believes the man has already sinned by failing to "will" his own healing (v. 7) and recognize the one who healed him, altering his life (v. 13).[20] An alternative offered by Tilborg reads Jesus' words as the command, "Do not continue carrying your bed and suffer the consequences of a Sabbath violator," understanding Jesus' words as "a protection...an expression of concern."[21] The indeterminacy of the meaning of Jesus' words is indicated by the multiple readings offered. Any reading interpreting Jesus' words as a universal statement of the cause and effect relationship between sin and human suffering will be corrected in the episode of the blind man (9:2-3).

After discovering Jesus' identity as his healer, the man bears witness to that fact before the Jews (v. 15). The man fits the paradigm of one who believes and responds to the word of Jesus without needing a sign prior to

---

[18] Ibid.
[19] Schnackenburg, II. 97.
[20] Brodie, 238.
[21] Tilborg, 218.

belief, then bears witness to others of what Jesus' word accomplished. His anonymity encourages and facilitates reader identification with his character in the narrative. This reading does not beg the question of the many readings pointing to the man's unwillingness to separate himself from non-believing Jews, and the function of his "witness" in "betraying" Jesus' identity and presence to his enemies.[22] I choose to retain the ambiguity of the man's portrayal, allowing the paradigm presented by the other anonymous characters to shape my understanding of this man.

The reading above offers a positive interpretation of the characterization of the infirm man, but when contrasted with the blind man's unwavering defense of Jesus in chapter 9, the infirm man's words appear ambiguous. Readers aware of the treachery of Jesus' enemies receiving the man's testimony might interpret his witness as part and parcel with their treachery. Culpepper is correct that "evidence" is lacking for this man's belief, but Culpepper's negative assessment, peppered with pejorative terminology including "blame," "complains," "culpable," and "dullness," also goes beyond what is narrated.[23] Another negative assessment of the man's portrayal is Brown's description of his "crotchety grumbling about the 'whippersnappers' who outrace him to the water."[24] Both Brown and Culpepper provide readings made possible by the ambiguity of the infirm man's characterization that place the responsibility for character assessment squarely on the reader. The contrast between positive and negative assessments of the man's actions reflects different extratextual choices by readers. Instead of relying on the actions of Jesus' enemies or a perceived contrast to the blind man in chapter 9 for the interpretive key to understand the infirm man, the reading offered here relies on the extent to which the man fits the response paradigm previously established in chapter 2.

A positive assessment of the infirm man is also advocated by Tilborg, who points to the verb narrating the man's report, claiming that ἀναγγέλλω is always used in the Fourth Gospel in the context of divine revelation.[25] In some locations this verb describes disclosures of ordinary human activity (i.e. Acts 19:18, where the practice of magical arts are revealed; 2 Cor. 7:7, where Titus reports the Corinthians' longing for Paul). But in its Fourth Gospel occurrences, it is always used of divine activity. In 4:25 the Samaritan woman describes the activity of the Messiah and in 5:15 the infirm man undeniably reports divine activity: Jesus' identity as

---

[22] Brown, 209; Haenchen, I, 247; Culpepper, *Anatomy*, 138; Culpepper, "Un exemple," 148; Martyn, 71.
[23] Culpepper, *Anatomy*, 138.
[24] Brown, *John*, I. 209.
[25] Tilborg, 218.

his healer. The man knows the identity of Jesus through divine revelation; Jesus discloses his own identity to the man. In chap. 16 Jesus uses ἀναγ-γέλλω to describe the activity of the Spirit he will send (vv. 13, 14, and 15). While it is true that three of these occurrences are still ahead, each one casts a favorable light back on this scene and its main character, for the reader who remembers its use here. This is particularly true for a reader predisposed to a positive assessment of this man's behavior by the previously established paradigm of anonymous characters who respond positively to Jesus' word.

Staley characterizes the infirm man as one who appears weak and ineffective, but who "in retrospect proves to be a daring and risk-taking individual, one who acts unquestioningly upon a stranger's Sabbath-breaking command."[26] He suggests the man's defense for carrying his bed in violation of the Sabbath could be a "profound theological argument for replacing the Torah with the words of a charismatic healer." Staley offers several possible understandings of the nature of the sin Jesus warns the man about ("flaunting" his healing, being in the Temple after Jesus speaks negatively of it, not fully revealing Jesus' identity when asked), but he admits it is impossible to make one option determinative. What is explicit is the immediacy of the man's response to Jesus' word when he returns to his interrogators to complete his identification of Jesus. In Staley's words, the man is "not a tattle-tale...(but) a faithful witness." The most compelling reason Staley offers for his positive assessment of the infirm man is "the fact that neither the narrator nor Jesus condemns him—either explicitly or implicitly."[27]

Perhaps the most that can be said is that we have here a man who receives Jesus' healing word, responds obediently, then reports what Jesus' word accomplished to others, whatever his motive for doing so and however limited his understanding. The understanding and belief of the Samaritan woman and the βασιλικός are also ambiguous, in their initial response to Jesus' word (μήτι 4:29, the two statements of his ἐπίστευσεν in 4:50, 53), yet they also fit the established paradigm of appropriate response and are offered as models for reader identification.

Reader identification with the infirm man is assisted by the extent of the match with the reader's own life experiences. Most readers are not so physically challenged as the infirm man, but many have experienced the frustration of an answer to their need remaining just out of reach, with no one to help them reach it, while others shove them aside and arrive there first. Because of the parallel structure of the account of the infirm man

---

[26] Staley, "Stumbling," 60.
[27] Ibid., 61-3.

and the episode of the blind man in chapter 9,[28] this episode prepares the reader for the episode of the blind man. The reader's experience with the narrative presentation of the episode of the infirm man functions to assist in the reader's assimilation and interpretation of the blind man and identification with him.

A Blind Man with no Place (of Worship)

Recent readings of the blind man in chapter 9 are shaped in response to the influential work of J. Louis Martyn. His understanding of this narrative as a two-level drama, grounded both in the historical setting of Jesus' ministry and in the historical setting of the community within which the Fourth Gospel was produced,[29] has influenced those following in his exegetical footsteps. His analysis of how this narrative accomplishes a "doubling" of Jesus with the figures of Christian witnesses in the community which produced it[30] may be seen as an example of how the first "readers" (probably "hearers") of the narrative of Jesus' origins and identity identified with and were able to enter into the narrative to encounter Jesus there, even to the extent of being placed within the Gospel themselves. The effect of staging (see chapter 4 above on episode of the Samaritan woman) has also been detected in Jesus' encounter with the blind man. On the back stage are Jesus and the blind man, while on an intermediate stage are the blind man and his neighbors. The front stage occupants consist of participants in three dialogues, two with the blind man and the Pharisees and one with the Pharisees and the man's parents.[31]

The themes of blindness and sight typify the concerns of the episode, and echo the earlier textual references to light and darkness (1:6-9, 3:19-21, and especially the revelatory ἐγώ εἰμι of 8:12 of which this narrative episode is a commentary[32]). The theologically weighty phrase ἐγώ εἰμι is echoed by the formerly blind man in verse 9 as his identity becomes a disputed issue, just as Jesus' identity is disputed. The episode is initiated by the disciples of Jesus seeking to ascertain the origin of the man's blindness, to which Jesus responds by disassociating the man's condition from the issue of sinfulness. This echoes an earlier reference to the infirm man concerning the relationship of sin and suffering, but it seems, however, to reverse that earlier statement (5:14). The reference here suggests

---

[28] see above.
[29] Martyn, 37-42.
[30] Ibid., 129.
[31] Ellis, 160.
[32] Talbert, 158.

to the reader that perhaps Jesus' statement in chapter 5 was not referring to the man's physical suffering, but a declaration that worse things than infirmity or blindness can befall a person, such as failing to respond appropriately to Jesus. Ironically, it is not the blind man but the Pharisees whose obtuseness unwittingly reveals the true origin of "blindness."[33]

This man's episode lacks the ambiguity of the infirm man's portrayal. The blind man's bold, consistent witness to Jesus in the face of hostility and his ultimate fate at the hands of the Pharisees place him decisively on Jesus' side in this dispute. From the moment of his return from his obedient faith response, he, in the words of J. Warren Holleran, "repeatedly, witnesses to the reality, the manner and the author of the healing." Moreover, he "stands out as a paradigm of what it is to be a disciple of Jesus."[34]

The assertion by Tanzer that the man is a "positive example of one whose faith grows genuinely out of a sign"[35] presumes a positive assessment of sign-produced faith that is counter to Jesus' caution against that kind of faith (2:23-25, 4:48, 6:26). It also overlooks the man's obedience to Jesus' word prior to his healing or the occurrence of any other "sign." Dodd notes that the journey to Siloam to wash "is in fact a measure of his faith, though John does not use the term."[36] The man's understanding of Jesus' identity develops, but it is not faith necessitating a sign as a prerequisite, but his personal encounter with Jesus that leads to that development. In the Fourth Gospel, sign-produced "faith" is something less than faith, and in this episode it is apparent that even a never before seen (verse 32) "sign" cannot compel faith.[37]

The blind man's healing is accomplished without a request on the part of the recipient, unlike the first two Cana signs. Jesus does not query the man, as he did the infirm man at Bethzatha. He uses physical manipulation for the second time in the narrative (making clay and anointing the man's eyes, verse 6). A reader might be reminded of Jesus' previous physical manipulation, writing in the dirt in the presence of the adulteress and her accusers (8:6,8). His instruction in verse 7 to go wash is reminiscent of previous instructions to the βασιλικός and the infirm man, also asked by Jesus to respond in faith prior to seeing any sign. These echoes of earlier episodes with anonymous characters who fit the established

---

[33] James L. Resseguie, "John 9: A Literary Critical Analysis." In *Literary Interpretation of Biblical Narratives*, ed. . Louis Gros and R. R. Kenneth, vol II. (Nashville: Abingdon, 1982), 296.

[34] J. Warren Holleran, "Seeing the Light: A Narrative Reading of John 9," *Ephemerides Theologicae Lovaniensis* 69 (1993): 20.

[35] Tanzer, 299.

[36] Dodd, *Tradition*, 183.

[37] Schnackenburg, II. 247.

paradigm of appropriate response assist readers in their positive evaluation of the blind man, even as his unambiguous stance on Jesus' side of the identity debate reflects back positively on the previous characters he parallels, especially the infirm man.

The nameless blind man's narrative is extended and dramatic; he responds to Jesus' command to wash and is healed; his faith response continues after Jesus' departure despite substantial risk. The scene climaxes with Jesus' return and the man's response of belief, bowing down before Jesus to worship him (v. 38; the only time this occurs in the Gospel).[38] The parallels to the healing of the infirm man at Bethzatha (see above) further shape readers' assessment of the infirm man. The inquiry of the Pharisees and the man's initial lack of full recognition of Jesus' identity cause the blind man's episode to sound familiar to the reader, almost an amplified re-reading.

A subtle shift occurs when compared to chapter 5 and the ambiguity of the infirm man's motives. The blind man's parallel episode has no ambiguity concerning on whose side he can be counted. His faith response to go and receive healing is promptly followed by testimony to the efficacy of Jesus' word. Immediately his faith in the identity and person of Jesus is recorded as he prostrates himself before Jesus. No gap exists requiring readers to decide whether this man is a faithful witness to the power of Jesus' word or a traitorous informer willing to "sell-out" his healer. The unambiguous response of this blind man will reflect favorably on the reader's remembrance of the episode of the infirm man's response, since they parallel one another in so many aspects.

The blind man's growing understanding of Jesus' identity is paralleled by the progressively revealed "blindness" of his inquisitors. While the man's testimony is bold and unshakable concerning what he knows, he is not afraid to confess his ignorance when applicable (οὐκ οἶδα vv. 12, 25; see also his admission that he does not know the identity of the Son of man in v. 36). In contrast, the Pharisees confidently assert what they think they know (v. 16, he is not from God; v. 24, we know that he is a sinner; and v. 29, we know God spoke to Moses but this man's origins are unknown).[39] Each of their confident assertions of "knowledge" are statements the reader knows to be patently untrue. When the Pharisees confront Jesus in verse 40, this contrast is again emphasized. The Pharisees ask what Paul Duke aptly labels a "sneering question" of Jesus to see if he will accuse them of blindness, and readers, whose expectations are shaped by the already apparent irony of this episode, expect an affirma-

---

[38] Brown, *John*, I. 376.
[39] Ibid., 377.

tive response. Instead, Jesus agrees they are not blind, and for that reason their guilt is magnified because instead of an acknowledged blindness, which would bring a recognition of dependency, they suffer from "an illusion of sight, which has led them to a far deeper darkness than they know."[40]

Again the focus is on the issue of identity, but the object of that focus, Jesus, is absent for most of the episode; his absence from vv. 8-34 is his longest in the Fourth Gospel's text.[41] The blind man's identity as a disciple is progressively revealed through his actions. As stated by Jan du Rand, "the blind man is characterized by what he does, namely witness about Jesus' σημεῖον and about Jesus' identity as well as through the deeds that were done to him: he was cast out. That shows that he was a believer in Jesus."[42] The blind man's growing understanding of Jesus' identity is expressed through a naming progression: man called Jesus (v.9), prophet (v.17), man from God (v.33), Lord (v.38). Although he is anonymous, the man undergoes his own naming progression: beggar (v.8), the man who had formerly been blind (v.13), the blind man (v.17), our son (v.20), the man who had been blind (v.24).[43] The positive forward movement of the progression becomes apparent when the reader realizes that after Jesus' return in v.35, the man's former state is no longer mentioned. His blindness is fully conquered through his understanding of and response to Jesus' identity. The restoration of his vision is complete when he comes to know his own identity. The man whose first textual appearance Resseguie characterizes "as a colorless object of theological speculation" now is portrayed "as a character in his own right."[44] The man's growing individuation occurs despite simultaneous attempts by the Pharisees to cast doubt on his identity. They initially identify him in direct address as "the one whose eyes Jesus has opened" (v. 17). But when addressing his parents, they will refer to him only as the one "allegedly born blind" ("who you say was born blind" v. 19). In verse 28 they accuse him of being a disciple of Jesus, ironic because this man's understanding is insufficient to allow him to be Jesus' disciple and because they intend this as a term of disparagement. Their expression of contempt is really their admission that they do not understand God's revelation in Jesus.[45]

---

[40] Paul D. Duke, *Irony in the Fourth Gospel* (Atlanta: John Knox Press, 1985), 124.
[41] Ibid., 119.
[42] Jan A. du Rand, "A Syntactical and Narratological Reading of John 10 in Coherence with Chapter 9," in *The Shepherd Discourse of John 10 and its Context*, ed. Johannes Beutler and Robert Fortna, Society for New Testament Studies Monograph Series 67, (Cambridge: Cambridge University Press, 1991), 113.
[43] Staley, "Stumbling," 66.
[44] Resseguie, 300.
[45] Schnackenburg, 251.

Their final designation for him is the harsh "in sin you were wholly born" (v. 34).

The blind man fits well the paradigm of appropriate response; he is challenged by Jesus to respond in faith prior to "seeing" any evidence of Jesus' power or ability (v. 7). He evinces the faith to go and wash as Jesus has commanded, and immediately follows his active faith response by witnessing to a progression of others concerning what Jesus' word has accomplished. First he identifies himself to "the neighbors and those who had seen him before," (v. 8) and testifies to what "the man called Jesus" said and did (v. 12). Then he is brought before the Pharisees and his testimony does not waver (vv. 15-17). His next witness contrasts him with the cowardly non-witness of his parents (vv. 18-23). In his second witness to the Pharisees he is emboldened to go beyond merely testifying to Jesus' word and deed: he challenges their unwillingness to accept his witness to the truth (vv. 24-34). The people who receive his witness respond in varied ways, some believe in the reality of the sign, others doubt that any healing even occurred (v. 9). Some of the Pharisees are even portrayed as considering the possibility of Jesus' divine origins through the man's testimony (v. 16), although they are heard from no more after the initial expression of openness to Jesus' identity claims. The final response of this man's hearers is to cast him out (v. 34). After the account of the man's faithful and consistent witness, he re-encounters Jesus, and he grows in understanding, not just of what Jesus has accomplished, but of the identity of Jesus; the man formerly in darkness prostrates himself before the light.

His witnessing without full comprehension of Jesus' identity is never criticized, it echoes the same phenomenon at Cana by Jesus' mother, the Samaritan woman, and the infirm man; none of whom fully understand Jesus' identity at the time they initially witness to the efficacy of his word. Yet he does not remain in partial understanding; his encounter with and response to Jesus is complete with his affirmation and prostration in verse 38. The identity formation on the part of the anonymous, formerly sightless man encourages readers' own identity re-formation through their identification with him. Resseguie notes that in recognizing Jesus' identity, "he also comes to the point of seeing who he himself is."[46] His development is "the development of a person, of a newfound selfhood that penetrates a stratified society and breaks down walls that divide."[47] Reader identification with the blind man is also assisted by the generic terms with which he is introduced. He is not τις ἄνθρωπος like the infirm

---

[46] Resseguie, 300.
[47] Ibid., 303.

man (5:5), or τις βασιλικὸς (4:46), "but simply ἄνθρωπος (a characteristic term for humanity), thus de-emphasizing his particularity."[48] The universality of the man's identity, together with the lack of any specification or physical description beyond the identification of his need, facilitates the reader's identification with this formerly blind anonymous man. Identification with him is enhanced for readers who themselves have been beggars of one sort or another, alienated from society, parents, or even their religious community. For readers who are able to identify with the man and enter into his circumstances, his characterization is "a social legitimization of their past and present history."[49] The sense of identification would increase for readers who have found the way of following Jesus to be costly, exacting a price.

A Dead Man With No Faith

What roles do the characters of Lazarus, Mary, and Martha play in the reader's experience of the Fourth Gospel? Their names alone cannot eliminate them from the paradigm of appropriate response to Jesus established at the Cana wine transformation. If any of them fits the paradigm of significant characters challenged to a faith response on the basis of Jesus' word without the prerequisite of a sign, and witness to others concerning the efficacy of his word, then the claim made here that anonymity is an essential element in the paradigm is called into question. An analysis of elements of their characterization apart from their names, however, reveals that they do not fit the paradigm of appropriate response.

The significance of chapter 11 is undeniable: it narrates Jesus' final σημεῖον, recognizable as the "great hinge" of the Fourth Gospel plot.[50] Together with chapter 12, it marks the turning point when Jesus' public ministry ceases, the plot against him intensifies, and he turns towards Jerusalem to begin his final journey. By most readers' estimation, this is the seventh and final sign of Jesus' public ministry. The reader is explicitly reminded of its place among the σημεῖα by the reference to the healing of the blind man (11:37). Appropriate to Jesus' coming passion, the mood of the first Cana σημεῖον is reversed: the festive wedding feast is replaced by the grief of a funeral procession.[51] The somber tone is in keeping with the darkening developments as exemplified by the increas-

---

[48] David S. Dockery, "John 9:1-41: A Narrative Discourse Study," *Occasional Papers in Translation and Textlinguistics* 2 (1988): 17.
[49] Stibbe, 112.
[50] Kermode, "John," 456.
[51] Mark W. G. Stibbe, "A Tomb with a View: John 11.1-44 in Narrative-Critical Perspective," *New Testament Studies* 40 (1994):39.

ing vehemence of Jesus' opponents; Jesus' conquest of Lazarus' death is the catalyst for his own death sentence (vv. 45-53).

A phrase used to identify Lazarus tantalizes readers concerning his relationship to Jesus and to the narrative. He is ὃν φιλεῖς (11:3), "he whom you love," a quality of relationship confirmed to the onlookers by Jesus' tears in verse 36. This may not surprise an uninformed reader, who might assume all disciples are among those Jesus loves. But to any re-reader of the Gospel, or reader whose extratext includes knowledge of the special role given to the disciple Jesus loved, the significance of the phrase is immediately recognized. It is used only here and in reference to the "disciple Jesus loved," who has not appeared yet, but who from chapter 13 on plays a primary role. Does this suggest Lazarus is the anonymous disciple Jesus loved? Certainly. But the suggestion is merely that, and cannot be taken as proof, as will be further examined in the next chapter. Lazarus is also connected to another Fourth Gospel character by proximity, John. In John's final reference, only three verses in length, he is named three times (10:40-42). In the verse immediately following, Lazarus is named for the first time, and within six verses is named twice more (11:1-6).[52] Johannes Beutler has suggested that there is an interrelationship between John, Lazarus, and the disciple Jesus loved, each taking over the narrative role of the one preceding them, and each making their first appearance in the narrative soon after the last reference to one of the others.[53]

Lazarus, although he is the focus of the episode, can quickly be eliminated from the pattern of the appropriate response paradigm. He never dialogues with Jesus, or speaks at all, and he cannot respond in faith to the life-giving word of Jesus, though at first glance he may appear to. He comes forth from death and the tomb at Jesus' word, but not as a human faith response because he is no longer a living member of humanity, capable of response, but rather an inanimate object with no will or decision making apparatus. He belongs in the category of the elements of nature Jesus has control over, like water transformed into wine or bread that multiplies. His is not a willful act of obedient response, but the involuntary response of an inanimate entity with no capacity to will or respond. As a representative figure, he may represent the disciple who has died and will be one day resurrected,[54] a symbol of hope, but not a model for reader imitation.

---

[52] Brodie, 386-7.
[53] Johannes Beutler, May 6, 1988 conversation with Thomas L. Brodie, cited in Brodie, 387.
[54] Collins, 46.

Mary of Bethany and her sister Martha must also be examined for their conformity to the paradigm of appropriate response. Mary's first reference reads like a re-introduction of a previously occurring character (11:2), "reminding" the reader of a narratively future event,[55] identifying her as the one who anointed Jesus. This is her first appearance, and seems to assume an extratextual knowledge of the tradition of Jesus' anointing. Most readers will be familiar with Jesus' anointing, but for a truly naive reader it reads as a reference to a particular person readers must know, further discouraging reader identification with her through its specification. Both sisters join in the message to Jesus, and their first words to him are identical (except for the location of μου), "Lord, if you had been here, my brother would not have died," (11:21, 32). Their responses to Jesus are not identical; Martha goes out to meet Jesus, Mary remains in the house and comes to him at the initiative of Jesus and Martha (11:28). She shows less reserve than Martha, falling at Jesus' feet (verse 32, the same physical association as in the anointing to follow in 12:3).[56]

Mary makes no faith response to Jesus nor does she witness to anyone, but that is not through any failure on her part. Martha is the only one to whom Jesus offers the opportunity to respond; all Jesus requires of Mary is for her to lead him to the tomb. Mary does not fit the paradigm of appropriate response to Jesus because she has no meaningful dialogue, response, or witness here.[57] Although her characterization is positive, her unsuitability for reader identification and imitation is due to her unique, unrepeatable witness to Jesus portrayed in the next chapter (as John's witness was unique and unrepeatable). She witnesses by anointing, preparing Jesus for his burial with a lavish outpouring of devotion (12:3-7), accomplishing in advance what Nicodemus attempts unnecessarily with his one hundred pounds of spices at the more conventional time after Jesus' death in 19:39-40. The anointing is given further positive appraisal by Jesus' parallel act when he too will wipe the feet of others (13:5).[58]

The structure of this narrative episode contrasts Mary with Martha. Their interaction with Jesus are both initiated by Jesus (his arrival in v. 17, his request in v. 28), both are portrayed surrounded by Jewish mourners (vv.18-19, 30-31), both go out to him (vv. 20, 29), both address him in identical words (vv. 21, 32), but Jesus responds to them in very different ways.[59] The similarity of construction invites comparison and reveals

---

[55] Culpepper, *Anatomy*, 60; Stibbe sees assumed here a reader "who follows the beginning and middle of the story always from the point of view of its end," "Tomb," 53.
[56] Brown, I, 435.
[57] Rena, 141.
[58] Seim, 73.
[59] Talbert, 172.

contrasts. Mary demonstrates her emotions by tears and falling at Jesus' feet. Martha, on the other hand, converses with Jesus, almost engaging him in theological debate. The other primary distinction is Jesus' response to their identical statements. There is no significant difference in their initial words, but they differ both in their posture (Mary at Jesus' feet in tears), and in Martha's addition to her statement, "and even now I know that whatever you ask from God, God will give you." The contrast between Jesus' response to Mary and his response to Martha is variously understood by different readers. Some readers believe Jesus' response differs because of the contrasting attitudes of his two dialogue partners. Stibbe understands Martha to be displaying a controlled grief with room for "growth in resurrection faith," while Mary's grief is "desperate, passionate and forlorn" and "wild and natural."[60] Others see the contrasting responses as positive but alternative responses, Martha representing the Christological confession of the later Johannine community while Mary represents the practical discipleship demonstrated in the anointing to follow.[61]

Almost all readers have viewed Martha's characterization positively, primarily on the basis of her "confession" in verse 27. This is the Fourth Gospel's parallel to Peter's confession in the Synoptics.[62] Many have stated this confession elevates her to apostleship, on an equal footing with other disciples in the Gospel,[63] a role she demonstrates by her witness to Mary (v. 28).[64] In a response to my earlier proposal of significant anonymous characters as the paradigm of appropriate response to Jesus in the Gospel, Evelyn Thibeux states that Martha represents a paradigm of appropriate response to Jesus and her "faith response is at least as strong as any character's but the beloved disciple's."[65]

Does Martha's response to Jesus fit the paradigm of appropriate response established at Cana? The answer depends on whether her confession is fully adequate and also her action definable as a "faith response," including bearing witness to the efficacy of Jesus' word. Byrne reads her faith as incomplete at this juncture, or else the sign which follows is superfluous.[66] His reading ignores the warnings against sign-produced faith in the Gospel. On close scrutiny, Martha's confession is at variance with

---

[60] Stibbe, "Tomb," 47; cf. Byrne, 56.
[61] Fiorenza, 330; Seim, 73.
[62] Culpepper, 141; Brown, *Community*, 190; Brodie, 394.
[63] Moltmann, 25-26; Seim, 71; Fiorenza (who suggests that the narrative may hint at her identification as the disciple Jesus loved, the author), 330.
[64] Fiorenza, 329; Stibbe, "Tomb," 47.
[65] Evelyn R. Thibeaux, "Response: Reading Readers Reading Characters," *Semeia* 63 (1993): 221.
[66] Byrne, 54.

the challenge expressed by Jesus in verses 25-26. In the ἐγώ εἰμι revelatory formula characteristic of the Fourth Gospel, Jesus declares that he is both resurrection and life, and that faith in him will completely overturn the process of life and death. He then asks Martha specifically, "Do you believe this?" The antecedent of "this" is Jesus' claim that he can reverse the natural order of life and death. The precise affirmation Jesus seeks from Martha is absent from her "confession." Within the context of Lazarus' death, Jesus says to Martha, "I have the power to invert this natural process, do you have the faith to believe that I can?" Martha answers, "Yes Lord, I have the faith to believe that you are the Messiah and identify you within the pre-existing christological categories of my belief system." What she does not seem capable of saying or believing is that he can meet her immediate need and restore life to her brother.

The discrepancy between Jesus' question and her response has not gone unnoticed. Barrett states that her "yes" expresses her belief in what Jesus has claimed, but not in its particular application in calling Lazarus out from the tomb. He suggests she "takes the discourse a step forward," raising it to new theological heights, a reading also shared by Brodie's assessment that although Martha does not answer Jesus specific question, "she goes beyond it."[67] Is "going beyond" Jesus' direct challenge a positive progression? Other readers are more cautious in their assessments. Schnackenburg notes that her "yes" does not imply her understanding of what Jesus said. Brown says that Jesus "does not reject her traditional titles, but he will demonstrate the deeper truth that lies behind them."[68] He is correct that her confession is never rejected or contradicted, yet each christological confession in the Gospel is shown to be inadequate when it stands alone. The christological formulations, with the exception of the prologue and Jesus' own statements, appear in the context of debate over Jesus' identity and origins (7:26, 27, 31, 41, and 42; 9:22; 10:24; and 12:34), or reveal incomplete or inadequate understanding (4:25, 29; 11:27; and 20:31). The confession of Thomas (see chapter 7 below) elicits an unenthusiastic response from Jesus, who regrets that "seeing" was a necessary prerequisite to confession (20:29).

Jesus never gives approval to Martha's "confession," and Martha never indicates that she believes Jesus' claim of authority over Lazarus' circumstances. When Jesus applies his ἐγώ εἰμι declaration to her present need, she specifically demonstrates her lack of faith and understanding. She discourages Jesus' demonstration of the truth of his words and displays her conviction of the finality of death's power. In the face of Jesus'

---

[67] Barrett, 396-7; Brodie, 394.
[68] Schnackenburg, 332; Brown, *John*, I. 434.

word revealing his power over death, she warns, "Lord, by now he smells," (12:39). At Jesus' command to remove the stone barrier to Lazarus' "forthcoming," Martha is given an opportunity to echo Jesus' mother, "Do whatever he tells you" (2:5), but instead she becomes the spokesperson for the doubters and naysayers. Her "witness" to Mary does not fit the paradigm of testimony to the power of Jesus' word, either before or after Lazarus' comes out of the tomb. She only relays Jesus' request to speak with Mary, never giving testimony of the power of Jesus' word. She fails to fit the paradigm the Gospel creates for appropriate response to Jesus, witnessing to the efficacy of Jesus' word. It was not her words of confession that were faulty, but her understanding of them and their significance in her life.

An Excursus:
A Woman With No Place (Textually)

The textual and canonical history of the episode of the adulteress (7:53-8:11) is so problematic that the decision to include it requires justification. On the other hand, ignoring it as if it never existed is considered acceptable practice, presuming readers are both aware of its history and agree that it does not belong either in the text or in an analysis of the text.[69] Others at least declare their intention not to consider it on the basis of inauthenticity.[70] Most readers deal with and interpret the episode, but only after making clear their assessment of its inauthenticity, usually bracketing it in some way or placing it in an appendix or an excursus. This is understandable, since even in its textual attestations, some witnesses bracket the episode, as if to indicate scribal awareness of the absence of strong manuscript attestation for the episode.[71]

Nonetheless, the pericope of the adulteress is a part of the text of the Fourth Gospel as read by most readers, from ancient times until now, within the interpretive communities of faith adherents in which they participate. Therefore, it is interesting that a commentary which has as its stated purpose to help its readers "towards a literary appreciation of each section of the Gospel," and which praised Culpepper for his emphasis on "what lies in front of our eyes as we look exclusively at the Fourth Gospel as a literary unity," gives no rationale for ignoring it.[72] This is particularly noteworthy since the text Stibbe says is literally in "front of his

---

[69] Bultmann, *John*; Stibbe, *John*.
[70] Talbert, 152; Haenchen, 21-22.
[71] Metzger, 221.
[72] Stibbe, *John*, 9,10.

eyes" throughout his analysis is The Greek New Testament (Aland, et al. U.B.S. 3rd ed.) and the NIV translation of the Gospel. Both contain the episode, although in brackets or footnotes. Its presence affects readers' responses to the narrative, even if they reject its authenticity. Any analysis of the Fourth Gospel needs to consider the episode, if only to justify its exclusion.

The evidence against its authenticity in the original text of the Fourth Gospel is well documented and includes its lack of attestation, excessive variant readings, its vocabulary and style foreign to the Gospel, and its disruption of the unity of chapters 7 and 8. The textual history of the pericope confirms its absence from the original text. It is not present in the earliest and most important witnesses including P^{66}, P^{75}, Sinaiticus, Vaticanus, the oldest form of the Syriac, and the Sahidic, among others. The only early Greek manuscript which includes it is D, though it is represented in several late Greek manuscripts (E (F) G H K M U Γ Π 28 700 892) and some old Latin manuscripts. Several witnesses that do include it mark the passage as though to bracket it from the rest of the text, indicating uncertainty of its authenticity, while some that omit it leave a space after 7:53 as if aware of an omitted pericope at that location.[73]

Until recently, it could also be said that "no Greek Church Father prior to Euthymius Zigabenus (twelfth century) comments on the passage, and the Euthymius reference declares that the accurate copies of the Gospel do not contain it."[74] This statement is no longer true. The 1941 discovery of the Biblical commentaries of Didymus the Blind, fourth-century Alexandrian exegete and educator, demonstrates knowledge of this pericope; he uses it to support his interpretation of Ecclesiastes 7:21-22a.[75] Didymus does not identify its source as the Fourth Gospel, but rather mentions it is located "in certain gospels," a curious phrase he uses nowhere else. The statement can be interpreted as Didymus' reflection of its non-canonicity. Bart Ehrman's analysis notes the absence of several details present in the Fourth Gospel textual tradition and suggests that Didymus' source for this episode was the now lost "Gospel according to the Hebrews." This was then conflated with the similar episode preserved in the third century Didascalia Apostolorum, which contains exactly the details lacking in Didymus' version, to form the more familiar Fourth Gospel version.[76] The discovery does not alter the non-authenticity of this epi-

---

[73] For a thorough discussion see Bruce M. Metzger, *A Textual Commentary on the Greek New Testament* (London: United Bible Societies, 1971 [1975]), 219-21.

[74] Ibid., 220.

[75] Bart D. Ehrman, "Jesus and the Adulteress," *New Testament Studies* 34 (1988): 24-5.

[76] Ibid., 25-38.

sode as a part of the original text, but offers more evidence for its existence as a well-known early piece of Jesus tradition. Ehrman's hypothesis, if correct, accounts for the form of the text extant in the Fourth Gospel textual tradition.

The evidence of vocabulary and style can be illustrated by the following phrases which are rare or non-existent in the rest of the Fourth Gospel narrative, but common in the Synoptics: v.1 Mount of Olives, v.2 παρεγένετο, v.2 πᾶς ὁ λαὸς, v.3 οἱ γραμματεῖς, v.10-11 κατακρίνω, and v.11 ἀπὸ τοῦ νῦν.[77] The disruption of the unity of chapters 7 and 8 by breaking up the discourses at the Feast of Tabernacles has also been offered to support the episode's inauthenticity.[78] But these discourses are already interrupted by the second Nicodemus episode. Brodie argues that in some ways, the episode "fits" its textual location very well. In chapter 7, Jesus has indicated that the Jews' mishandling of the law of Moses makes an instrument of death from it, while in Jesus' hand it is a source of life; and this point "finds vivid expression in the scene around the woman."[79] An examination of chapter 8 for echoes paralleling the themes in the adulterous woman's episode, reveals the theme of judgment. Jesus denies that he judges anyone while accusing the Jews of judging falsely (vv. 15, 26, 46), a truth just illustrated in his dealings with the woman.[80] This gives the episode a sense of "fit" with its narrative environment, suiting the "judging" and "condemning" themes of chapter 8. It appropriately follows the debate concerning Jesus' teaching, the questioning of his teaching authority (7:15), and Nicodemus' reference to the legality of using the law to judge him without a hearing.[81]

What cannot be granted to this pericope is its rightful place in the narrative. If there can be no serious attempt to refute the evidence of this episode's non-authenticity, why include it in an analysis of the narrative effect of characters on the reading process? The reason is identical to the explanation for its inclusion in critical texts of the Fourth Gospel: its textual tradition within communities of believers, one of the interpretive communities of most of its readers, is too strong to justify ignoring it. Instead, while admitting its non-authenticity, just as the editors of the critical texts accomplish with their brackets, this study will examine two questions. What effect does this episode have on readers who include it in their reading experience? Secondly, does anything in the language or de-

---

[77] Talbert, 152.
[78] Brown, *John*, I. 336.
[79] Brodie, 338.
[80] Brown, *John*, 336; Beasley-Murray, 144; Ehrman, 27.
[81] John Paul Heil, "The Story of Jesus and the Adulteress (John 7,53-8,11) Reconsidered," *Biblica* 72 (1991): 186-91.

tails of this episode help explain how this independent piece of Jesus tradition would come late to be attached to this particular Gospel?

Gail O'Day's recent examination of what she terms the "misreadings" of this text looks at its most common lines of interpretation.[82] She notes that in its rhetorical shape, the woman and her accusers are placed on an equal level. This is accomplished primarily through Jesus' language, action, and attitude towards both.[83] The common interpretations of the woman's episode generally follow one of three directions. Some readers follow Augustine and focus on the woman's dialogue with Jesus; some follow Calvin and recast Jesus' words for fear of advocating leniency towards sin; for others the focus lies in recreating what Jesus wrote on the ground.[84]

Readers possess an amazing confidence in their ability to re-create what Jesus' wrote, in spite of a total lack of textual specification. Recent examples of readings that "read" Jesus' written words include those of Dom Andrew Nugent and James Sanders.[85] Nugent claims Jesus' challenge "Let him who is without sin..." is insufficient to halt the woman's accusers. It is not a legal requirement, and it is precisely the law on which they take their stand. Jesus' only authority and power, therefore, "resides not in what he says, but what he does."[86] The gap created by Jesus' unspecified writing begs readers to take notice, process information from their extratexts, and fill this blank. Both Nugent and Sanders supply similar information from their extratext, reading here a reference to the giving of the Law. It fits the context of a dispute on a point of law both within the episode itself, and in chapter 7 which precedes it. Nugent reads the reference to the "writing with the finger" (8:6) as significant; its only other canonical use is Exodus 31:18 and Deuteronomy 9:10. Writing a second time (8:8) echoes God's second writing of the decalogue "to reaffirm the Law after the 'adultery' of his people."[87] Similarly, Sanders suggests Jesus' first act of writing (8:6) was to write the first half of the decalogue. When he bent down the second time (8:8), he finished the decalogue.[88]

---

[82] Gail O'Day, "John 7:53-8:11: A Study in Misreading," *Journal of Biblical Literature* 111 (1992): 631-40.

[83] Ibid., 633.

[84] Ibid., 633-6.

[85] Dom Andrew Nugent, "What Did Jesus Write? (John 7, 53-8,11)," *The Downside Review* 108 (1990): 193-8; James Sanders, "'Nor Do I...': A Canonical Reading of the Challenge to Jesus in John 8," in *The Conversation Continues: Studies in Paul and John in Honor of J. Louis Martyn*, ed. Robert T. Fortna and Beverly Gaventa, (Nashville: Abingdon, 1990), 337-47.

[86] Nugent, 194.

[87] Ibid., 195-6.

[88] Sanders, 343-5.

It is difficult to avoid speculation on the content of Jesus' writing, but O'Day is correct in her assessment that allowing the speculation to control the understanding of the woman's episode leads to an entirely extratextually based reading. She suggests an alternative reading focusing on Jesus' behavior pattern: his initial silence, his bending down and writing, then standing to address his conversation partner. The pattern is identical for the woman and for her accusers, placing the woman and her accusers on the same level in relation to Jesus. He transforms the conflict from condemnation and death (8:7) to acquittal and life (8:11), a transformation applying equally to both parties. Both the woman and her accusers "are invited to give up old ways and enter a new way of life".[89] The reader is left with another gap concerning whether either party in this dialogue will respond affirmatively to Jesus, break free of the past, and begin anew. The answer is not explicit within the text, indeterminacy again prevails.

How does the presence of this episode affect the readers of the Fourth Gospel? Does the adulterous woman fit the established paradigm of anonymous characters given significant textual space, challenged to respond in faith to Jesus' word without a prior sign, and bearing witness to others of the efficacy of Jesus' word? The woman shares anonymity and significant textual space with other paradigmatic characters, and is challenged to respond to Jesus' life-changing word; but unlike the others, her narrative ends without a recorded response or witness. Unlike Nicodemus, she does not disappear from a scene where Jesus' presence continues. Verse 12 is a definitive intermission, with scene change, prior to the resumption of Jesus' ongoing dispute with the Pharisees.

The woman's episode is dense with indeterminacy; most notably the woman's anonymity and the concealment of Jesus' writing. For the first time readers encounter someone writing. Most references to "writing" in the Fourth Gospel refer to the writings of Hebrew Scripture. The only other time someone performs the act of writing is in chapter 19, where Pilate prepares the inscription for Jesus' cross (19:19). Both instances of writing are in the context of a trial and execution, share the same accusers, and the one who writes desires to acquit, or at least commute, the sentence of the accused. The above parallels shed little light on the origin of the adulteress' episode, but offer insight into how the presence of her pericope might effect a reader's experience of the Fourth Gospel. Without speculating on the content of the writing and determining the episode's

---

[89] O'Day, "Misreading," 636-8.

meanings from an entirely extratextual invention, the reading offered here focuses on the significance of the act, regardless of the content.[90]

The episode also impacts the reader by its location, interpolated between two disputes concerning Jesus' origins. In 7:27-28 Jesus warns his accusers that they only think they know his origins. In 7:41-43 a division occurs, with its identified starting point in a dispute over the town of Jesus' birth, and in 7:52 the Pharisees deny his origins based on his Galilean roots. In 8:14 Jesus tells the people they have no clue as to his comings and goings, then declares that they are forbidden to come where he is going (verse 21). The genealogy of his accusers are also called into question in the debate over the true definition of "children of Abraham" (8:33-59). Jesus inverts the focus on origins in the episode of the adulteress, located in the midst of the ongoing dispute about origins. His word to the woman is to stop looking back to her origins, but go forward in her life narrative, neither condemned nor controlled by her past.

The woman's fit in the paradigm is not fully comfortable. The absence of a recorded response and witness makes her parallel to Nicodemus. Few textual clues are provided to help fill the gaps, and readers must be content to choose between accepting the ambiguity of her characterization or assuming an almost totally extratextual basis for understanding her ultimate response to Jesus. The presence of an independent piece of tradition "finding" a particular place in a narrative makes the context noteworthy. In her context, was Jesus writing the narrative of her accusers? Could it be the next chapter in the woman's own narrative? The indeterminacy of the woman's episode solicits reader participation; the indeterminacy of Jesus' writing invites readers to permit Jesus to (re)write their own narrative as they respond in faith to his word.

What prompted this independent floating piece of Jesus tradition to find a home, albeit an insecure one, at this particular point, or anywhere else, in the Fourth Gospel? The disjuncture between chapters 7 and 8, the common Pharisaic enemies in 8:3 and 8:13, and the familiar narrative pattern of encounter with Jesus followed by dialogue, may have contributed to the tradition finding its way into this Gospel at this point. The theme of judgment and the disputes concerning Jesus' origins help connect this episode thematically to the disputes concerning Jesus' origins preceding and following it. The role of women characters in the Fourth Gospel might also have drawn this episode to merge into the text "which places women at crucial points of development and confrontation."[91] As table 3 in chapter 2 illustrates, extensive narrative space is not granted to

---

[90] Ibid., 636.
[91] Fiorenza, 326.

anonymous characters in the Synoptics, making this narrative more appealing than other available alternatives as a home for the woman's pericope. The woman's partial fit in the appropriate response paradigm, including her anonymity, gives her a commonality with other Fourth Gospel characters fitting that paradigm.

CHAPTER 7

THE DISCIPLE JESUS LOVED

History of Interpretation

The interpretation of the disciple Jesus loved in the Fourth Gospel has focused primarily on his historicity, identity, role within the Fourth Gospel community, and his paradigmatic function in the narrative. Early attempts to identify this figure focused on John, son of Zebedee, and can be traced back to the second century through the writings of Eusebius.[1] Readers favoring this identification today are a minority[2] and several alternative identifications have been suggested. These include John Mark,[3] an elder John, who is not the Apostlic son of Zebedee but a Palestinian Jew,[4] Matthias,[5] a disciple of the Baptist from a priestly family not one of the twelve,[6] an Essene monk from Jerusalem who was probably a priest,[7] and even Paul.[8]

Recently James H. Charlesworth has argued that the identity of the disciple Jesus loved is textually determinable, "that anonymity moves to an epithet and finally to a revelation of the identity of the Beloved Disciple." Rather than an anonymous character whose identity is not revealed by the narrative, according to his reading this figure is instead "an enigma

---

[1] Eusebius *Ecclesiastical History*, V.8.4; V.24.3.

[2] e.g. Donald Guthrie, *New Testament Introduction*, rev. ed. (Downers Grove, Illinois: Inter-Varsity Press, 1990), 252-60; D. A. Carson, Douglas J. Moo and Leon Morris, *An Introduction to the New Testament* (Grand Rapids, Michigan: Zondervan, 1992), 138-47. Both Brown (John, 1:xcviii) and Schnackenburg (I. 101-4) have since retreated from their earlier hesitant identification of the apostle John as the disciple Jesus loved.

[3] Lewis Johnson, "Who Was the Beloved Disciple?" *Expository Times* 77 (1966): 157-8.

[4] Hartwig Thyen, "Entwicklungen innerhalb der johannischen Theologie und Kirche im Spiegel von Joh 21 und der Lieblingsjümgertexte des Evangeliums," in *L'Evangile de Jean: Sources, rédaction, théologie*, ed. M de Jong. Bibliotheca ephemiridum theologicarum lovaniensium (Louvain: University Press, 1977): 259-99.

[5] Eric L. Titus, "The Identity of the Beloved Disciple," *Journal of Biblical Literature* 69 (1950): 323-8.

[6] Joseph A. Grassi, *The Secret Identity of the Beloved Disciple* (New York: Paulist Press, 1992), 115.

[7] Eugen Ruckstuhl, *Jesus im Horizont der Evangelien*. Stutgarter Biblische Aufsatzbände 3 (Stuttgart: Katholisches Bibelwerk, 1988), 31-65.

[8] B. W. Bacon, *The Fourth Gospel in Research and Debate* (London: T. Fisher Unwin, 1910), 301-31.

that is gradually disclosed."⁹ His extensive research into previous attempts to identify this character is of inestimable value for its thoroughness. His examination of the passages in which the disciple Jesus loved is present leads him to conclude "the one name that alone looms large as the Beloved Disciple seems to be Thomas, the Twin–the one to whom the Evangelist gives the spotlight in the final and concluding scene in the GosJn."¹⁰ If Charlesworth is correct, the thesis that the function of the anonymity of the disciple Jesus loved is narratively necessary to enable and facilitate reader identification with the character, is dealt a severe blow. A careful examination of Charlesworth's argument is necessary. His exegetical conclusions will be carefully evaluated below as each of the textual occurrences of the disciple Jesus loved are investigated.

Lazarus is frequently suggested as the disciple Jesus loved, primarily on the basis of the references to him in chapter 11 identifying him as loved by Jesus, the only other male follower of Jesus so designated except for the anonymous disciple Jesus loved who first appears in the 13th chapter of this narrative. This is not a new suggestion, but continues to find several proponents.¹¹ The primary reasons for identifying Lazarus as this disciple, besides the designation of "ὃν φιλεῖς," include Bethany's proximity to Jerusalem correlated to the disciple's familiarity with that city and how his own resurrection experience would both enable his quick acceptance of Jesus' resurrection (20:8) and cause confusion concerning his death (21:22-23).¹²

Recently Vernard Eller attempts to identify Lazarus as the disciple Jesus loved, making a novel presentation for his case for excluding the external evidence from his investigation. "I'm going all the way with Sherlock himself—namely, working the case entirely from 'internal evidence', fathoming the truth simply from the clues at hand. Did Holmes ever have to resort to help from outside experts?"¹³ The "evidence" for his "deductions" include the identification of Lazarus as loved by Jesus,

---

⁹ James H. Charlesworth, *The Beloved Disciple: Whose Witness Validates the Gospel of John?* (Valley Forge: Trinity Press International, 1995), xv.

¹⁰ Ibid., 48.

¹¹ Robert Eisler, *The Enigma of the 4G: Its Author and Its Writer* (London: Methuen, 1937); Floyd Filson, "Who Was the Beloved Disciple," *Journal of Biblical Literature* 68 (1949): 83-88; Karl A. Eckhardt, *Der Tod des Johannes als Schüssel zum Verständnis der johanneischen Schriften*, Studien zur Rechts - und Religionsgeschichte 3 (Berlin: De Gruyter, 1961); J. N. Sanders, "Those Whom Jesus Loved," *New Testament Studies* 1 (1954) 29-41 and *A Commentary on the Gospel According to St. John*. ed. and completed by B. A. Mastin, Harper's New Testament Commentaries (New York: Harper & Row, 1968), 31-32.

¹² Sanders, *John*, 31-32.

¹³ Vernard Eller, *The Beloved Disciple: His Name, His Story, His Thought* (Grand Rapids: Eerdmans, 1987), ix.

the crucial narrative turning point at chapters 11-12, Lazarus' inclusion among the Jewish intelligentsia (as indicated by his mourners), the absence of any overlap in the appearances of the disciple Jesus loved and Lazarus in the Gospel, and his own positive assessment of Lazarus' "fit" in each passage that refers to the disciple Jesus loved.[14] Despite Eller's claim that the fictional detective inspired his exclusion of external evidence in formulating his solution, the reality is that no such corroborating external evidence exists.[15]

As plausible as the identification of Lazarus as the disciple Jesus loved appears because of his characterization, David Hawkin's refutation of its proponents is convincing:

> The identification of Lazarus as the Beloved Disciple begins with the assumption that somewhere the Evangelist would indicate the identity of the Beloved Disciple...However, this argument *still* leaves the difficulty of why the Beloved Disciple is not named in chapters 13, 19 and 20...what they seem unable to accept is the fact that the Evangelist simply does not tell us (for whatever reason) who the Beloved Disciple is.[16]

Hawkin's argument focuses on the reality of the anonymity of the disciple Jesus loved; accepting the indeterminacy that accompanies him. It is an appropriate critique not only of attempts to identify the disciple Jesus loved as Lazarus, but also of every attempt to claim that the narrative indicates the identity and name of this character. The disciple Jesus loved is unnamed, and that absence functions in specific ways within the narrative. The point at issue is not whether the disciple Jesus loved could historically be Lazarus or any of the other named characters in this Gospel; that possibility is certainly reasonable. The fact remains that the narrative carefully avoids making any such identification.

The narratively prescribed anonymity of this loved disciple has been subverted by many interpreters of the Fourth Gospel in their choice of how to identify this character as they write about him. Every time his designation as "the disciple whom Jesus loved" is replaced with "Beloved Disciple," the capitalization, for all practical purposes, makes a name of it.[17] Culpepper notes "the reference to the Beloved Disciple is a relative

---

[14] Ibid, 53-72.

[15] R. Alan Culpepper, *John, the Son of Zebedee: The Life of a Legend*, Studies on Personalities of the New Testament, ed. D. Moody Smith (Columbia, South Carolina: University of South Carolina Press, 1994), 76.

[16] David J. Hawkin, "The Function of the Beloved Disciple Motif in the Johannine Redaction," *Laval theologique et philosophique* 33 (1977): 140, n. 24.

[17] Not all scholars are guilty of this practice. Among those who do not capitalize the designation beloved disciple are Barrett, Kysar, Talbert, Stibbe, Kurz, Segovia, Brodie, Grassi, Pamment, Agourides, and Watty.

clause,"[18] but contradicts his own accurate grammatical analysis even within that statement by capitalizing the designation, thereby creating a proper noun. Even worse is the occasional reader who refers to the disciple Jesus loved by his "initials" as a scholarly shorthand, "BD".[19] Others speak of his identifying designation as a title,[20] which is grammatically just a step away from a name. Some readers refer to his designating clause "the disciple Jesus loved" *as* his name, denying him his narrated anonymity.[21]

Given the anonymity of the disciple loved by Jesus, the search for the purpose behind his anonymity has led to a variety of proposals. It has been suggested he was unknown to the audience of the Gospel,[22] or not held in high enough esteem to fill the crucial role of authenticator of the Fourth Gospel tradition.[23] His anonymity has been understood as a deliberate heightening of the contrast between him and other characters, such as Peter, the Qumran Teacher of Righteousness, or other characters in general by setting him apart "in a different category from the others."[24] Watty suggests that the anonymity of the disciple Jesus loved is a reflection of concern for readers with no close ties to the original apostolic group who exerted so great an influence. Through the anonymous disciple loved by Jesus the Fourth Evangelist "attempts to break up the magic circle which was in the making...'Names' are rendered futile and superfluous so as to enable a unity and continuity in spite of the barriers of time and space."[25] One certain aspect of the anonymous disciple Jesus loved is his indeterminacy, which provides ample fodder for exegetical exercise. Frank Kermode spotlights the ambiguity of the characterization of the disciple Jesus loved when he refers to him as a "producer of enigmas."[26]

Tilborg maintains that the relationship between Jesus and the disciple he loved establishes Jesus' social identity by which all of his other rela-

---

[18] Culpepper, John, 57.
[19] e.g. Pryor, 185, passim; Charlesworth, xxiii, passim.
[20] "Peter does not enjoy the intimacy and loving relationship with Jesus that the Beloved Disciple (as his very title implies) enjoys," Quast, 69.
[21] "The Beloved Disciple appears (by name) for the first time at the farewell supper," Painter, 70; cf. Beasley-Murray, lxxiii.
[22] Painter, 64n.116.
[23] J.J. Gunther, "The Relationship of the Beloved Disciple to the 12," *Theologische Zeitschrift* 37 (1981): 141.
[24] Stibbe, 98; Jürgen Roloff, "Der johanneische 'Lieblingsjünger' und der Lehrer der Gerechtigkeit," *New Testament Studies* 15 (1968): 105; Richard Bauckham, "The Beloved Disciple as Ideal Author," *Journal for the Study of the New Testament* 49 (1993): 43.
[25] William W. Watty, "The Significance of Anonymity in the Fourth Gospel," *The Expository Times* 90 (1979): 212.
[26] Kermode, "John," 463.

tionships, including those with his "mother, brothers and sisters, with his disciples in general and with particular women and men, derive their color and content."[27] The representative role of the disciple Jesus loved strengthens the connection between the reader and Jesus, as well as between the reader and the disciple himself. It is by means of the representational quality of his characterization that "the reader is able to see that the Beloved Disciple, and hence the Johannine community, can and does enjoy a direct, intimate relationship with Christ."[28] His intimacy with Jesus and his role as special recipient of Jesus' love qualifies him as the witness to Jesus for his community and later readers.[29] Through him his community experienced the continuation of Jesus' ministry. Being entrusted with the care of Jesus' mother has been read as effectively making him the executor of Jesus' earthly program.[30] Culpepper says that in the work and witness of the disciple Jesus loved, "the Johannine community saw the Paraclete at work among them ...he was their link with the earthly Jesus and their witness to the risen Lord."[31]

Textual Appearances

The first appearance of the disciple Jesus loved that is explicitly stated within the narrative of the Fourth Gospel occurs at the supper in chapter 13. The scene begins with Jesus' dialogue with Peter (13:1-11) as he washes the feet of the disciples, once more demonstrating Peter's failure to understand what Jesus says or is doing. Jesus then teaches on servanthood and obedience (13:12-17). He then uses a citation from Psalm 41 (13:18) to predict his betrayal. For the reader who is unaware of Jesus' betrayal, and for his disciples who in the Fourth Gospel are always unaware of what he is talking about prior to his resurrection, Jesus speaks plainly, "one of you will betray me." This leads to the scene in which the reader first explicitly encounters the disciple "whom Jesus loved." There is no explanation of who he is or where he came from. It is almost as if the reader is to assume he has been there all along, but with no indication he is to be identified with any particular disciple previously encoun-

---

[27] Tilborg, 2.
[28] Quast, 70.
[29] Collins, 131.
[30] J. Kügler, *Der Jünger, den Jesus liebte. Literarische, theologische und historische Untersuchungen zu einer Schlüsselgestalt johanneischer Theologie und Geschichte. Mit einem Exkurs über die Brotrede in Joh 6*, Stuttgarter biblische Beiträge 16 (Stuttgart: Verlag katholisches Bibelwerk, 1988), 254.
[31] Culpepper, John, 84.

tered.³² There is no introduction to detail anything of his personality traits, background, family, or the circumstances which led to his following Jesus. He is simply stated to be "one of his disciples," (13:23). In his initial introduction in chapter 13 the narrative gives the impression that "the beloved disciple participates in the supper with Jesus, but that nothing he says or does effects the events. He seems to be both present and absent, so to speak."³³ Yet the very uniqueness of his designation as a recipient of Jesus' love and his position in relation to Jesus make it inaccurate to say he is "insignificant."³⁴

The only two noteworthy items in his first narrative description are his designation and his position. It has been noted that his position, ἐν τῷ κόλπῳ τοῦ Ἰησοῦ, "on the breast of Jesus", precedes the descriptive phrase, ὃν ἠγάπα ὁ Ἰησοῦς, "the one whom Jesus loved."³⁵ Many interpreters have attempted to understand this designation in terms of the position of honor around the table.³⁶ These attempts miss the fact that whatever extratextual knowledge of first century seating arrangements are applied to this scene, the text is silent on this disciple's position at the table, focusing instead on his *position toward Jesus*. Instead of providing information concerning the loved disciple's honored position among the disciples, the Fourth Gospel guides the reader to an understanding about his special relationship to Jesus. The description of the disciple Jesus loved—ἐν τῷ κόλπῳ τοῦ Ἰησοῦ (13:23)—echoes the earlier description of Jesus—ὁ ὢν εἰς τὸν κόλπον τοῦ πατρὸς (1:18)—and "implies that Jesus' relationship to the Father was a model for the Beloved Disciple's relationship to Jesus."³⁷

The text immediately informs the reader of the role this disciple plays in presenting Peter's query to Jesus. These two brief statements of his position with Jesus and his relay of Peter's question are the only information narrated concerning him in this briefest of glimpses that initiates the narrative presence of this enigmatic figure. Many questions concerning him are left unanswered. Does he understand Jesus' identification of Judas as the betrayer? Some interpreters insist that he must,³⁸ but this re-

---

³² Contra Charlesworth.
³³ Margaret Pamment, "The Fourth Gospel's Beloved Disciple," *The Expository Times* 94 (1983): 366.
³⁴ Haenchen, 112.
³⁵ Beasley-Murray, 237.
³⁶ e.g. Barrett, 446; Brown, 574, but Brown admits "the above reconstruction is highly speculative."
³⁷ Culpepper, *John*, 60; cf. Hawkin, 142; Quast, 58.
³⁸ Haenchen, 111; David J. Hawkin, *The Johannine World: Reflections on the Theology of the Fourth Gospel and Contemporary Society*, SUNY Series in Religious Studies, (Albany: State University of New York Press, 1996), 82; D. A. Carson, *The Gospel According to John* (Grand Rapids: Wm. B. Eerdmans, Publishing Company, 1991), 474.

quires understanding verse 28, "no one at the table knew why Jesus had said this to him," to mean something other than its most natural reading. Then narrator says "no one" and this includes the disciple Jesus loved. To understand "why" as referring to anything other than the significance of Jesus' action as an answer to their request for the betrayer's identity is without textual support. Does the disciple Jesus loved relay any information to Peter who prompted his initial query to Jesus? The text simply refuses to fill this gap, requiring readers to fill it from their extratext or live with the ambiguity.[39]

The supper episode (13:21-30) does not portray a mediatory role for the disciple Jesus loved, toward Peter or any of the disciples, because he mediates nothing to Peter or any other character.[40] Neither can it support the claim that the disciple Jesus loved was the only one to share the intimacy of the knowledge of the betrayer's identity with Jesus; verse 28 specifically refutes the claim that anyone other than Jesus shared that knowledge.[41] Instead, the indeterminacy of this scene raises the issue of utmost import for the reader. The statement by Jesus that one of his *disciples* will betray him, together with the indeterminacy of this introduction to the disciple Jesus loved, addresses each reader with her/his loyalty to and relationship with Jesus. As Brodie states it, "The phrasing, as well as being open-ended, is also overlapping (from betrayer to beloved) and it all indicates a single idea: any of them could be the betrayer and any of them could be the beloved."[42]

The next time the reader encounters the disciple explicitly identified as loved by Jesus is at the cross in chapter 19.[43] This is his only appearance without Peter alongside him. Instead he appears here with the mother of Jesus, the anonymous character whose initial encounter with Jesus in chapter 2 establishes the paradigm of appropriate response. The narrative entrance of both is abrupt, with no explanation of how or why, they are suddenly present "standing by the cross," (19:25-27). Their appearance is again notably brief. Jesus again addresses his mother as γύναι, reinforcing his prior challenge to reconfigure her understanding of their relationship in other than filial terms. [44] At the same time, he points her to another, the disciple he loved, to consider as her son, and instructs that disciple to look on her as his mother. We are then informed of the

---

[39] Culpepper, *John*, 60.
[40] Hawkin, "Function," 143.
[41] Contra Tilborg, 91.
[42] Brodie, 453.
[43] See below for a discussion of the identification of the "other disciple" with Peter in 18:15 as the disciple Jesus loved.
[44] See discussion above in chapter 5.

immediacy his obedience. What are we to make of this second and equally brief appearance of the disciple Jesus loved?

The symbolic understandings of this scene are numerous. For Bultmann Jesus' mother represented Jewish Christianity while the disciple Jesus loved was representative of Gentile Christianity which incorporated what had been a Jewish sectarian movement into its fold. Brown understands the mother of Jesus as the church who now has oversight of the Christian, represented by the disciple.[45] Many have followed their lead in approaching the meaning of this scene allegorically. A more narrative shaped reading would remind the reader of chapter 2, where the challenge Jesus offered his mother was accepted. Here we have a narrative portrayal of her presence with the disciple on an equal footing before Jesus, as she necessarily stands before the cross not as Jesus' mother, but as his disciple.[46] The entrusting of her care to the disciple reinforces the intimacy of his relationship with Jesus, whose mother is now to become his mother.[47] The presence of the disciple Jesus loved at the cross is a narrative affirmation of the eyewitness claim made in verse 35,[48] a claim upon which the veracity and authenticity of his witness rests.

It is in the third scene in chapter 20 where the disciple Jesus loved is present at the tomb that he is first said to believe. As in chapter 13 he is once more in the company of Peter. They are informed by Mary that things are not as expected at the tomb. The narrative quotes her saying, "They have taken the Lord out of the tomb, and we do not know where they have laid him," (20:2). The use of the we may indicate she is a spokesperson for a larger group, but narratively it suggests she speaks not only for herself, but "as though she represented others."[49] The symbolism to be found in the disciple Jesus loved outpacing Peter to the tomb, yet not going in, while Peter enters without hesitating is primarily dependent on the extratext of the reader. So too the detail of the burial cloths lying separate from the head wrapping. These have been seen as indicating Christ's ascension leaving behind the worldly trappings or as a symbol of the unity that Jesus' ascension provides for all humanity.[50] An interpretation that is more focused on the Fourth Gospel narrative hears an echo of the raising of Lazarus. There he came out still bound in his grave wrappings, dependent on others to set him free (11:44). In contrast, Jesus has

---

[45] Bultmann, *John*, 673; Brown, *John*, 926.
[46] Carson, 619.
[47] Barrett, 552.
[48] See below.
[49] Brodie, 561.
[50] Schnackenburg, 3:311; Brodie, 563.

departed from the tomb unencumbered by those same confinements.[51] The detail concern the priority of arrival and entry serves to contrast the disciple Jesus loved with Peter. If "competitors" is too strong a description for their narrative juxtapostioning, a contrast is present, nonetheless. Instead of their actions being simultaneous—they ran, they arrived, they went in—we have two distinct sets of actions narrated. This prepares the reader for the distinctiveness of their responses. The only verbs describing Peter's response are "went in" and "saw" (20:6). An additional verb is employed to narrate the response of the disciple Jesus loved. He also "went in" and "saw," but his response goes further than Peter's, he also "believed," (20:8).

This belief is explicitly narrated in 20:8, but the exact content of that belief as well as what prompted it has been the focus of much debate. Arthur H. Maynard reads with particular significance the three distinct words for seeing used in narrating this discovery at the tomb: βλέπει (v. 5), θεωρεῖ (v. 6) and εἶδεν (v. 8). "Before he enters the tomb, the other disciple 'sees' in a general sense. Peter, when he enters, only 'observes' the physical scene, but the Beloved Disciple upon entering 'sees with spiritual insight' and the result is faith."[52] The difficulty with this appealing symbolism (besides the Fourth Gospel's penchant for synonyms), is that verse 8 does not specify what he believed and verse 9 explicitly states that "as yet, they did not know the Scripture, that he must rise from the dead." It has been suggested that what is narrated in verse 8 is an incomplete faith on the part of the disciple Jesus loved that will be developed further as the narrative advances.[53] Bultmann, while rejecting the authenticity of this verse by declaring it an ecclesiastical redactor's gloss, nonetheless suggests its meaning is simply that prior to that moment, they had not believed because of their failure to understand Scripture, but now belief has come.[54] Barrett understands the statement as an explanation that, unlike the community of the first readers, the disciple Jesus loved had a faith based only on what he saw at the tomb, not a conviction concerning what the Scripture had foretold concerning Jesus.[55]

There is no indication whether Peter also came to faith at this time.[56] Only one of these two disciples is narratively portrayed coming to believe, the disciple Jesus loved. His is a faith without the prerequisite of a

---

[51] Brown, *John*, 1008; Carson, 637.
[52] Arthur H. Maynard, "The Role of Peter in the Fourth Gospel," *New Testament Studies* 30 (1984): 540.
[53] Brown, *John*, 2:987; cf. Minear, 127.
[54] Bultmann, 685.
[55] Barrett, 564; cf. Haenchen 2, 208.
[56] Quast, 119; contra Bultmann, 684: "Clearly, it is presupposed that Peter before him was likewise brought to faith through the sight of the empty grave."

visible sign, a faith produced precisely by that which is not seen. The significance of the empty tomb is not what was seen, but what was absent. Brendan Byrne identifies a link between 20:9 and 20:29 where "the point is not that of 'not seeing and yet believing', but rather of 'not seeing *Jesus* and yet believing'."[57] The narrative does not concern itself with Peter's faith at this moment, but rather offers the disciple Jesus loved as a model of faith response "for the purpose of encouraging the readers to respond in a similar act of faith."[58]

The appearance at the tomb in chapter 20 is the primary text that convinces Charlesworth that the narrative of the Fourth Gospel provides a gradual unveiling of the identity of the disciple Jesus loved, revealing him to be Thomas. He faults commentators for their misinterpretation of chapter 20 that prevents them from recognizing the textual identitification of the disciple Jesus loved as Thomas. It is his contention that it is inaccurate to read this chapter to be declaring that this disciple, seeing the empty tomb and the grave-clothes, believes that Jesus is risen from the dead. In spite of the impressive consensus among readers to this effect, which Charlesworth thoroughly surveys, he "dares to go against the formidable force of such an armada of experts" and question their conclusion that 20:8 denotes resurrection faith on the part of the disciple Jesus loved.[59] He maintains that they have failed to adequately consider 20:9 and its contextual implications that indicate both Peter and the disciple Jesus loved do not in fact yet believe that Jesus is risen from the dead.

In an extremely detailed and thorough (50 pages) discussion of the meaning of 20:8, Charlesworth provides insightful exegesis which remains true to both the narrative revelation of the Fourth Gospel and the immediate context of this verse, carefully examining exactly what the narrative does and does not say. He rightly notes that in 20:8 the narrative is again ambiguous, never stating the content of what the disciple came to believe. He points out that morphologically, the most common (36 occurrences) pattern for this verb in the Fourth Gospel is πιστεύειν εἰς, to believe in something. The Evangelist could easily have written that the disciple Jesus loved believed in Jesus' resurrection. "He chose not to do so."[60] Charlesworth suggests that rather than read into the text a preconceived idea of this disciples experience, it is more faithful to the narrative to understand ἐπίστευσεν as an inceptive aorist, "implying that the Beloved Disciple, as he went into the empty tomb and saw the clothes and

---

[57] Brendan Byrne, "The Faith of the Beloved Disciple and the Community in John 20," *Journal for the Study of the New Testament* 23 (1985): 90.
[58] Quast, 120; cf. Lindars, 602.
[59] Charlesworth, 77.
[60] Ibid., 93.

face-cloth, began to develop a belief that culminated in a full awareness that Jesus had been raised."[61]

If the disciple Jesus loved believed in the resurrection at this moment, his failure to show compassion and alleviate Mary's grief makes him a less than ideal figure for model discipleship.[62] Instead, at this moment, his beginning belief does not include a clear understanding that Jesus is risen from the dead (as 20:9 makes clear). Instead, 20:8 "may signify in ways uncomprehended by the Beloved Disciple that Jesus has done exactly what he had claimed,"—going back to his Father—and he would return as he also promised.[63] This interpretation maintains the integrity of the statement in 20:9 that neither Peter nor the disciple Jesus loved understood the Scripture concerning Jesus' resurrection. It also maintains the narrative integrity of the statement in 20:8 that sets apart the disciple Jesus' loved because "he saw and believed," contrasting him with Peter for whom no belief is indicated. This is preferable to the alternative of maintaining the integrity of the statement of 20:9 by reducing the meaning of ἐπίστευσεν in 20:8 to believing that Mary had reported accurately the situation at the tomb, that the tomb was empty after all. This interpretation is as ancient as Augustine, but it has also had recent proponents who either advocate it or at least consider it a possibility.[64] This reading falls short in three areas. It neglects the theological significance of πιστεύω as established by the narrative of the Fourth Gospel, and it ignores the contrast with Peter, who surely also "saw and believed" that Jesus' body was gone as Mary had reported. The third shortcoming of this view, however, is that this is not what she reported, she declared Jesus' body "taken." To read as if she simply declared the tomb empty ignores the narrated content of Mary's statement. It is inconceivable that the perpetrators of a grave robbery, regardless of their identity and motives, would have taken the time to remove the grave wrappings. The narration of these details serves to *disprove* Mary's account of what has happened, and if the narrator is only commenting on the accuracy of her report, the disciple would not believe it but find it in error.

The final scene in which the disciple Jesus loved is explicitly present is chapter 21. This chapter has long been the subject of exegetical debate concerning its place in the Fourth Gospel and its authorship in relation to the rest of the Gospel. This study will not examine those questions, since

---

[61] Ibid., 95.
[62] Ibid., 89.
[63] Ibid., 81.
[64] Augustine, *Homilies on the Gospel of John*, in Nicene and Post Nicene Fathers, ed. Phillip Schaff (Edinburgh: T & T Clark, 1986) 7:436; William Countryman, *The Mystical Way in the Fourth Gospel* (Philadelphia: Fortress, 1987), 123; and Morris, *John*, 833-34.

its position in the text makes it a part of the reading experience of every reader of the extant text. There is no manuscript evidence for the Gospel ever existing without this chapter, regardless of whether it is an integral conclusion to the Gospel or a later appendix. In its opening list of seven disciples, two anonymous "other disciples" conclude the list. The appearance of the disciple Jesus loved later in this episode leads the reader to conclude that he is one of the disciples in this list, usually assumed to be one of the four who are unnamed. He is either one of the sons of Zebedee, mentioned only here in the Fourth Gospel, or one of the two "other disciples." It has even been suggested that the other of the two is a redactor/colleague of the disciple Jesus loved who is responsible for the authorship of this chapter.[65]

Not until verse 7 is the reader aware that the disciple Jesus loved is among this group fishing. He again is in the company of Peter, this time informing Peter that the one whose instructions have just provided a hugely successful catch is the one whose tomb they have so recently viewed empty, and whose resurrection appearance confronted them unhindered by the barricade of closed doors (20:19). "It is the Lord!" The significance of the disciple's identification of Jesus is not made explicit. The obvious impact on the reader is that it is this disciple Jesus loved who is best able to recognize Jesus when he is encountered. Furthermore, it is a confirmation of the declaration of veracity already encountered in 19:35 and soon to be restated in 21:24. The witness of this disciple is trustworthy and reliable. You can base the activity of your life on it, as Peter does here.

The latter part of this chapter contains the final appearance of this disciple, as the one Peter sees "following" (21:20), the Johannine "term par excellence for the dedication of discipleship,"[66] after his "feed my sheep" restoration dialogue with Jesus. Immediately preceding his appearance, Jesus concluded his comments to Peter with the command "follow me," (20:19). After Jesus rebukes Peter's inappropriate concern for the consequences of discipleship for someone else, the reader is confronted with the final words Jesus speaks in this Gospel, the repetition of his command to Peter, "Follow me!" (21:22). Interpolated between the two admonitions to Peter concerning the content of discipleship, the disciple Jesus loved is

---

[65] John K. Thornecroft, "The Redactor and the 'Beloved' in John," *The Expository Times* 98 (1987): 136; cf. Oscar Cullmann, *The Johannine Circle*, trans. by John Bowden (Philadelphia: Westnminster, 1976), 76; and Martin Hengel, *The Johannine Question*, trans. by John Bowden (London: SCM Press, 1989; Philadelphia: Trinity Press International, 1989) who declares "The editors—like the author—want the riddle to remain unsolved, the issue to be left open," 128.

[66] Brown, *John*, 78.

portrayed doing exactly that, with a reminder of both his designation as one loved by Jesus and the intimacy of his position toward Jesus, "who had lain upon his breast," (21:20).[67] The closing verses of this Gospel testify to the role of the disciple as the witness par excellence to Jesus. These will be discussed in some detail below.

Before we move into an analysis of the disciple Jesus loved and his contrast to other characters the reader encounters after his arrival in the narrative, what assessment can be made concerning the "other disciple" with Peter in chapter 18? Is this the disciple Jesus loved? The identification of the "other disciple" of chapter 18 with the disciple Jesus loved is problematic, yet enticing and many continue to assume that they are one and the same. The bases for the identification include his association with Peter and, more recently, the notable parallel literary constructions noted between 18:15-16 and 20:3-20:3-8.[68] Unlike the "other disciple" of chapter 1, the reader already has a familiarity with this disciple through his introduction at the supper in chapter 13. Combined with his companionship with Peter, it might be said that this identification is probable. But since the disciple Jesus loved has already been introduced by his identifying clause in chapter 13 there is no compelling reason why he should not be identified by it here, if this is indeed he.[69] However, identifying him with any other specific figure from the Fourth Gospel narrative is equally as problematic, and subject to the same criticisms.[70]

If the anonymous disciple in chapter 18 is to be identified with the disciple Jesus loved, then Culpepper rightly notes that this is the only reference to him that reveals anything "apart from his relationship to Jesus, Peter, Jesus' mother, or the later Christian community;"[71] specifically his acquaintance with the high priest, allowing him to be Peter's access to the courtyard. However, it is better with Barrett to accept the ambiguity of this text and recognize that "it is quite possible to identify him as the disciple 'whom Jesus loved', but there is no definite ground for doing so."[72] He stands in the text as another anonymous disciple who remains a shadowy figure leaving readers uncertain whether they have met before.

---

[67] Carson, 681.

[68] Frans Neirynck, "The 'Other Disciple' in Jn 18:15-16," *Ephemerides theologicae lovaniensis* 51 (1975): 113-41. Others who hold to at least the probability of this traditional identification include Brown, *John*, 2:822; Collins, 129; Beasley-Murray, 324; Lindars, 548; Quast, 80; Talbert, 236; Ellis, 256; Culpepper, *John*, 58.

[69] For arguments against the identification of this "other disciple" with the disciple Jesus loved see Bultmann, John, 645; Schnackenburg, III, 235; Barrett, 525.

[70] Contra Brodie, 529; Gunther, 146-7, where it is argued that Judas is this other disciple.

[71] Culpepper, *John*, 61.

[72] Barrett, 525.

The Disciple Jesus Loved and Named Characters

Judas

Although the disciple Jesus loved is the only significant anonymous character appearing in the Fourth Gospel passion narrative, several named characters are present. In the portrayal of Judas no ambiguity is encountered; he is identified as a devil and betrayer (6:70-71). In chapter 12, he is again called a betrayer (12:5). When he reappears, he again bears the double designation of betrayer and one whose heart is accessible to the devil (13:2). He next appears when the disciple Jesus loved is introduced, and that disciple's query prompts Jesus' public, if not comprehended, identification of Judas as betrayer (13:23-30). In Judas' final appearance he commits the betrayal already marking his identity (18:2-5). He is the only disciple singled out by Jesus for preferential attention, apart from the disciple Jesus loved, and therefore is in Tilborg's assessment, "the anti-type to the love relationship between Jesus and the beloved disciple."[73]

Pilate

Another named character juxtaposed in the passion narrative with the disciple Jesus loved is Pilate. He is characterized more ambiguously than Judas. Initially responding to Jesus' accusers by asking to have no part in the proceedings (18:29), he is forced to play a role in the proceedings and he responds to Jesus with the philosophical question, "What is truth?" (18:38), and a pronouncement of innocence (18:38). Nonetheless, he is unwilling to do what is just and release the one he proclaims innocent, preferring instead to shun responsibility and let others determine his actions. He again proclaims Jesus' innocence (19:4) and reinitiates a dialogue that is more a philosophical debate than a courtroom interrogation. He does bear public, written witness to Jesus' identity, against the protests of Jesus' accusers (19:19-22), and he allows Joseph and Nicodemus (another man whose characterization is fraught with ambiguity) to take Jesus' body for burial. The reader's negative perception of Pilate, however, is assured by the stark reality that "he handed him over to be crucified," (19:16).

Mary Magdalene

Two named characters that appear in textual proximity to the disciple Jesus loved are described much more positively; Mary Magdalene and

---

[73] Tilborg, 93.

Thomas. Mary Magdalene's experience with Jesus demonstrates her loyalty and devotion, and in obedience to Jesus' command she bears good news to the disciples, a task which has caused her to be perceived by some as attaining apostolic status.[74] Despite the positive elements of her characterization, several factors disqualify her as a candidate for reader identification and imitation. She serves a necessary, yet temporary, role of eye-witness to the risen Jesus. There is no possibility nor need for a continuation of this role by modern readers, or even later first century readers. Prior to fulfilling her "apostolic" function, she misunderstands Jesus' mission and person, even in her post-resurrection encounter. She seeks his continued physical presence (20:17) while he offers a discipleship that necessitates returning to his Father (chapters 14, 16). Her declaration to the disciples records a message somewhat different from what Jesus told her to report. While 20:18 can be read as an indication that Mary's quoted statement conveys the meaning Jesus intended, or is only a summary statement of a longer message, the first words narratively present, spoken by Mary to the disciples, present a different emphasis than what Jesus said, an emphasis on seeing ("I have seen the Lord,"). Mary Magdalene plays the role of witness, reporting her encounter with Jesus to his disciples, but the directly quoted portion of her testimony demonstrates her need of a visual prerequisite to belief (20:18), in contrast to the disciple Jesus loved.[75] This, together with Jesus' rebuke of her desire to cling to his presence, reminds the reader of Jesus' correction. Brodie suggests that her characterization not only puts her in a negative light when contrasted with Jesus' mother, the Samaritan woman, and other Fourth Gospel figures, "in this gospel at least, she in some way represents those Jews who did not believe."[76]

Thomas

Thomas' confession, like Martha's in chapter 11,[77] is also limited to a verbal statement of belief with no active response of faith. His confession exemplifies a faith that requires first-hand observation. The inadequacy is

---

[74] Brown, *Community*, 189-90, notes that in the Western Church the creed was recited on her feast day precisely because she was considered "the apostle to the apostles." He cites the ninth century biography of her by Rabanus Maurus for its frequent references to her as "apostle"; cf. Fiorenza, 332.
[75] Rena, 143-4.
[76] Brodie, 549.
[77] See chapter 6 above.

not with the confession itself but with the prerequisite of "seeing" before he could believe. Jesus' response to Thomas' confession shows he is unimpressed with its prerequisite. Jesus never calls Thomas' or his confession blessed. It is those textually absent ones who are not eyewitnesses (i.e. potentially all future readers?) but yet believe whose confessions prompts Jesus to approvingly designate them as blessed (μακάριοι). As Collins states, "the reader of the Fourth Gospel knows that he has encountered in Thomas a leading disciple who epitomizes both the bravado and the ignorance of the disciples."[78]

An opposing reading of Thomas is that of James Charlesworth who asserts that an accurate reading of John 20 indicates that this narrative intends Thomas to be identified by the reader as the disciple Jesus loved. A primary basis for this reading of the text is his understanding of the boundaries of the original narrative. Rather than focus on the narrative as we have received it (chapters 1-21)—the form that has been passed on from generation to generation, the only form for which their is any manuscript evidence supporting it—Charlesworth accepts the common scholarly assertion that the Fourth Gospel originally ended with chapter 20, making Jesus' final encounter with any character the episode with Thomas.[79] Having chosen to read as if chapter 21 were not present, he is able to declare that if Thomas is not the disciple Jesus loved, then that character makes his final exit from the narrative stage with no narrated encounter with the risen Jesus and hence without resurrection faith.[80] He rightly recognizes this as contradicting the paradigmatic presentation of the disciple Jesus loved in the Fourth Gospel which models for the reader the appropriate response to Jesus. Since it is impossible the reader is intended to model the failure to understand declared in 20:9, the only conclusion remaining is that Thomas' encounter with the risen Jesus, culminating in his confession "ὁ κύριός μου καὶ ὁ θεός μου," becomes the model of appropriate response to the risen Jesus, strongly suggesting the identification of Thomas as the disciple Jesus loved. This reading is based on faulty premises which are refuted below.[81]

Peter

The disciple Jesus loved is juxtaposed with Peter in each of his appearances but one, and while it is perhaps reading more into the text than

---

[78] Collins, 125; contra Thompson, 75, who says that "Jesus' command to Thomas, 'Do not be faithless,' should not be taken as a negative assessment of Thomas' statements in 20:25."
[79] Charlesworth, *Beloved Disciple*, 3, 33-4.
[80] Ibid., 88.
[81] See excursus at the end of this section.

what is narratively demonstrable to "hear an echo of the not unfriendly rivalry of primitive Christian communities,"[82] their textual proximity makes it impossible for readers not to contrast them with one another. In 13:24 the loved disciple is Peter's mouthpiece and, if he is the 'other disciple' with Peter in chapter 18, he is Peter's "key" that unlocks closed doors and permits him entry. In 19:26-27 he becomes Jesus' appointed guardian for his mother. By his very presence at the cross, this disciple stands in contrast to Peter (and all the other male disciples) whose absence is glaring when contrasted with the women's presence. In chapter 20 he is Peter's opposite who arrives first but only looks in, yet when he does enter advances beyond Peter in response and sees and believes. In the epilogue of chapter 21, the disciple Jesus loved first identifies Jesus' presence to Peter (v. 7), then provides the example of one who is already following Jesus as Peter is instructed to do (v. 20).

The question whether this indicates an opposition between these two figures and groups they represent has not received a consensus answer among scholars. Some readers believe the contrast casts a totally negative light on Peter, who is portrayed in opposition to the paradigm of the disciple Jesus loved. Raymond Collins sees in "their 'competition' a crux interpretum for the student of the Fourth Gospel," and William Watty believes that the name 'Peter' in the Fourth Gospel "focuses and highlights precisely what the evangelist wishes to correct."[83] The dissenting view is represented by Kevin Quast who believes Peter's response to Jesus in 6:68-69 "typifies the response of faith" in contrast with the followers who now fall away. He also notes that, contrary to the Synoptics, the identification with Satan here is Judas', not Peter's.[84] These attempts to either "redeem" Peter or set him in direct opposition to the paradigm of discipleship presented in the disciple Jesus loved both require extratextual evidence and move beyond what the Fourth Gospel narrates.

Peter's only public testimony to Jesus in the Fourth Gospel (beyond the circle of Jesus' disciples in 6:68-69) is a negative testimony of denial. His most remembered textual appearance is his declaration denying any acquaintance with Jesus or involvement with him (18:17, 25-27). The intertwining of his denial with Jesus' unhesitating self-witness at his trial, places Peter's negative witness in direct opposition to Jesus' self revelation. At his arrest Jesus repeatedly declares "ἐγώ εἰμι" (18:5, 6, 8), a recognizably pregnant utterance in the Fourth Gospel with soteriological

---

[82] Brown, 1121.
[83] Collins, 127; Watty, 211; cf. Savas C. Agourides, "Peter and John in the Fourth Gospel," in *Studia Evangelica* ed. Frank L. Cross (Berlin: Akademie, 1968): 3-7.
[84] Quast, 52; cf. Okure, 226; Hawkin, 146.

implications.[85] In the middle of the narration of Peter's denial Jesus responds to his accusers that nothing he has taught has been secret or hidden (18:20-21). In contrast, Peter's failure to testify to the truth of Jesus and his attempts to hide his association with Jesus when the opportunity for witnessing concerning Jesus' identity arises, is all the more glaring. As Kevin Quast succinctly states, "A dramatic contrast is created wherein Jesus denies nothing and Peter denies everything."[86]

Peter's initial response to Jesus' arrest prompts a rebuke from Jesus and indicates Peter's failure to understand Jesus' purpose, a failure Arthur Droge has termed "a fundamental misunderstanding of Jesus." Droge goes on to claim that Peter's swordplay puts him so at odds with Jesus that it "confirms the truth of his 'denial' of being Jesus' disciple. Peter's denial is really his confession."[87] Peter remains silent throughout the account of Mary's announcement of the empty tomb and his own race to examine the evidence for himself (20:2-10). The episode focuses on the distinction between the actions of Peter and the disciple Jesus loved. After receiving the news from Mary, both run to the tomb, but twice the Gospel specifies that the other disciple outran Peter and arrived first. Barrett sees no significance in the repetition,[88] but for the reader the repetition at least places emphasis on the earlier arrival of the disciple Jesus loved. "The point must be taken with the same emphasis it is given,"[89] but the significance will be what readers assign to it, since no specific reason for this emphasis is stated. There seems here a preview of the beginning of faith for the disciple Jesus' loved; the disciple who arrived first also becomes the first to believe.[90]

After Peter's denial in chapter 18, his next words follow the (non-) conclusion of 20:30-31 and its strong Christological affirmation. In contrast, Peter makes the jarringly mundane announcement, "I am going fishing" (21:3). Many readers see this as merely a way to introduce the story of the miraculous catch of fish.[91] Barrett entertains the possibility that the words convey a symbolic double meaning, referring also to the apostolic commission of "catching men".[92] Others see it indicating the

---

[85] David Mark Ball, *"I Am" in John's Gospel: Literary Function, Background and Theological Implications,* Journal for the Study of the New Testament-Supplement Series 124 (Sheffield: JSOT Press, 1996), 282.

[86] Quast, 97-98.

[87] Arthur J. Droge, "The Status of Peter in the Fourth Gospel: John 18:10-11," *Journal of Biblical Literature* 109 (1990): 311.

[88] Barrett, 563.

[89] Quast, 111.

[90] Lindars, 600; cf. Brown, *John*, 2:1007.

[91] Haenchen, 2: 222; Schnackenburg, 3:353;

[92] Barrett, 579.

restoration of Peter to a leadership role among the disciples.[93] Beasley-Murray and Brodie both read the words as the appropriate activity of daily living that does not imply an abandonment of their commissioning in chapter 20.[94] A harsher judgment of Peter's words is present in Brown, who perceives here "aimless activity undertaken in desperation," and similarly in Stibbe's analysis that Peter, in a psychological state of denying his denial, makes an "attempt to fill his 'hole in the soul' with work and fails miserably."[95] The sheer variety of readings of the significance of Peter's statement demonstrates their dependence on readers' extratexts and prior assessment of his characterization. Undeniably, Peter's first recorded post-resurrection utterance concerns fishing, while the disciple Jesus loved speaks recognition of Jesus, and bears witness of his presence to others ("It is the Lord!" 21:7).

Peter next speaks in his restorative dialogue with Jesus. Jesus' command for Peter to feed his lambs may hint at a future witnessing role, one readers may be able to supply from extratextual knowledge. Watty, however, goes too far in suggesting that in 21:15-19 "Peter is 'un-named' by reverting to the identity of 'Son of John'."[96] Peter declares his love for Jesus, is commissioned a shepherd, has his future foretold, and is commanded to follow (21:15-19). The act of "following" is a primary theme of this chapter, and it is required of Peter that he now follow Jesus (21:19, 22), something the disciple Jesus loved is already doing (21:20). By following Jesus and Peter in 21:20, the disciple Jesus loved appears as the "ideal follower, the epitome of what it means to be a believer."[97] Peter's obtuseness is not eliminated; his final words express his concern about the consequences of following for someone else, a concern Jesus tells him is totally inappropriate (21:21-23). The warning here is that following Jesus may lead even to death for some, but not others, and of whom it will require death is of no concern to the others, who need to focus instead on their own "following."[98] Readers familiar with Peter's role in church tradition as part of their extratext will find in Peter's commission to feed Jesus' sheep a suggestion of his potential as a witness to Jesus. Nowhere in this narrative, however, does Peter fulfill that potential by witnessing to anyone concerning Jesus. In the final words of the Gospel, the narrative makes clear that the real witness to Jesus, the one whose

---

[93] Quast, 138, 163; Ellis, 300; Brodie, 580.
[94] Beasley-Murray, 399; Brodie, 582-3.
[95] Brown, *John*, 2: 1096; Stibbe, 210.
[96] Watty, 211.
[97] John F. O'Grady, "The Role of the Beloved Disciple," *Biblical Theology Bulletin* 9 (1979): 60; cf. Collins, 130; Quast, 160.
[98] Fernando F. Segovia, "The Final Farewell of Jesus: A Reading of John 20:30-21:25," *Semeia* 53 (1991): 182.

witness the reader can trust as true, is the disciple Jesus loved, never named but always present through his testimony that is the Fourth Gospel.

An Excursus:
Charlesworth's Identification of Thomas as the Disciple Jesus Loved

Charlesworth's monograph is a most significant contribution to the inquiry into the enigmatic figure of the disciple Jesus loved and is noteworthy for its thoroughness and exegetical precision, leaving very few stones unturned. He contends that the identification of the disciple Jesus loved must meet eight criteria. He maintains that this is necessary whether this figure is identified as someone named in this Gospel, someone who is anonymous, or even a symbolic theme. The first is the criterion of love. Why is he identified by the phrase "the disciple whom Jesus loved"? The second is anonymity. Why is he not named, at least in the pericopes that reference him as "the disciple whom Jesus loved"? The third criterion is an explanation of his closeness to Jesus and the authority thereby implied. The fourth criterion is lateness, explaining why the disciple Jesus loved is not mentioned prior to the narration of Jesus' final week. The fifth criterion is the cross, with the intent of explaining why only he and no other disciple is portrayed as present at the cross. Charlesworth's sixth criterion is commendation, to account for the narrative's endorsement of this disciple's witness in chapter 21. The seventh criterion is fear and death, to explain the fear Charlesworth believes is addressed by the final chapter, fear caused by the death of the disciple Jesus loved, fear that Jesus' words were false and he would not return, and fear that the witness of this disciple is not authentic. The final criterion is Peter and his close link with the disciple Jesus loved in the Fourth Gospel.[99]

Chapter 21 is understood by Charlesworth to be an early Appendix written by one who shares the Evangelist's perspective and it provides the strongest evidence for narrowing the identity of the disciple Jesus loved. He agrees with the commonly held assumption that this disciple is included in the list in 21:2. Peter is obviously not a candidate since the two characters are so frequently juxtaposed in this narrative. Rejecting the attempts to identify him as one of the sons of Zebedee, Charlesworth limits the possibilities to Nathanael, Thomas, or one of the two "others." He eliminates the two unnamed disciples on the grounds that the author's purpose in chapter 21 is to reveal the identity of this disciple and the un-

---

[99] Charlesworth, xiv-xviii.

fruitful consequences of identifying him as unnamed.[100] Both of these assumptions are suspect. The double entendre Charlesworth suggests (that the second of the repetitive occurrences of ἐφανέρωσεν in 21:2 may mean both that Jesus "showed" himself, and that the identity of the disciple Jesus loved is being "shown" to the reader)[101] is tenuous at best. Furthermore, the argument that the results are unfruitful is only valid based on the prior tenuous suggestion that the narrative in some way indicates an intention to reveal the identity of this enigmatic figure, and only necessary if the ambiguity of anonymity is undesirable. Nathanael is rejected on the grounds he is too peripheral a character in the Fourth Gospel to be the disciple Jesus loved.[102]

This leaves Thomas for consideration, and Charlesworth finds this option most appealing. He bases this on the confessional use of κύριός in both 20:28 (by Thomas) and in 21:7 (by the disciple Jesus loved) with only 11 verses separating them. In each instance it is the final recorded words of that character. A second factor leading to this conclusion is the successive placement of the two scenes in 20:24-28 and 21:1-14 with Thomas having center stage in the first and the disciple Jesus loved having that focal place in the immediately following scene.[103] These indications are sufficient for Charlesworth to claim "the one name that alone looms large as the Beloved Disciple seems to be Thomas."[104] Reviewing the other passages in the Fourth gospel where the disciple Jesus loved is narratively present, Charlesworth believes he finds further confirmation for this conclusion. He reasons that the identification of the disciple Jesus loved as Thomas permits a fuller perception of the pathos of the story, for "his willingness to die with Jesus (ἄγωμεν καὶ ἡμεῖς ἵνα ἀποθάνωμεν μετ' αὐτοῦ)—uttered in 11:16—was experienced empathetically beneath Jesus' cross."[105]

Having already arrived at this conclusion, Charlesworth finds support for this identification in the parallels he sees in the narration of Thomas and the disciple Jesus loved in the two scenes in chapter 20, the empty tomb (1-10) and the resurrection appearances (19-29). He charts the schema as follows:

---

[100] Ibid., 38
[101] Ibid.
[102] Ibid., 40.
[103] Ibid., 41.
[104] Ibid., 48.
[105] Ibid., 68.

Empty Tomb	*Resurrection Appearances*
Mary Magdalene's report	Mary Magdalene's report
Peter "saw"	The disciples "saw"
BD's need for verification of both	Thomas's need for verification of both
BD's seeing and believing	Thomas's seeing and believing[106]

Charlesworth sees in each a character "not easily persuaded" to believe. The "hard-won and examined knowledge and belief" enables the trustworthiness of Thomas' witness to his community.

> ...they believed because one among them, Thomas the Beloved Disciple, did not believe unsubstantiated reports. He demanded empirical proof. Only after checking them out and proving they were worthy of trusting did he confess.[107]

Having been persuaded that the text reveals that Thomas is the disciple Jesus loved, Charlesworth finds several other exegetical insights to affirm this identification. Two are particularly intriguing. The first of these is Thomas' demand to physically handle the wound in the side of Jesus, yet the only disciple narratively present to witness the spear thrust was the one Jesus loved.[108] This "evidence" is not conclusive since while it is not a narrated part of the conversation, the contact with the other disciples (20:25) is sufficient to explain his knowledge of the wound. The text explicitly states that in his first resurrection appearance to the disciples, Jesus "showed them his hands *and his side*" (20:20).

The second interesting parallel between Thomas and the disciple Jesus loved referenced by Charlesworth is the call to martyrdom. According to his reconstruction of the historical situation behind chapter 21, the Johannine community is shaken by the death of the disciple Jesus loved because it is not martyrdom. In contrast, Peter, his rival, has been called on to give a martyr's sacrifice. The response to the crisis brought on by this death of the disciple Jesus loved on the part of the author of the Fourth Gospel is the introduction of Thomas to the narrative in 11:16, "Let us also go, that we may die with him." With these words he exhorts all the disciples to put their lives on the line for Jesus. "What better way to portray him than as one who enters on the scene of the drama, the narrative of the GosJn, as the spokesman who leads in being willing to die for Christ.[109] Although he was not called to offer a martyr's sacrifice, he

---

[106] Ibid., 113.
[107] Ibid., 121.
[108] Ibid., 227.
[109] Ibid., 238.

nonetheless willingly faced potential martyrdom, urging the others to follow. If he is the disciple Jesus loved, only he had the courage to be present to witness Jesus' death, regardless of what it might cost to do so.

Given the premise that Thomas is the disciple Jesus loved, these become fascinating parallels in the characterization of that figure. I have no quarrel with Charlesworth at this point, as he recognizes that these are only confirming evidence at best, and only so if his premise is accepted. It is his premise that the text has already indicated that Thomas is to be identified as the disciple Jesus loved that I take issue with. This identification arises from his reading of chapter 20 and has three key assertions that buttress his interpretation of the evidence. The first of these is his contention that if Thomas is not the disciple Jesus loved, then that figure disappears from the narrative never having been an eye-witness to the risen Jesus and never having expressed resurrection faith. This is based entirely on his arbitrary choice to stop reading the narrative at the end of chapter 20. Whatever internal evidence can be garnered to support the contention that this was the "original" ending, there is no manuscript evidence to support the claim that anyone in the history of the church ever knew this "original" narrative.[110] For twenty centuries of transmission history the narrative of the Fourth Gospel has included the twenty-one chapters we know at present. I choose to read this extant narrative, rather than one whose actual existence is entirely undocumenteable.

The second foundation supporting his identification of Thomas as the disciple Jesus loved is his rejection of any intent to contrast these two figures in chapter 20 in terms of the model for reader response they present. It is Charlesworth's claim that any interpretation that understands Thomas' characterization as antithetical to the characterization of the disciple Jesus loved is "without exegetical support."[111] He may be correct that rebuke is too strong to be an accurate description of Jesus' response in 20:29 to Thomas' confession. The response of Jesus to Thomas' confession does not explicitly rebuke Thomas; the content of his confession is never questioned or corrected.[112] As F. F. Bruce has rightly noted concerning the delay in Thomas' coming to believe in contrast to the other disciples, "if they believed a week earlier than Thomas, that was because they saw a week earlier than he," not because they believed without seeing.[113] None of this overcomes the direct statement of Jesus in 20:29 which says in effect, "you needed to see to believe; the blessed ones are

---

[110] See arguments above.

[111] Charlesworth, 112.

[112] D. A. Carson, *The Gospel According to John* (Grand Rapids: Eerdmans, 1991), 659.

[113] F. F. Bruce, *The Gospel of John* (Grand Rapids: Eerdmans, 1983), 394.

those who do not require seeing to believe," contrasting Thomas with the "blessed ones."

The final key support to his interpretation is Charlesworth's assertion that the Fourth Gospel "opens and closes with an emphasis upon the necessity of seeing for believing."[114] If this were true, it either eliminates readers from any potential for "believing," or it requires one kind of "seeing" for the first disciples and second-hand "seeing" for all future believers, creating a second category of discipleship for future generations of believers, the very thing that Jesus' words to Thomas in 20:29 refute. The reading presented in the above analysis of the narrative of the Fourth Gospel has demonstrated the opposite to be true. The paradigm of appropriate response established by Jesus' encounter with his mother and present throughout each subsequent encounter with anonymous Fourth Gospel characters indicate that the model offered the reader is the necessity of a faith response *prior* to any "seeing." This is consistent with a straight forward reading of Jesus' response to Thomas in 20:29 and with the experience of future generations of believers

Paradigm of Appropriate Response

The indeterminacy of the characterization of the disciple Jesus loved is appropriate to his paradigmatic role in modeling an appropriate response to Jesus for readers of the Fourth Gospel. The specifics of his identity, occupation, family life, and initial encounter with Jesus remain unnarrated. Lindars points out his eventual fate is also not specified, "his end is in obscurity, without the glamour of a martyr's crown."[115] The universality about his portrayal is particularly appropriate for his representative role. In his study of the representative figures in the Gospel, Raymond Collins notes that in the figure of the loved disciple the positive responses of other characters are gathered:

> the tradition of the Fourth Gospel capsualizes in the single person of the Beloved Disciple the testimony of John, the receptivity of Mary, the faith of Nathanael as well as that of the man born blind, Peter, Mary Magdalene, and Thomas...he is *the* representative figure, the one who epitomizes all that faith in Jesus Christ implies.[116]

Furthermore, the insight of the disciple Jesus loved, his correct understanding, and his faithfulness to Jesus, are unwavering in each of his appearances. He is the only one present at every stage of Jesus' passion: the

---

[114] Charlesworth, 114.
[115] Lindars, 622.
[116] Collins, 132.

last supper, possibly the courtyard with Peter (see discussion above), the cross, the empty tomb, and the appearance in Galilee.[117]

The paradigm of ideal discipleship presented by the disciple Jesus loved is not founded upon a confession, but upon his believing, a belief not based on signs and requiring no "seeing," and on his function as witness par excellence. The disciple's belief is not based on physical sight; in Collins' words: "His is a resurrection faith in its purest state. Unlike Thomas whose faith was dependent on a 'physical' vision of the risen Jesus, the Beloved comes to faith without seeing the risen Christ."[118]

In his textual appearances in the Gospel, the disciple Jesus loved is never portrayed bearing witness to anyone concerning Jesus, nor is any statement of confession placed upon his lips. Yet, according to Culpepper, the narration of his presence at key moments in the passion narrative "is a way of affirming both his authority as a true witness and, by implication, the authority and credibility of the Gospel."[119] This, together with his special intimacy with Jesus and the portrayal of his insight into what he sees, "qualifies him to be the ideal witness to Jesus, his story, and its meaning."[120] William Kurz notes that in Jesus' prayer in chapter 17, the reader of the Fourth Gospel is specifically referenced, among "those who believe in me through their word" (17:20). Later generations of believers have a faith dependent upon the witness of the first followers of Jesus, and especially the disciple Jesus loved. Kurz notes that Jesus actually prays for his followers to become "disciples Jesus loves" themselves, fully identifying with the one upon whose witness the narrative, and their faith, is based.[121]

In chapter 19 the disciple Jesus loved is at the cross, the only male disciple of Jesus present at the cross in any Gospel.[122] He witnesses the words of Jesus on the cross, as well as his death.[123] The statement of 19:35 focuses the reader's attention on his witnessing function. It is one of only two places in the Fourth Gospel where the reader is directly addressed, the other being 20:30-31. In both instances, the emphasis is on the witness of the Fourth Gospel, and states its specific purpose with the same words, ἵνα πιστεύσητε, "in order that you might believe." The address to readers "speaks of the beloved disciple's activity of bearing wit-

---

[117] Culpepper, *John*, 72.
[118] Collins, 130.
[119] Culpepper, *John*, 65.
[120] Bauckham, 36.
[121] William S Kurz, "The Beloved Disciple and Implied Readers," *Biblical Theology Bulletin* 19 (1989): 102.
[122] Paul Minear, "The Beloved Disciple in the Gospel of John: Some Clues and Conjectures," *Novum Testamentum* 19 (1977): 119.
[123] Quast, 96.

ness to what he then saw, an activity which takes place not within the story the Gospel tells, but beyond it,"[124] beyond it to the experience of every reader. Kügler suggests Jesus himself as the reference of ἐκεῖνος in 19:35, that is, Jesus is the one who verifies the witness of the disciple he loved.[125] Hawkin recognizes that in 19:26-27 "the Evangelist is inviting his readership to identify with the Beloved Disciple, the disciple who was commissioned by the dying Jesus to be a witness and propagator of the new salvific dispensation, born under the shadow of the cross."[126]

In contrast to the mostly silent portrayal of the disciple singled out as a special recipient of Jesus' love, the reader is informed in the final verses that his testimony is heard throughout the text from the prologue onward (21:24). Exactly what this statement reveals about authorship is uncertain. Culpepper states that "the author attributed a prior and formative role to the Beloved Disciple," while Bauckham claims "21:24 designates this disciple Jesus loved as the *author* of the Gospel," not just the guarantor of the tradition.[127] Whichever understanding is correct, it is the witness of the disciple Jesus loved that stands as the backdrop and basis for the entire portrayal of Jesus in the Fourth Gospel. The reader is given *his* testimony in each episode of Jesus' encounter with various characters, both named and anonymous; and the text boldly claims that the veracity of his witness is without question; it is ἀληθής (21:24). The disciple's identification of Jesus for Peter, and presumably for the other disciples in 21:7, can be seen to initiate his witnessing function.[128] But it is not in the role of mediator between Jesus and Peter, or the other disciples, that the disciple Jesus loved has his primary witness. "Rather he is represented as the disciple who was so related to Jesus and the events of Jesus' story that he can bear witness *to the readers/hearers of the Gospel.*"[129]

Reader Identification With the Disciple Jesus Loved

The characters in the first portion of the Fourth Gospel who fit the established paradigm of appropriate response to Jesus (an active faith response to Jesus' word without a sign or the need to "see" and bearing witness to the efficacy of Jesus' word to others) are anonymous. All of the named characters are inappropriate models for readers to identify with. Some are negative characters who oppose Jesus (e.g. Judas); others are ambiguous

---

[124] Bauckham, 40.
[125] Kügler, 276.
[126] Hawkin, 144.
[127] Culpepper, *John*, 71; Bauckham, 29.
[128] Tilborg, 104.
[129] Bauckham, 39.

in their response and never maker a commitment to follow Jesus (e.g. Nicodemus); others are somewhat positive examples of followering Jesus, but there remains something inadequate about their faith response (e.g. Martha, Mary Magdalene, Thomas); others have completely positive characterizations, but their roles are unique and unrepeatable (e.g. John, Mary of Bethany). The significant anonymous characters are offered as models because their faith response is appropriate and repeatable. Their positive portrayal encourages empathy and invites reader identification with them, especially in their response to Jesus. Certain specifications may act as barriers to reader identification with characters if readers do not share those experiences. These might include gender, parenting, or disenfranchisement, etc. One specification that can block reader identification is a name. A specific, named character has an identity the reader may relate to, but the name may function as a barrier to a total appropriation of the character's identity. The variety among the anonymous characters in the first 9 chapters of the Gospel increase the opportunity for readers to find commonality with at least some of the characters, thus facilitating identification and participation in their narrative encounters with Jesus.

The faith response of the disciple Jesus loved is seen when he takes Jesus' mother into his home, when he runs to the tomb and believes without the need to see, and by his consistent portrayal in the posture of "following" Jesus, "perhaps the most basic characteristic of the Beloved Disciple," one that defines discipleship in the narrative.[130] He begins to believe at the empty tomb, a belief not based on what he sees or any other tangible sign, but a belief born in the absence of Jesus, an absence that is a part of the reality of readers who are called by the Gospel to believe in one who is "absent" from their tangible experience.[131] The disciple Jesus loved is contrasted to Thomas, the named disciple who needs to "see," as the Samaritan woman is to Nicodemus. Through his faith response that does not require "seeing" or need any sign, the disciple Jesus loved meets one of the criteria of appropriate response established in the narrative (see chapter 5 above). He fills the remaining criterion when his faith response to Jesus culminates in his bearing witness to the words and deeds of Jesus with his true testimony. It is not others within the "story" of the Fourth Gospel who are the primary recipients of his witness, though he is the first in this narrative to verbalize his recognition of the risen Jesus (21:7).[132] He fulfills his primary witnessing function through the Fourth

---

[130] Quast, 160.
[131] Byrne, "Faith," 90.
[132] Culpepper, *John*, 69.

Gospel itself; his is the testimony guaranteeing its veracity. Whether we accept his specific identification of the disciple Jesus loved as the actual author who penned the Gospel, Bauckham's assessment is accurate:

> What the beloved disciple has to do after the events of chapter 20 is precisely to tell the story which the Gospel tells up to and including chapter 20. If he has done so orally for a lifetime, at the end of his life he does so finally as the author of the Gospel.[133]

The keys to the reader's ability to identify with the paradigm of discipleship offered in the person of the disciple Jesus loved includes his unambiguous positive textual portrayal, his always faithful "following" of Jesus, the indeterminacy of his characterization, and his anonymity.[134] The lack of "background" details of his life creates an indeterminacy of identity permitting readers to identify with him purely on the basis of his appropriate response to Jesus, without necessitating a match between the details of his life and readers' lives. Anonymity is both part of his fit in the discipleship paradigm and part of the indeterminacy of his identity.

Watty argues that the anonymity of the disciple Jesus loved was for the sake of unity and continuity in the shaping of this late Gospel. As long as the disciple is not named, any disciple at any point in history may be the one whom Jesus loved.[135] Yet Watty's theological and historical understanding of the anonymity of the disciple Jesus loved needs supplementation. An analysis of the reader's experience helps clarify how the characterizations of unnamed persons whose encounter with Jesus produces life-changing responses enables readers from any era, including our own, to make what Kurz describes as "their spontaneous identification with what happens in the narrative." This includes the reader's acceptance of and participation in the discipleship paradigm embodied in the disciple Jesus loves.[136]

Brendan Byrne understands the purpose of the Fourth Gospel to be to provide access for subsequent generations within the Christian community to the events of Jesus' life, death, and resurrection. The Gospel narrative assures them that "they can have an encounter with Jesus every bit as valid and indeed more fruitful" than even his own contemporaries. This is accomplished through the agency of the disciple Jesus loved, "the point of insertion for the later generations" into the narrative world inhabited by Jesus in the Gospel.[137] His anonymity is one element enabling reader identification with him and entry into his narrative world. His

---

[133] Bauckham, 41.
[134] Kurz, 101, 105; cf. Quast, 160.
[135] Watty, 212.
[136] Kurz, 106.
[137] Byrne, "Faith," 93.

identity has greater indeterminacy than the preceding anonymous characters. Nothing is revealed of his familial relationships, social standing, occupation, physical condition, or his past. The only aspect of his story initially revealed is Jesus' love for him. This greater indeterminacy facilitates readers' ability to fill the identity gaps in his characterization with their own identity, entering and accepting the paradigm of discipleship presented by him. The disciple Jesus loved is, for the reader, not only "the disciple par excellence, but he is also the interpreter par excellence,"[138] guiding readers in their faith response to the words and deeds of Jesus in the Fourth Gospel. He stands in the narrative as the embodiment of discipleship characterized by intimacy with Jesus, an active faith response that needs no "sign," and witnessing to Jesus' identity and the power of his word.[139]

---

[138] Schuyler Brown, 376.
[139] Okure, 226.

CHAPTER 8

CONCLUSION

Genuine discipleship in the Fourth Gospel consists of an active faith response to Jesus' word, without the prerequisite of a "sign" or any visible demonstration. One aspect of an appropriate response to Jesus is a witness to the power of Jesus' word and what it accomplishes. The paradigm of appropriate response is first established at Cana by the mother of Jesus prior to his first sign. Other characters fitting the paradigm are the woman of Samaria, the βασιλικός, the infirm man, and the blind man; a partial fit is present in the adulterous woman. The characters who fit the paradigm are portrayed positively in their response to Jesus and in contrast to his opponents. Moreover, some characters readers might expect to respond appropriately to Jesus, do not. The ambiguous portrayal of the infirm man gains a more positive assessment by his participation in the appropriate response paradigm and the parallels between his episode and that of the blind man. The adulteress' portrayal is more incomplete than ambiguous. The contrast with her accusers and the equivalence with which Jesus addresses her prompt readers to include her among the favorably portrayed respondents to Jesus word, even though her response must be assumed since it is not explicit.

The appropriate response paradigm culminates in the characterization of the disciple Jesus loved. By the time of his appearance in chapter 13 the paradigm is well established and readers know what constitutes appropriate response. He is the only character fitting the paradigm who continually reappears. Each time he is present readers are reminded of Jesus' love for him. His response to Jesus is seen in his intimacy (ἐν τῷ κόλπῳ) with Jesus (chapter 13), in his accepting responsibility for Jesus' mother (chapter 18), in his race to the tomb and his subsequent belief (chapter 20), in his post-resurrection recognition of Jesus (chapter 21), and in his following Jesus (chapter 21). Nowhere is he portrayed witnessing to any particular person, unless the identification of Jesus in chapter 21 is understood as witness, but it is not necessary to search the Gospel for the witness of the disciple Jesus loved; the Fourth Gospel *is* his witness (19:35, 21:24).

The characters who fit the appropriate response paradigm share another common feature, their anonymity. In this Gospel, it is anonymous characters with extended portrayals and narrative significance who consistently respond appropriately to Jesus. Most readers approach the Gospel desiring to identify with the protagonist and with characters who positively respond to him because of the influence of their interpretive communities where Jesus is venerated. The positive characterization of the persons fitting the appropriate response paradigm make them appealing to readers and facilitates reader identification with them. Indeterminacy in characterization assists the identification process, since specific details (i.e. gender, ethnicity, experiences) could hinder identification for readers not sharing these specifics in common with the character. The disciple Jesus loved is portrayed with the greatest indeterminacy, appropriate to the extent of his paradigmatic role. One element of indeterminacy is anonymity, which removes the barrier a name creates in making a distinction between the character's identity and the reader's, hindering the reader's ability to identify fully with a character.

One objection to the reading of character proposed by this study is that it assigns a role of non-significance or at least declares non-paradigmatic the named characters who are portrayed at least somewhat positively. Among these are John (the witness to the λόγος), Peter, Nathanael, Thomas, Mary Magdalene, Mary of Bethany, and Martha. If the purpose of the Gospel's characters is to entice and facilitate reader identification by confronting readers with a life-changing encounter with Jesus through the portrayal of characters' encounters with Jesus, how is it that named characters with a degree of positive portrayal are inappropriate models for reader identification and imitation?

The named characters who receive significant attention either fail to witness to anyone concerning Jesus, give a unique unrepeatable testimony, or else give negative testimony. John's testimony falls in the middle category. His witness to Jesus is from the perspective of the unique "voice of one crying in the wilderness" (1:23), the narratively prior one who accepts his secondary role and prominence. His unique function of contemporaneous witness to Jesus is unrepeatable and not a role readers can share. John's place in the history of the early Christian community was so firmly established that it extended to the Fourth Gospel community.

Mary's anointing of Jesus (12:2-3) is a non-verbal witness, but an undeniably positive witness. Jesus' own words in 12:7-8 declare the uniqueness of her testimonial act. She prepares his body for burial, in contrast to Nicodemus who also silently concerns himself with Jesus' burial preparation (19:39-41), but the value and significance of his act is ambiguous at best. The next attention the narrative gives to Jesus' burial is its erasure by his resurrection (20:1-8, 13). Mary's preparatory role in the burial of Jesus, like John's, is unique and unrepeatable.

The narrative portrayal of some named characters preclude them as models for reader imitation. Nathanael, Martha, and Thomas all make significant Christological statements. In the Fourth Gospel, however, confessions of faith alone, no matter how accurate, are not acceptable measures of discipleship and alone do not constitute a faith response.[1] The recognition of the disciple Jesus loved as the ideal paradigm of discipleship is not based on confession, but on his faith (not requiring signs or "seeing") and his function as witness par excellence. Jesus does not ask Nathanael for an active faith response, but says in effect, "You haven't seen anything yet." Thomas' confession is only verbal with no accompanying active response of faith. His is a faith requiring sight and his confession shares Martha's inadequacy. Jesus' response to Thomas' confession precludes readers' imitating the error of need to "see" prior to believeing.

Martha does not even affirm the faith Jesus asked for in his question that prompts her confession. He asks, "Do you believe I am the resurrection and the life; and he who believes in me, though he die, yet shall he live?" (11:25). Removed from its immediate context, Martha's confession appears to be a fully adequate Christological confession of the Christian community: "You are the Christ, the Son of God, who is coming into the world," (11:27). Within the boundaries of its immediate textual confines, it is less. Instead of faith in Jesus' power to answer her immediate need and restore life to her brother, she responds with a theological statement without relevance to her present circumstances. The inadequacy is not inherent within the confession, but in Martha's understanding of it. Jesus gives her an opportunity to respond in faith by either joining in the effort to remove the stone or directing others to do so, (i.e. speaking words of witness to the need of others to heed Jesus' word). Martha's response, instead, reveals her concern for the odoriferous consequences of obedience, thus demonstrating her lack of faith.

Mary Magdalene's experience with Jesus demonstrates her loyalty and devotion to him, and her obedience to Jesus' command to bear witness to the good news to his disciples, causing some to identify her as an apostle. In spite of these positive aspects of her portrayal, there remain several factors disqualifying her for reader identification and imitation. Hers was a necessary, yet temporary role of eye-witness to the risen Jesus. There is no possibility nor need for a continuation of this role by modern readers, or even later first-century readers. Prior to her witness-bearing function, she indicates her misunderstanding of Jesus' mission and person, even in her post-resurrection encounter. She sought his continued physical pres-

---

[1] Contra Thibeaux, 221.

ence while he offered a discipleship that necessitated his return to his Father (chapters 14, 16).

One element present in significant anonymous characters making them appropriate models for reader identification and imitation is a faith response. In the Fourth Gospel, confession alone, as found on the lips of Nathanael in chapter 1, Martha in chapter 11, or Thomas in chapter 20, is an insufficient response to Jesus' revelation of his identity. In each significant anonymous character examined above, no confession is recorded; instead they make an active faith response, with the exception of the adulterous woman noted above. All of their responses share in common a witness to Jesus and the efficacy of his words.

Jesus' mother responds to the challenge implied by Jesus' surprising address (γύναι) by instructing the servants to obey unquestioningly anything he might require of them (2:5). The Samaritan woman testifies to her fellow townspeople of one to whom secrets are laid bare, and raises the possibility (albeit hesitantly) that he might be the Messiah (4:29). The βασιλικός first responds by believing Jesus' word of hope enough to depart from Jesus without insisting on being accompanied by Jesus, and when he learns of his son's recovery, his belief is deepened along with his household's (4:50, 53). The belief of his household implicitly assumes the man's witness to them concerning Jesus' identity and the power of his word. The infirm man testified to the Jews both what Jesus did and where he could be found (5:11-15), though his motive is not without ambiguity. The blind man's testimony is extensive, with indication of his growing understanding of Jesus' identity (9:15-34).

The adulterous woman is the only anonymous character given significant textual space without a recorded faith response. Jesus challenges her to move beyond mere gratitude at her deliverance to repentance expressed in altered behavior. Any explication of her response to this challenge, whether it be exegetical, hermeneutical, or homeletical; is extratextual. Nevertheless, her pericope is presented in the context of testimony concerning Jesus. Immediately beforehand, the Gospel records division among people, some of whom are quoted as bearing witness to Jesus' Messiahship (7:41). Immediately following, Jesus is accused of giving self-testimony, a charge he does not deny (8:13); he only denies that his testimony is untrue.

The disciple Jesus loved is not explicitly portrayed bearing testimony to anyone concerning Jesus, nor is any statement of confession placed upon his lips. In contrast to the rather quiet presence of the disciple singled out as a special recipient of Jesus' love, the reader is informed in the final verses that his testimony is heard throughout the text from the prologue forward (21:24). It is *his* witness that stands as the backdrop and basis for the Fourth Gospel. It is *his* testimony the reader receives in each account of Jesus' encounter with various characters, both named and anonymous, and the text boldly proclaims the veracity of his witness: it is ἀληθής.

Nicodemus, on the other hand, completely fails to bear witness to Jesus. His progressive textual silencing has been documented above. The statement before the council that some read as a witness/defense for Jesus is actually only a hesitant legal question phrased in the hypothetical generic (7:51). Far from a witness to Jesus, it does not even exclusively nor necessarily apply to him. Judas' witness to Jesus is an act of betrayal, identifying his location for his enemies (20: 2-3). Pilate bears witness of Jesus' innocence (18:38, 19:4), but in a cowardly manner which only serves to heighten his culpability. His testimony to Jesus' kingship is ironic, placed on the cross at Jesus' death scene.[2]

Lazarus has no recorded speech in the Gospel, or any other response to Jesus after having his life restored. If he is identified as the disciple Jesus loved, it is an extratextual identification, and involves the loss of his identity as he becomes anonymous for the remainder of the Gospel. Martha's "confession" in 11:27 is followed by her telling Mary Jesus is present, but not witnessing to the efficacy of his word. Mary gives no testimony to Jesus at this time, and Martha's next words are an expression of doubt that Jesus' earlier words to her could really be understood as relevant to the immediate need in the life of her family (11:39). Thomas is another example of one who verbally confesses, and whose confession is never corrected by Jesus or the narrative (20:28). But Jesus expresses disappointment at the visual prerequisite to Thomas' belief, and Thomas is not a witness bearer to anyone else.

Peter's only "testimony," and most memorable appearance, is when he denies any acquaintance or involvement with Jesus (18:17, 25-27). The intertwining of his denial with Jesus' unhesitating self-witness places his words in direct opposition to Jesus' self revelation. Peter remains silent throughout Mary's announcement and his own race to examine the empty tomb for himself (20:2-10). His next recorded words, following immediately upon the (non-)conclusion of 20:30-31 with its strong Christological affirmation, constitute the mundane announcement, "I am going fishing," (21:3). He next speaks in his restorative dialogue with Jesus. He declares his love, is commissioned a shepherd, has his future foretold, and is commanded to follow (21:15-19). His obtuseness is not eliminated; his final words express concern about the consequences of following for someone else, a concern Jesus considers totally inappropriate (21:21-23).

---

[2] Duke, 89, 136-7.

Peter's potential witness to Jesus is suggested by his commission to feed Jesus' sheep, especially for readers whose extratext includes familiarity with his role in the tradition of the church (e.g. Acts). Nowhere in the Fourth Gospel does Peter fulfill that potential by witnessing to anyone concerning Jesus.

Throughout the discourse passages of 13-17 the Gospel reinforces the importance of bearing witness to Jesus, what Teresa Okure calls "the missionary task,"[3] but only the disciple Jesus loved faithfully fulfills that function, and he does not accomplish his witness *in* the narrative; his witness to Jesus *is* the Fourth Gospel.

The Conclusion That Does not Conclude

Readers of the Gospel have given much attention to the premature conclusion of 20:30-31. It is used to bolster the argument that chapter 21 is a later addition to the Gospel, an appendix to an already completed narrative.[4] Others argue that this ending only concludes the twentieth chapter and was never intended to indicate closure of the narrative as a whole.[5] The lack of support for this minority viewpoint indicates that most readers do experience a sense of closure upon finishing chapter 20, a feeling frustrated by chapter 21. The continuation of the Gospel beyond the conclusory statement of 20:30-31 undermines the closure and signals readers the narrative of Jesus presented by the Gospel is not easily concluded. When another attempt at closure occurs in 21:25, a reluctance to end is again sensed. Readers are informed the narrative is not exhaustive, and no narrative could accomplish an all-inclusive record of everything Jesus did. Any attempt would fail, because "the world itself could not contain the books that would be written."

The open-endedness of the final statements concurs with other ambiguous closures within the Fourth Gospel narrative. For instance, the reappearance and unanswered fate of Nicodemus remains an open question. Jesus' writing before the condemned woman's accusers is still unrevealed, as is her response to Jesus' word to begin a new life-direction. Lazarus' life after the return from the grave is unnarrated. The specifics of the disciple Jesus loved, including his identity, occupation, family life, initial encounter with Jesus and eventual fate, remain a mystery. The finale of the Gospel declares the impossibility of a closed narrative of Je-

---

[3] Okure, 196
[4] E.g. Brown, *John*, II, 1057.
[5] Paul Minear, "The Original Function of John 21," *Journal of Biblical Literature* 102 (1983): 87.

sus. The absence of closure prepares readers for the continuation of Jesus' working in their own life narrative. Jesus, encountered in the Fourth Gospel through reader identification with characters, is revealed as the one still available to those blessed "who have not seen and yet believe."

Implications for Future Study

The attention to the reading experience that has been the focus of this study has produced important insights for understanding the function and meaning of characterization in the Fourth Gospel. The method, however, has not exhausted its usefulness with this analysis. Several areas for further study suggest themselves. Useful for confirming the results of my study and the reading it produced would be inquiry into the responses of real readers to the Gospel narrative. A two-fold difficulty in this type of investigation, however, concerns the subjects for the study. What type of readers would be included? The elusive "naive first-time" reader some reader response practitioners have favored in their interpretive method would be difficult to locate since the claims of the Gospel permeate the culture dominant in our world for much of the time since its production. If readers are chosen who are already consciously familiar with the text through their participation in Christian communities, another difficulty is faced: how could it be determined whether their responses were a product of their experience within those communities or responses to the narrative itself?

In responding to reader-oriented interpretations of Mark, literary critic Temma Berg professes to be a first-time reader of that narrative, but by her own admission illustrates how illusive the assumption of "naive" as an adjective preceding "first-time reader" becomes for us in the twentieth century. "I have, of course, read about it and read others' experiences of it."[6] One wonders to what extent her responses are formed and influenced by her secondary familiarity with the narrative of Mark, rather than by a true "first-reading." Further, she confesses that she is not one who assents to the faith claims the narrative presents. To what extent is her reading of Mark's narrative necessarily influenced by her experiences with others who do assent to these claims? This brings us full circle to the reality of the social location of all readers, be they trained reader/critics, naive first-time readers, or members of communities who value the Fourth Gospel as a sacred text. I can certainly engage in self-assessment to become more aware of my own social location and how my reading differs from those

---

[6] Temma Berg, "Reading In/to Mark," *Semeia* 58 (1989): 197.

who do not share that location, but am I or any reader capable of reading from a social location that is not my own?

This study has only focused on individual characters, and reveals that the characters offered as models for discipleship are anonymous. Does the appropriate response paradigm hold true for character groups as well? Is there a parallel with the function of individual characters who have been the focus of this study? What is the interrelationship of the discourses to the narrative presentations of significant anonymous characters? Do the discursive passages confirm the emphasis on discipleship as witness bearing discovered through the anonymous characters fitting the appropriate response paradigm?

Reader Participation in the Fourth Gospel Narrative

The Fourth Gospel claims that with Jesus' entry into the world to participate in the lives of first-century persons, God is made available to them as never before experienced. The narrative refers to people who would later come to believe through the testimony of the characters whose life narratives are glimpsed by readers (17:20, 20:29). Together with the accounts of people who believe on the basis of second hand testimony (e.g. the Samaritan townspeople and the household of the βασιλικός), and the criticism of belief requiring signs or "seeing," readers discovery of specific references to themselves (i.e. the second person address in the purpose statement 20:31) alert them to their potential for encountering Jesus in the Fourth Gospel and for allowing him participation in their own life narrative.

The established paradigm of appropriate response to Jesus fits a particular group of Fourth Gospel characters: anonymous individuals who receive more than just a brief mention and who have significant encounters with Jesus. Why are they all portrayed anonymously, including some whose identities might well have been known at least by first-century readers (Jesus' mother, the disciple Jesus loved)? Elements of their characterization combine to make them attractive models for reader identification; through them readers may experience Jesus. Identification with a narrative character is facilitated by the indeterminacy of the character. The less determinate the characterization, the easier for readers to enter the narrative world through participation in the character's episode with Jesus. Anonymity is a major facet of a character's indeterminacy, since names can distinguish, as well as identify. The Fourth Gospel does not encourage bystanders, but rather invites "readers to enter into the revelatory dynamic themselves,"⁷ and some narrative elements facilitate reader participation. One literary aspect of the Gospel that assists reader participation is the art of characterization and the role of anonymity as one element of positive paradigmatic character portrayal.

The Fourth Gospel ends without a distinct conclusion or accomplishing closure. Instead, the reader is informed that the narrative of Jesus is not complete with the portraits, snapshots, and sketches of various characters and their encounters with Jesus—indeed, it cannot yet be completed. To narrate all of Jesus' life changing encounters with individuals is impossible because it is a continuing occurrence. John bore his unique witness to Jesus; Jesus' mother, the Samaritan woman, the βασιλικός, the lame man, and the blind man all testified to others concerning their encounters with Jesus. The disciple Jesus loved bears witness concerning Jesus to all readers through the Fourth Gospel text. Many readers throughout the history of the communities preserving and treasuring the Gospel were first directed to it by the testimony of others, who encountered Jesus through their encounters with the Gospel's characters. In the only direct address to the reader in the narrative, the text challenges the reader to move beyond being informed or entertained. This narrative was written and passed on for the purpose that through dynamic participation in its encounters and claims, "you (the reader) may believe that Jesus is the Christ, the Son of God, and believing you might have life in his name."

---

⁷ O'Day, 95.

BIBLIOGRAPHY

Agourides, Savas C. "Peter and John in the Fourth Gospel," in *Studia Evangelica* Fourth ed. Frank L. Cross (Berlin: Akademie, 1968): 3-7

Aland, Kurt. *Synopsis of the Fourth Gospel: Greek-English Edition of the Synopsis Quattuor Evangeliorum.* Stuttgart: UBS, 1975.

Alcorn, Marshall W., and Mark Bracher. "Literature, Psychoanalysis, and the Re-Formation of the Self: A New Direction for Reader-Response Theory." *Publications of the Modern Language Association of America* 100 (May 1985): 342-54.

Allen, Thomas G. "God the Namer: A Note on Ephesians 1:21b." *New Testament Studies* 32.3 (1986): 470-5.

Alter, Robert. *The Art of Biblical Narrative.* New York: Basic Books, 1981.

Alter, Robert and Frank Kermode. *The Literary Guide to the Bible.* Cambridge: Harvard University Press, 1987.

Ashton, John. *Studying John: Approaches to the Fourth Gospel.* Oxford: Claredon Press, 1994.

Aune, David. *Greco-Roman Literature and the New Testament.* Society of Biblical Literature Sources for Biblical Studies 21. Atlanta: Scholars Press, 1988.

Bacon, B. W. "Displacement of John xiv." *Journal of Biblical Literature* 13 (1894): 64-75.

———. *The Fourth Gospel in Research and Debate.* London: T. Fisher Unwin, 1910.

Bal, Mieke. "Dealing/With/Women: Daughters in the Book of Judges." In *The Book and the Text: The Bible and Literary Theory.* Edited by Regina Schwartz, 16-39. Cambridge, MA: Basil Blackwell, 1990.

———. *Narratology: Introduction to the Theory of Narrative.* Translated by Christine van Boheemen. Toronto: University of Toronto Press, 1985.

Ball, David Mark. *"I Am" in John's Gospel: Literary Function, Background and Theological Implications.* Journal for the Study of the New Testament-Supplement Series 124. Sheffield: JSOT Press, 1996.

Bar-Efrat, Shimon. *Narrative Art in the Bible.* Bible and Literature Series 17. Journal for the Study of the Old Testament-Supplement Series 70. Decatur, GA: Almond Press, 1989.

Barrett, C. K. *The Gospel According to St. John: An Introduction with Commentary and Notes on the Greek Text.* 2nd rev. ed. Philadelphia: Westminster, 1978.

Barrose, T. "The Seven Days of New Creation in St. John's Gospel." *Catholic Biblical Quarterly* 21 (1959): 507-16.

Bassler, Jouette M. "Mixed Signals: Nicodemus in the Fourth Gospel." *Journal of Biblical Literature* 108 (1989): 635-46.

Bauckham, Richard. "The Beloved Disciple as Ideal Author." *Journal for the Study of the New Testament* 49 (1993): 21-44.

Beardslee, William A. *Margins of Belonging: Essays on the New Testament and Theology.* American Academy of Religion Studies in Religion 58. Atlanta: Scholars Press, 1991.

Beasley-Murray, George R. *John.* Vol. 36, Word Biblical Commentary. Waco, Texas: Word Books, 1987.

———. "John 3:3, 5: Baptism, Spirit and the Kingdom." *The Expository Times* 97 (1986): 167-70.

Beck, David R. "The Narrative Function of Anonymity in Fourth Gospel Characterization." *Semeia* 63 (1993): 143-158.

Berlin, Adele. *Poetics and Interpretation of Biblical Narrative.* Bible and Literature Series 9. Sheffield: Almond Press, 1983.

Bernard, John H. *A Critical and Exegetical Commentary on the Gospel According to St. John*, 2 vols. Edited by A. H. McNeile. Edinburgh: T & T Clark, 1928.
Bernstein, Charles. "Characterization." In *Writing/Talks*. Edited by Bob Perelman, 7-30. Carbondale: Southern Illinois University Press, 1985.
Blass, Friedrich, and Albert Debrunner. *A Greek Grammar of the New Testament and Other Early Christian Literature*. Translated by Robert W. Funk. Chicago: University of Chicago Press, 1961.
Bligh, John. "Jesus in Samaria." *Heythrop Journal* 3 (1962): 329-46.
Boers, Hendrikus. *Neither on this Mountain nor in Jerusalem: A Study of John 4*. Society of Biblical Literature Monograph Series 35. Atlanta: Scholars Press, 1988.
Boismard, M.-E. *Du Baptême à Cana (Jean 1:19-2:11)*. Lectio divina 18. Paris: Editions du Cerf, 1956.
——. "Les traditions johanniques concernant le Baptiste." *Revue biblique* 70 (1963): 5-42.
Botha, J. Eugene. *Jesus and the Samaritan Woman: A Speech Act Reading of John 4:1-42*. Novum Testamentum Supplements 65. Leiden: E.J. Brill, 1991.
——. "Reader 'Entrapment' as Literary Device in John 4:1-42." *Neotestimentica* 24 (1990): 37-47.
Booth, Steve. *Selected Peak Marking Features in the Gospel of John*. American University Studies, Series 7, Theology and Religion, vol. 178. New York: Peter Lang Publishing, Inc., 1996.
Braun, Willi. "Resisting John: Ambivalent Redactor and Defensive Reader of the Fourth Gospel." *Studies in Religion/Sciences religieuses* 19.1 (1990): 59-71.
Brewer, William F. and Keisuke Ohtsuka. "Story Structure, Characterization, Just World Organization, and Reader Affect in American and Hungarian Short Stories." *Poetics* 17 (1988): 395-415.
Briggs, Sheila. "'Buried with Christ': The Politics of Identity and the Poverty of Interpretation." In *The Book and the Text: The Bible and Literary Theory*. Edited by Regina Schwartz, 276-303. Cambridge, MA: Basil Blackwell, 1990.
Brodie, Thomas L. *The Gospel According to John: A Literary and Theological Commentary*. New York: Oxford University Press, 1993.
Broer, Ingo. "Noch einmal: Zur religionsgeschichtlichen 'Ableitung' von Jo 1, 1-11." *Studien zum Neuen Testament und seiner Umwelt* 8 (1983): 103-23.
Brown, Raymond E. *The Community of the Beloved Disciple*. New York: Paulist, 1979.
——. *The Gospel According to John: Introduction, Translation and Notes*. Anchor Bible. 2 vols. Garden City, N.Y.: Doubleday, 1966, 1970.
——. "Jesus and Elijah." *Perspectives* 12 (1971): 85-104.
Brown, Raymond E., Karl P. Donfried, Joseph A. Fitzmyer, and John Reumann. Edited by *Mary in the New Testament: A Collaborative Assessment by Protestant and Roman Catholic Scholars*. Philadelphia: Fortress, 1978; New York: Paulist, 1978.
Brown, Raymond E., Karl P. Donfried, John Reumann. *Peter in the New Testament: A Collaborative Assessment by Protestants and Roman Catholic Scholars*. Minneapolis: Augsburg, 1973; New York: Paulist, 1973.
Brown, Schuyler. "The Beloved Disciple: A Jungian View." In *The Conversation Continues: Studies in Paul & John*. Edited by Robert T. Fortna and Beverly R. Gaventa, 366-78. Nashville: Abingdon, 1990.
——. "Apostleship in the New Testament as an Historical and Theological Problem." *New Testament Studies* 30 (1984): 474-80.
Bruce, F. F. *The Gospel of John*. Grand Rapids: Eerdmanns, 1983.
Bultmann, Rudolf. *The Gospel of John: A Commentary*. Translated by G. R. Beasley-Murray et al. Philadelphia: Westminster, 1971.

———. "The History of Religions Background of the Prologue to the Gospel of John." Translated by John Ashton. In *The Interpretation of John*. Edited by John Ashton, 18-35. Issues in Religion and Theology 9. Philadelphia: Fortress, 1986.
Byrne, Brendan. "The Faith of the Beloved Disciple and the Community in John 20." *Journal for the Study of the New Testament* 23 (1985): 83-97.
———. *Lazarus: A Contemporary Reading of John 11:1-46*. Zacchaeus Studies: New Testament. Edited by Mary Ann Getty.Collegeville, Minnesota: The Liturgical Press, 1991.
Cahill, P. Joseph. "Narrative Art in John IV." *Religious Studies Bulletin* 2 (1982): 41-48.
Campbell-Sposito, Mary. "Onomastics as a Defamiliarizing Device in Raymond Queneau's Novels." *French Review* 5 (April 1988): 724-33.
Carr, David. "Narrativity and the Real World: An Argument for Continuity." *History and Theory* 25.2 (1986): 117-31.
Carson, D. A., *The Gospel According to John*. Grand Rapids: Wm. B. Eerdmans, Publishing Company, 1991.
Carson, D. A., Douglas J. Moo, and Leon Morris. *An Introduction to the New Testament*. Grand Rapids, Michigan: Zondervan, 1992.
Cassidy, Richard J. *John's Gospel in New Perspective: Christology and Roman Power*. Maryknoll, New York: Orbis Books, 1992.
Chapman, J. Harley. *Jung's Three Theories of Religious Experience*. Studies in the Psychology of Religion, Vol. 3. Lewiston: The Edwin Mellon Press, 1988.
Charles, J. Daryl. "Will the Court Please Call in the Prime Witness?': John 1:29-34 and the 'Witness'- Motif." *Trinity Journal* 10 NS (1989):71-83.
Charlesworth, James H. *The Beloved Disciple: Whose Witness Validates the Gospel of John?* Valley Forge, Pennsylvania: Trinity Press International, 1995.
Chatman, Seymour. *Story and Discourse: Narrative Structure in Fiction and Film*. Ithaca: Cornell University Press, 1978.
Colley, Ann C. "The Quest for the 'Nameless' in Tennyson's 'The Lady of Shallot'." *Victorian Poetry* 23.4 (1985): 369-78.
Collins, Matthew S. "The Question of *Doxa*: A Socioliterary Reading of the Wedding at Cana." *Biblical Theology Bulletin* 23:3 (1995): 100-9.
Collins, Raymond F. "From John to the Beloved Disciple: An Essay on Johannine Characters." *Interpretation* 49:4 (1995): 359-69.
———. "Representative Figures in the Fourth Gospel." *The Downside Review* 94 (1976): 26-46, 118-32.
Cottam, Thomas. "Some Displacements in the Fourth Gospel." *Expository Times* 38 (1926): 91-92.
Cottrell, F. P. "The Nicodemus Conversation: A Fresh Appraisal." *The Expository Times* 96 (1985): 237-42.
Countryman, L. William *The Mystical Way in the Fourth Gospel*. Philadelphia: Fortress, 1987.
Culbertson, Diana. "Are You also Deceived?: Reforming the Reader in John 7." In *Proceedings: Eastern Great Lakes and Midwest Bible Societies* 9 (1989): 148-60.
———. *The Poetics of Revelation: Recognition and the Narrative Tradition*. Studies in American Biblical Hermeneutics 4. Macon: Mercer University Press, 1989.
Cullmann, Oscar. *The Johannine Circle*. Translated by John Bowden. Philadelphia: Westminster Press, 1976.
Culpepper, R. Alan. *Anatomy of the Forth Gospel: A Study in Literary Design*. Foundations and Facets: New Testament. Philadelphia: Fortress, 1983.

———. *John, the Son of Zebedee: The Life of a Legend.* Studies on Personalities of the New Testament. Edited by D. Moody Smith. Columbia, South Carolina: University of South Carolina Press, 1994.

———. "The Pivot of John's Prologue." *New Testament Studies* 27 (1980): 1-31.

———. "The Plot of John's Story of Jesus." *Interpretation* 49:4 (1995):347-58.

———. "Reading Johannine Irony." In *Exploring the Gospel of John: in Honor of D. Moody Smith*, ed. R. Alan Culpepper and D. Clifton Black, 193-207. Louisville: Westminster John Knox Press, 1996.

———. "Un exemple de commentaire fond, sur la critique narrative: Jean 5,1-18." In *La communaut, johannique et son histoire: La trajectoire de l'évangile de Jean aux deux premiers siècles.* Edited by Jean-Daniel Kaestli, Jean-Michel Poffet, and Jean Zumstein, 135-51. Geneva: Labor et Fides, 1990.

Cutting-Gray, Joanne L. *Revelation and Concealment: Woman and the Novels of Fanny Burney.* Ph.D. diss. Marquette University, 1986. Ann Arbor: UMI, 1987.

Cuvillier, Élian. "La Figure des Disciples en Jean 4." *New Testament Studies* 42 (1996): 245-59.

Darr, John A. *On Character Building: The Reader and the Rhetoric of Characterization in Luke-Acts.* Literary Currents in Biblical Interpretation. Louisville: Westminster/John Knox Press, 1992.

Deil, Paul and Jeannine Solotareff. *Symbolism in the Gospel of John.* Translated by Nelly Marans. San Francisco: Harper & Row, 1988.

DeJean, Joan. "Lafayette's Ellipses: The Privileges of Anonymity." *Publications of the Modern Language Association* 99.5 (1984): 884-902.

de Jonge, Marinus. "The Beloved Disciple and the Date of the Gospel of John." In *Text and Interpretation: Studies in the New Testament presented to Matthew Black.* Edited by E. Best and R. McL Wilson, 99-114. Cambridge: Cambridge University Press, 1979.

———. "John the Baptist and Elijah in the Fourth Gospel." In *The Conversation Continues: Studies in Paul and John in Honor of J. Louis Martyn.* Edited by Robert T. Fortna and Beverly Gaventa, 299-308. Nashville: Abingdon, 1990.

Detwiler, Andreas. "Le prologue johannique (Jean 1,1-18)." In *La communaut, johannique et son histoire: La trajectoire de l'évangile de Jean aux deux premiers siècles.* Edited by Jean-Daniel Kaestli, Jean-Michel Poffet, and Jean Zumstein, 185-203. Geneva: Labor et Fides, 1990.

Dixon, John and Leslie Stratta. "Developing Responses to Character in Literature." *Passages to Literature: Essays on Teaching in Australia, Canada, England, theUnited States and Wales.* Edited by Joseph O'Beirne and Lucy Floyd Murdock. Urbana: National Council of Teachers of England, 1989.

Docherty, Thomas. *Reading (Absent) Character: Towards A Theory of Characterization in Fiction.* Oxford: Clarendon, 1983.

Dockery, David S. "John 9:1-41: A Narrative Discourse Study." *Occasional Papers in Translation and Textlinguistics* 2 (1988): 14-26.

Dodd, C. H. *Historical Tradition in the Fourth Gospel.* Cambridge: Cambridge University Press, 1963.

———. *The Interpretation of the Fourth Gospel.* Cambridge: Cambridge University Press, 1968.

Domeris, William R. "The Johannine Drama." *Journal of Theology for Southern Africa* 42 (1983): 29-35.

Droge, Arthur J. "The Status of Peter in the Fourth Gospel: John 18:10-11." *Journal of Biblical Literature* 109 (1990): 307-11.

D'Sa, Francis X. "The Language of God and the God of Language: The Relation Between God, Human Beings, World, and Language in St. John." In *God in Lan-*

guage. Edited by Robert P. Scharlemann and Gilbert E. M. Ogutu, 35-59. New York: Paragon House, 1987.
Duke, Paul D. *Irony in the Fourth Gospel.* Atlanta: John Knox Press, 1985.
du Rand, Jan A. "The Characterization of Jesus as Depicted in the Narrative of the Fourth Gospel." *Neotestamentica* 19 (1985): 18-35.
———. "A Syntactical and Narratological Reading of John 10 in Coherence with Chapter 9." In *The Shepherd Discourse of John 10 and its Context.* Edited by Johannes Beutler and Robert Fortna, 94-115. Society for New Testament Studies Monograph Series 67. Cambridge: Cambridge University Press, 1991.
Dunn, James D. G. "John and the Oral Gospel Tradition." In *Jesus and the Oral Gospel Tradition.* Edited by Henry Wansbrough, 351-79. Journal for the Study of the New Testament Supplement Series 64. Sheffield: JSOT Press, 1991.
———. "Let John Be John: A Gospel for Its Time." In *The Gospel and the Gospels.* Edited by Peter Stuhlmacher, 293-322. Grand Rapids, Mich.: Eerdmans, 1991.
Eckhardt, Karl A. *Der Tod des Johannes als Schlssel zum Verständnis der johanneischen Schriften.* Studien zur Rechts - und Religionsgeschichte 3; Berlin: Walter de Gruyter, 1961.
Eckle, Wolfgang. *Den der Herr liebhatte: Rätsel um den Evangelisten Johannes: zum historischen Verständnis seiner autobiographischen Andeutungen.* Hamburg: Kovac, 1991.
Eco, Umberto. *A Theory of Semiotics.* Bloomington, Indiana: Indiana University Press, 1976.
Edwards, Michael. "The World Could not Contain the Books." In *The Bible as Rhetoric: Studies in Biblical Persuasion and Credibility.* Warwick Studies in Philosophy and Literature. Edited by Martin Warner, 178-94. London: Routledge, 1990.
Ehrman, Bart D. "Jesus and the Adulteress." *New Testament Studies* 34 (1988): 24-44.
Eisler, Robert. *The Enigma of the Fourth Gospel: Its Author and Its Writer.* London: Methuen, 1937.
Eller, Vernard. *The Beloved Disciple: His Name, His Story, His Thought.* Grand Rapids, Mich.: Eerdmans, 1987.
Ellis, Peter F. *The Genius of John: A Composition-Critical Commentary on the Fourth Gospel.* Collegeville, Minn.: Liturgical Press, 1984.
Enz, Jacob J. "The Book of Exodus as a Literary Type for the Gospel of John." *Journal of Biblical Literature* 76 (1957): 208-15.
Eslinger, Lyle. "The Wooing of the Woman at the Well: Jesus, The Reader and Reader-Response Criticism." *Journal of Literature and Theology* 1 (1987): 167-83.
Evans, Craig A. *Word and Glory: On the Exegetical and Theological Background of John's Prologue.* Journal for the Study of the New Testament-Supplement Series 89. Sheffield: JSOT Press, 1993.
Fewell, Danna Nolan and David Miller Gunn. *Compromising Redemption: Relating Characters in the Book of Ruth.* Currents in Biblical Interpretation. Louisville: Westminster/John Knox Press, 1990.
Farmer, Kathleen. "Ungodly Habits of Identification." *Journal of Theology* 91 (1987): 59-66.
Filson, Floyd V. "Who Was the Beloved Disciple?" *Journal of Biblical Literature* 68 (1949): 83-88.
Fiorenza, Elizabeth Schüssler. In Memory of Her: *A Feminist Theological Reconstruction of Christian Origins.* New York: Crossroads, 1983.
Fish, Stanley. *Is There a Text in This Class: The Authority of Interpretive Communities.* Cambridge: Harvard University Press, 1980.

Flanagan, Owen and Amilie Oksenberg Rorty. *Identity, Character and Morality: Essays in Moral Psychology.* Cambridge: MIT Press, 1990.

Flesch, William. "Anonymity and Unhappiness in Proust and Wittgenstein." *Criticism* 29.4 (1987): 459-76.

Fokkema, Aleid. *Postmodern Characters: A Study of Characterization in British and Postmodern Fiction.* Postmodern Studies 4. Amsterdam: Rodopi, 1991.

Forster, E. M. *Aspects of the Novel.* New York: Harcourt, Brace and World, 1927.

Fortna, Robert Tomson. *The Fourth Gospel and its Predecessor: From Narrative Source to Present Gospel.* Philadelphia: Fortress, 1988.

Foster, Donald. "John Come Lately: The Belated Evangelist." *The Bible and the Narrative Tradition.* Edited by F. McConnell. Oxford: Oxford University Press, 1986. 113-31.

Fowler, Robert M. *Let the Reader Understand: Reader-Response Criticism and the Gospel of Mark.* Minneapolis: Augsburg Fortress, 1991.

Freed, Edwin D. "Variations in the Language and Thought of John." *Zeitschrift für die neutestamentliche Wissenschaft* 55 (1964): 167-97.

Funk, Robert W. *The Poetics of Biblical Narrative.* Foundations and Facets. Sonoma, CA: Polebridge Press, 1988.

Gaventa, Beverly Roberts. "The Archive of Excess: John 21 and the Problem of Narrative Closure." In *Exploring the Gospel of John: in Honor of D. Moody Smith*, ed. R. Alan Culpepper and D. Clifton Black, 240-52. Louisville: Westminster John Knox Press, 1996.

Gennette, Girard. *Narrative Discourses.* Translated by Jane Lewin. Ithaca, NY: Cornell University Press, 1980.

Geyser, A. "The Semeion at Cana of the Galilee." In *Studies in John: Presented to Professor Dr. J. N. Sevenster on the Occasion of his Seventieth Birthday*, 12-21. Novum Testamentum Supplements 24. Leiden: E. J. Brill, 1970.

Gibbons, Debbie. "Nicodemus: Character Development, Irony and Repetition in the Fourth Gospel." In *Proceedings: Eastern Great Lakes and Midwest Biblical Societies* 11 (1991): 116-28.

Giblin, Charles H. "Suggestion, Negative Response, and Positive Action in St. John's Portrayal of Jesus." *New Testament Studies* 26 (1980): 197-211.

Gill, Christopher. "The Character-Personality Distinction." In *Characterization and Individuality in Greek Literature.* Edited by Christopher Pelling, 1-31. Oxford: Clarendon, 1990.

Ginsberg, Warren. *The Cast of Character: The Representation of Personality in Ancient and Medieval Literature.* Toronto: The University of Toronto Press, 1983.

Girard, M. "La composition structurale des sept signes dans le quartième évangile." *Sciences religieuses* 9 (1980): 315-24.

Grassi, Joseph A. "The Role of Jesus' Mother in John's Gospel: A Reappraisal." *Catholic Biblical Quarterly* 48 (1986): 67-80.

———. *The Secret Identity of the Beloved Disciple.* New York: Paulist, 1992.

Green, Eugene. "Power, Commitment and the Right to a Name in Beowulf." In *Persons in Groups: Social Behavior as Identity Formation in Medieval and Renaissance Europe.* Edited by Richard C. Trexler, 133-40. Binghamton, NY: Medieval & Renaissance Texts & Studies, 1985.

Greimas, A. J. *Sémantique structurale: récherche de méthode.* Paris: Librairie Larousse, 1966.

Gunther, J. J. "The Relationship of the Beloved Disciple to the Twelve." *Theologische Zeitschrift* 37 (1981): 129-48.

Guthrie, Donald. *New Testament Introduction*, rev. ed. Downers Grove, Illinois: Inter-Varsity Press, 1990.

Hadas, Moses. *Three Greek Romances: Longus, Xenophon, Dio Chrysostom.* New York: Bobbs-Merrill, 1953.
Haenchen, Ernst. *John 1: A Commentary on the Gospel of John Chapters 1-6* and *John 2: A Commentary on the Gospel of John Chapters 7-21.* Translated by Robert W. Funk., Ulrich Busse. Hermeneia. Philadelphia: Fortress, 1984.
Hägg, Thomas. *The Novel in Antiquity.* Berkeley: University of California Press, 1983.
Halász, László. "Affective Structural Effect and the Character's Perception in Reception of Short Stories: An American-Hungarian Cross-Cultural Study." *Poetics* 17 (1988): 417-38.
———. "Self Relevant Reading in Literary Understanding." Chap. 11 in *Reader Response to Literature: The Empirical Dimension.* Edited by Elaine F. Nardocchio, 229-45. Approaches to Semiotics 108. New York: Mouton de Gruyter, 1992.
Hartin, P. J. "The Role of Peter in the Fourth Gospel." *Neotestimentica* 24 (1990): 49-61.
Hartman, Lars. "An Attempt at a Text-Centered Exegesis of John 21." *Studia Theologica* 38 (1984): 29-45.
Hawkin, David J. "The Function of the Beloved Disciple Motif in the Johannine Redaction." *Laval theologique et philosophique* 33 (1977): 135-50.
———. *The Johannine World: Reflections on the Theology of the Fourth Gospel and Contemporary Society.* SUNY Series in Religious Studies. Albany: State University of New York Press, 1996.
Heil, John Paul. "The Story of Jesus and the Adulteress (John 7,53-8,11) Reconsidered." *Biblica* 72 (1991): 182-91.
Henaut, Barry W. "John 4:43-54 and the Ambivalent Narrator. A Response to Culpepper's *Anatomy of the Fourth Gospel.*" *Studies in Religion* 19 (1990): 287-304.
Hengel, Martin. "The Interpretation of the Wine Miracle at Cana: John 2:1-11." Translated by G. Schmidt. In *The Glory of Christ in the New Testament: Studies in Christology in Memory of George Bradford Caird.* Edited by L. D. Hurst and N. T. Wright, 83-112. Oxford: Clarendon, 1987.
———. *The Johannine Question.* Translated by John Bowden. London: SCM Press, 1989; Philadelphia: Trinty Press International, 1989.
Highie, Robert. *Character & Structure in the English Novel.* Gainesville: University of Florida Press, 1984.
Hirsch, E. D., Jr. *Cultural Literacy: What Every American Needs to Know.* New York: Vantage Books, 1988.
Hoare, Frederick R. *The Original Order and Chapters of St. John's Gospel.* London: Burns, Oates & Washbourne, 1944.
Hochman, Baruch. *Character in Literature.* Ithaca: Cornell University Press, 1985.
Holland, Norman. "Unity Identity Text Self." In *Reader-Response Criticism: From Formalism to Post-Structuralism.* Edited by Jane P. Thompkins, 118-33. Baltimore: John Hopkins University Press, 1980.
Holleran, J. Warren. "Seeing the Light: A Narrative Reading of John 9." *Ephemerides theologicae lovaniensis* 69 (1993):5-26, 354-82.
Hyman, Ronald T. "Questions and Changing Identities in the Book of Ruth." *Union Seminary Quarterly Review* 39.3 (1984): 189-201.
Iser, Wolfgang. *The Act of Reading: A Theory of Aesthetic Response.* Baltimore: John Hopkins University Press, 1978.
Izevbaye, D. S. "Naming and the Character of African Fiction." *Research in African Literatures* 12.2 (1983): 162-84.

Johnson, Lewis. "Who Was the Beloved Disciple?" *Expository Times* 77 (1966): 157-8.
Jose, Paul E "The Role of Gender and Gender Role Similarity in Reader's Identification with Story Characters." *Sex Roles* 21 (1989): 697-713.
Jose, Paul E, and William F. Brewer. "Development of Story Liking: Character Identification, Suspense and Resolution." *Developmental Psychology* 20 (1984): 911-24.
Jouve, Vincent. *L'effet-personnage dans le roman*. Paris: Presses Universitaires de France, 1992.
Käsemann, Ernst. "The Structure and Purpose of the Prologue to John's Gospel." In *New Testament Questions of Today*, 138-67. London: SCM Press, 1969.
Kaufman, Philip S. *The Beloved Disciple: Witness Against Anti-Semitism*. Collegeville, Minnesota: The Liturgical Press, 1991.
Kelber, Werner H. "The Birth of a Beginning: John 1:1-18." *Semeia* 52 (1990): 121-44.
Kermode, Frank. *The Genesis of Secrecy: On the Interpretation of Narrative*. Cambridge: Harvard University Press, 1979.
———. "New Ways with Bible Stories." In *Parable and Story in Judaism and Christianity*. Edited by Clemons Thoma and Michael Whschogrod, 121-35. New York: Paulist, 1989.
Kilmartin, Edward J. "The Mother of Jesus was there: The Significance of Mary in Jn 2, 3-5 and Jn 19, 25-27." *Sciences Ecclesiastiques* 15 (1963): 213-26.
Kitzberger, Ingrid Rosa. "Mary of Bethany and Mary of Magdala – Two Female Characters in the Johannine Passion Narrative: A Feminist, Narrative-Critical Reader-Response." *New Testament Studies* 41 (1995): 564-86.
Koester, Craig. "'The Savior of the World' (John 4:42)." *Journal of Biblical Literature* 109 (1990): 665-80.
———. "Messianic Exegesis and the Call of Nathanael (John 1.45-51)." *Journal for the Study of the New Testament* 39 (1990): 23-34.
———. *Symbolism in the Fourth Gospel: Meaning, Mystery, Community*. Minneapolis: Fortress Press, 1995.
Kopas, Jane. "Critic's Corner: Jesus and Women: John's Gospel." *Theology Today* 41 (1984): 201-5.
Kort, Wesley A. *Story, Text, and Scripture: Literary Interests in Biblical Narrative*. University Park: Pennsylvania State University Press, 1988.
Kotz, P.P.A. "John and Reader's Response." *Neotestimentica* 19 (1985): 50-63.
Kraabel, A. Thomas. "The God-Fearers Meet the Beloved Disciple." In *The Future of Early Christianity*. Edited by B. Pearson, et al, 276-84. Minneapolis: Fortress, 1991.
Kreitler, Hans, and Shulamith Kreitler. *The Psychology of the Arts*. Durham: Duke University Press, 1972.
Kügler, J. *Der Jünger, den Jesus liebte. Literarische, theologische und historische Untersuchungen zu einer Schlüsselgestalt johanneischer Theologie und Geshichte. Mit einem Exkurs über die Brotrede in Joh 6*. Stuttgarter biblische Beiträge 16. Stuttgart: Verlag katholisches Bibelwerk, 1988.
Kurz, William S. "The Beloved Disciple and Implied Readers." *Biblical Theology Bulletin* 19 (1989):100-07.
Kysar, Robert. *John*. Augsburg Commentary on the New Testament. Minneapolis: Augsburg, 1986.
———. *John's Story of Jesus*. Philadelphia: Fortress, 1984.
Lee, Dorothy A. *The Symbolic Narratives of the Fourth Gospel: The Interplay of Form and Meaning*, Journal for the Study of the New Testament Supplement Series 95, Sheffield: JSOT Press, 1994.

———. "Partnership in Easter Faith: The Role of Mary Magdalene and Thomas in John 20." *Journal for the Study of the New Testament* 58 (1995): 37-49.
———. "The Story of the Woman at the Well: A Symbolic Reading (John 4:1-42)." *Australian Biblical Review* 41 (1993): 35-48.
Leonard, John. *Naming in Paradise: Milton and the Language of Adam and Eve*. Oxford: Clarendon, 1990.
Levenson, Michael. *Modernism and the Fate of Individuality: Character and Novelistic Form from Conrad to Woolf*. Cambridge: Cambridge University Press, 1991.
Lewis, Frank W. *Disarrangements in the Fourth Gospel*. Cambridge: Cambridge University Press, 1910.
Lightfoot, Robert Henry. *St. John's Gospel. A Commentary*. Edited by C. F. Evans. Oxford: Clarendon Press, 1956.
Lindars, Barnabas. *The Gospel of John*. New Century Bible Commentary. Grand Rapids, Mich.: Eerdmans, 1972.
Litt, Dorothy E. "Namelessness in English Renaissance Drama." *Literary Onomastics Studies* 13 (1986): 1-24.
Long, Burke O. "The Shunammite Woman: In the Shadow of the Prophet?" *Bible Review* 7 (1991): 12-19, 42.
Mahoney, Robert K. *Two Disciples at the Tomb: The Background and Message of John 20,1-10*. Theologie und Wirklichkeit 6. Frankfurt: Lang, 1974.
Mangolin, Uri. "The Doer and the Deed: Action as a Basis for Characterization in Narrative." *Poetics Today* 7.2 (1986): 205-25.
Manno, Bruce. "Michael Polanyi and Erik Erikson: Towards a Post-critical Perspective on Human Identity." *Religious Education* 75 (1980): 205-14.
Maurer, Warren R. "Trends in Literary Scholarship: German Literary Onomastics: An Overview." *The German Quarterly* 56.1 (1983): 89-105.
Martyn, J. Louis. *History and Theology in the Fourth Gospel*, Rev. ed. Nashville: Abingdon, 1979.
Maynard, Arthur H. "ΤΙ ΕΜΟΙ ΚΑΙ ΣΟΙ." *New Testament Studies* 31 (1985): 582-86.
———. "The Role of Peter in the Fourth Gospel." *New Testament Studies* 30 (1984): 531-48.
McDonald, J. Ian. "The So-Called *Pericope de adultera*." *New Testament Studies* 41:3 (1995): 415-27.
McGann, Diarmuid. *Journeying Within Transcendence: The Gospel of John Through a Jungian Perspective*. New York: Paulist, 1988.
Mead, A. H. "The βασιλικός" in John 4:46-53. *Journal for the Study of the New Testament* 23 (1985): 69-72.
Meeks, Wayne. "The Man from Heaven in Johannine Sectarianism." *Journal of Biblical Literature* 91 (1972): 44-72.
Menken, M. J. J. "The Quotation from Isaiah 40,3 in John 1,23." *Biblical* 66:2 (1985): 190-205.
Merkelbach, Reinhold. *Roman und Mysterium in der Antike*. Munich: C. H. Beck, 1962.
Metzger, Bruce M. "Names for the Nameless in the New Testament: A Study in the Growth of Christian Tradition." *Kyriakon: Festschrift Johannes Quasten*. Vol. 1. Edited by Patrick Granfield and Josef A. Jungmann, 79-99. Munster, Westfalen: Aschendorff, 1970.
———. *A Textual Commentary on the Greek New Testament*. London: United Bible Societies, 1971 [1975]
Miller, Ed. L. "The Johannine Origins of the Johannine Logos." *Journal of Biblical Literature* 112 (1993): 445-57.

Minear, Paul. "The Beloved Disciple in the Gospel of John: Some Clues and Conjectures." *Novum Testamentum* 19 (1977): 105-23.

———. "The Original Function of John 21." *Journal of Biblical Literature* 102 (1983): 85-98.

———. "'We don't know where...' John 20:2." *Interpretation* 30 (1976): 125-39.

Miscall, Peter D. *The Workings of Old Testament Narrative*. Philadelphia: Fortress, 1983.

Moloney, Francis J. *Belief in the Word: Reading John 1-4*. Minneapolis: Fortress, 1993.

———. "From Cana to Cana (John 2:1-4:54) and the Fourth Evangelist's Concept of Correct (and Incorrect) Faith." In *Studia Biblica 1978: II*. Edited by E. A. Livingstone, 185-213. Journal for the Study of the New Testament-Supplement Series 2. Sheffield: JSOT Press, 1980.

Moltmann, Elizabeth. *The Women Around Jesus*. Translated by John Bowden. New York: Crossroad, 1987.

Moorton, Richard F. "What's in a Name? The Significance of 'Mannon' in Mourning Becomes Electra." *The Eugene O'Neill Newsletter* 12.3 (1988): 42-4.

Moore, Stephen D. *Literary Criticism and the Gospels: The Theoretical Challenge*. New Haven: Yale University Press, 1989.

Morris, Leon. *The Gospel According to John*. The New International Commentary on the New Testament. Grand Rapids: Wm. B. Eerdmanns Publishing Co., 1971.

Neirynck, Frans. "The 'Other Disciple' in Jn 18:15-16." *Ephemerides theologicae lovaniensis* 51 (1975): 113-41.

———. "The Anonymous Disciple in John 1." *Ephemerides theologicae lovanienses* 66 (1990): 5-37.

Nohrnberg, James C. "Princely Characters." In *"Not in Heaven": Coherence and Complexity in Biblical Narrative*. Edited by Jason P. Rosenblatt and Joseph C. Sitterson, Jr., 58-97. Indiana Studies in Biblical Literature. Bloomington: Indiana University Press, 1991.

Nugent, Dom Andrew. "What Did Jesus Write? (John 7, 53-8,11)." *The Downside Review* 108 (1990): 193-8.

O'Day, Gail R. "John 7:53-8:11: A Study in Misreading." *Journal of Biblical Litearature* 111 (1992): 631-40.

———. *Revelation in the Fourth Gospel: Narrative Mode and Theological Claim*. Philadelphia: Fortress, 1986.

———. "Toward a Narrative-Critical Study of John." *Interpretation* 49:4 (1995):341-6.

O'Grady, J. "The Role of the Beloved Disciple." *Biblical Theology Bulletin* 9 (1979): 58-65.

Okure, Teresa. *The Johannine Approach to Mission: A Contextual Study of John 4:1-42*. Wissenschaftliche Untersuchungen zum Neuen Testament 2. Reihe 31. Tübingen: J.C.B. Mohr, 1988.

Olsson, Birger. *Structure and Meaning in the Fourth Gospel: A Text-Linguistic Analysis of John 2:1-11 and 4:1-42*. Coniectanea biblica, New Testament 6. Lund, Sweeden: CWK Gleerup, 1974.

Painter, John. *The Quest for the Messiah: The History, Literature and Theology of the Johannine Community*. 2nd ed. Nashville: Abingdon, 1993.

———. "Text and Context in John 5." *Australian Biblical Review* 35 (1987): 28-34.

Pamment, Margaret. "Focus in the Fourth Gospel." *The Expository Times* 97 (1985): 71-4.

———. "The Fourth Gospel's Beloved Disciple." *The Expository Times* 94 (1983): 363-7.

Passage, Charles E. *Character Names in Dostoevsky's Fiction*. Ann Arbor: Ardis, 1982.

Pathrapankal, Joseph. "Jesus and the Greeks: Reflections on a Theology of Religous Identity." *Journal of Dharma: An International Quarterly of World Religions* 10.4 (1985): 392-403.
Pazdan, Mary Margaret. "Nicodemus and the Samaritan Woman: Contrasting Models of Discipleship." *Biblical Theology Bulletin* 17 (1987): 145-8.
Pelling, Christopher, ed. *Characterization and Individuality in Greek Literature*. Oxford: Clarendon, 1990.
Perkins, Pheme. "Mary in Johannine Traditions." In *Mary, Woman of Nazareth: Biblical and Theological Perspectives*. Edited by Doris Donnelly, 109-22. New York: Paulist, 1989.
Peterson, Norman R. *The Gospel of John and the Sociology of Light: Language and Characterization in the Fourth Gospel*. Valley Forge, PA: Trinity Press International, 1993.
Pfitzner, Victor C. "The Charm of Biblical Narrative." *Lutheran Theological Journal* 17 (1983): 1-12.
Phelan, James. *Reading People, Reading Plots: Character, Progression, and the Interpretation of Narrative*. Chicago: University of Chicago Press, 1989.
Potterie, Ignace de la. "Le témoin qui demeure: le disciple que Jésus aimait." *Biblica* 67 (1986): 343-59.
———. "Structure du prologue de Saint Jean." *New Testament Studies* 30 (1984): 354-81.
Pryor, John W. *John: Evangelist of the Covenant People: The Narrative and Themes of the Fourth Gospel*. Downers Grove, Illinois, 1992.
Quast, Kevin. *Peter and the Beloved Disciple: Figures for a Community in Crisis*. Journal for the Study of the New Testament-Supplement Series 32. Sheffield: JSOT Press, 1989.
Queneau, Raymond. *Le dimanche de la vie*. Paris: Gallimard, 1952.
Radway, Janice A. *Reading the Romance: Women Patriarchy, and Popular Literature*. Chapel Hill: University of North Carolina Press, 1984.
Ramsey, George W. "Is Name-Giving an Act of Domination in Genesis 2:23 and Elsewhere?" *Catholic Biblical Quarterly* 50 (1988): 24-35.
Reardon, B. P., ed. *Collected Ancient Greek Novels*. Berkeley: University of California Press, 1989.
Reinhartz, Adele. "Anonymity and Character in the Books of Samuel." *Semeia* 63 (1993): 117-41.
———. "Great Expectations: A Reader-Oriented Approach to Johannine Christology and Eschatology." *Journal of Theology and Literature* 3 (1989): 61-76.
———. "Jesus as Prophet: Predictive Prolepses in the Fourth Gospel." *Journal for the Study of the New Testament* 36 (1989): 3-16.
———. *The Word in the World: The Cosmological Tale in the Fourth Gospel*. Society of Biblical Literature Monograph Series 45. Atlanta: Scholars Press, 1992.
Rena, John. "Women in the Gospel of John." *Église et Théologie* 17 (1986): 131-47.
Rensberger, David. *Johannine Faith and Liberating Community*. Philadelphia: Westminster, 1988.
Resseguie, James L. "John 9: A Literary Critical Analysis." In *Literary Interpretation of Biblical Narratives*. Ed. Louis Gros and R. R. Kenneth, 295-303, vol. II. Nashville: Abingdon, 1982.
Ricoeur, Paul. "L'identité Narrative." In *La Narration: Quand le Récit Devient Communication*. Lieux Théologiques, no. 12. Edited by P. Bühler et J. F. Habermacher, 287-300. Geneva: L'Université de Neuchâtel, 1988.
Rissi, Matthew. "Der Aufbau des vierten Evangeliums." *New Testament Studies* 29 (1983): 48-54.

———. "Die Hochzeit in Kana (Joh 2, 1-11)." In *Oikonomia: Oscar Cullmann gewidmet*. Edited by F. Christ, 76-92, Hamburg: Reich, 1967.

Robinson, John A. T. "His Witness is True: A Test of the Johannine Claim." In *Jesus and the Politics of his Day*. Edited by Ernst Bammel and C. F. D. Moule, 453-76. Cambridge: Cambridge University Press, 1984.

Rogers, Thomas F. "The Gospel of John as Literature." *Brigham Young University Studies* 28 (1988): 67-80.

Roloff, Jürgen. "Der johanneische 'Lieblingsjünger' und der Lehrer der Gerechtigkeit." *New Testament Studies* 15 (1968): 129-51.

Ruckstuhl, Eugen. *Jesus im Horizont der Evangelien*. Stuttgarter Biblische Aufsatzbände 3. Stuttgart: Katholisches Bibelwerk, 1988.

Russell, D. A. "*Ethos* in Oratory and Rhetoric." In *Characterization and Individuality in Greek Litertature*. Edited by Christopher Pelling, 207-9. Oxford: Clarendon, 1990.

Sanders, E. P. *The Tendancies of the Synoptic Tradition*. Society for New Testament Studies Monograph Series 9. Cambridge: Cambridge University Press, 1969.

Sanders, J. N. *A Commentary on the Gospel According to St. John*. Edited and completed by B. A. Mastin. Harper's New Testament Commentaries. New York: Harper & Row, 1968.

———. "Those Whom Jesus Loved." *New Testament Studies* 1 (1954) 29-41.

Sanders, James. "'Nor Do I...': A Canonical Reading of the Challenge to Jesus in John 8." In *The Conversation Continues: Studies in Paul and John in Honor of J. Louis Martyn*. Edited by Robert T. Fortna and Beverly Gaventa, 337-47. Nashville: Abingdon, 1990.

Schencke, Hans-Martin. "The Function and Background of the Beloved Disciple in the Gospel of John." In *Nag Hammadi, Gnosticism and Early Christianity*. ed. C. H. Hedrick and R Hodgson Jr. Peabody, MA: Hendrickson, 1986.

Schnackenburg, Rudolf. *The Gospel According to John*. 3 vols., Translated by Kevin Smyth et al. New York: Crossroad, 1968-82.

Schneiders, Sandra M. "Born Anew." *Theology Today* 44:2 (1987): 189-96.

Scholes, Robert and Robert Kellogg. *The Nature of Narrative*. Oxford: Oxford University Press, 1966.

Seeley, David. *Deconstructing the New Testament*. Biblical Interpretation Series 5. Edited by R. Alan Culpepper & Rolf Rendtorf. Leiden: E. J. Brill, 1994.

Segovia, Fernando F. "And They bgan to Speak in Other Tongues': Competing Modes of Disocurse in Contemporary Biblical Criticism." In *Reading from this Place*. Vol. 1, *Social Location and Biblical Interpretation in the United States*, ed. Fernando F. Segovia and Mary Ann Tolbert, 1-32. Minneapolis: Fortress Press, 1994.

———."The Final Farewell of Jesus: A Reading of John 20:30-21:25." *Semeia* 53 (1991): 167-90.

———. "The Journey(s) of the Word of God: A Reading of the Plot of the Fourth Gospel." *Semeia* 53 (1991): 23-54.

———. "Peace I leave with you; My Peace I Give unto You: Discipleship in the Fourth Gospel." In *Discipleship in the New Testament*, ed. with an Introduction Fernando F. Segovia, 79-102. Philadelphia: Fortress, 1985.

———. "The Significance of Social Location in Reading John's Story." *Interpretation* 49:4 (1995): 370-8.

Seim, Turid Karlsen. "Roles of Women in the Gospel of John." In *Aspects on the Johannine Literature: Papers Presented at a Conference of Scandinavian New Testament Exegetes at Uppsala, June 16-19, 1986*. Edited by Lars Hartman and Birger Olsson, 56-73. Coniectanea biblica, New Testament 18. Uppsala: Almquist and Wiksell International, 1987.

Selvidge, Marla J. "Nicodemus and the Woman with Five Husbands." In *Proceedings, Eastern Great Lakes Biblical Society* 2. Edited by P. Sigal. (1982): 63-75.

Shelley, Steven M. "Lift Up Your Eyes: John 4:4-42." *Review and Expositor* 92 (1995): 81-8.

Shepherd, William H. Jr. *The Narrative Function of the Holy Spirit as a Character in Luke-Acts*. SBL Dissertation Series 147. Atlanta: Scholars Press, 1994.

Simon, Uriel. "Minor Characters in Biblical Narrative." *Journal for the Study of the Old Testament* 46 (1990): 11-19.

Smalley, Stephen S. *John: Evangelist and Interpreter*. Exeter, England: The Paternoster Press, 1978.

Smelik, K. A. D. "The Literary Function of 1 Kings 17.8-24." In *Penteteuchal and Deuteronomistic Studies: Papers Read at the XIIth IOSOT Congress Leuven 1989*. Edited by C. Brekelmans and J. Lust, 239-43. Leuven: Leuven University Press, 1990.

Smith, D. Moody. *John*. 2d rev. ed. Proclamation Commentaries. Philadelphia: Fortress, 1986.

———. *John Among the Gospels: The Relationship in Twentieth- Century Research*. Minneapolis: Fortress, 1991.

Smith, Robert H. "'Seeking Jesus' in the Gospel of John." *Currents in Theology and Mission* 15 (1988): 48-55.

Sobejano-Moran, Antonio. "Ambiguity and Destruction Through the Naming Process in *Reivindicion del conde don Julian and Recuento*." *Literary Onomastic Studies* 15 (1988): 31-7.

Solages, Bruno de. *Jean et les Synoptiques*. Leiden: E. J. Brill, 1979.

Staley, Jeffrey Lloyd. *The Print's First Kiss: A Rhetorical Investigation of the Implied Reader in the Fourth Gospel*. Society of Biblical Literature Dissertation Series 82. Atlanta: Scholars Press, 1988.

———. "Stumbling in the Dark, Reaching for the Light: Reading Character in John 5 and 9." *Semeia* 53 (1991): 55-80.

Sternberg, Meir. *The Poetics of Biblical Narrative: Ideological Literature and the Drama of Reading*. Bloomington: Indiana University Press, 1985.

Stewart, Claude Y., Jr. "Redoing the First Work of Adam: A Creation-Conscious Perspective on Naming and Misnaming." *Encounter* (Indianapolis) 48 (1987): 351-66.

Stibbe, Mark W. G. *John*. Readings: A New Biblical Commentary. Sheffield: JSOT Press, 1993.

———. *John as Storyteller: Narrative Criticism and the Fourth Gospel*. Society for New Testament Studies Monograph Series 73. Cambridge: Cambridge University Press, 1992.

———. "A Tomb with a View: John 11.1-44 in Narrative-Critical Perspective." *New Testament Studies* 40 (1994): 38-54.

Sylva, Dennis D. "Nicodemus and His Spices." *New Testament Studies* 34 (1988): 148-51.

Talbert, Charles H. Reading John: *A Literary and Theological Commentary on the Fourth Gospel and the Johannine Epistles*. Reading the New Testament Series. New York: Crossroad, 1992.

Tanzer, Sarah J. "Salvation is of the Jews: Secret Christians in the Gospel of John." In *The Future of Early Christianity: Essays in Honor of Helmut Koester*. Edited by Birger A. Pearson, 285-300. Minneapolis: Fortress, 1991.

Theilman, Frank. "The Style of the Fourth Gospel and Ancient Literary Critical Concepts of Religious Discourse." In *Persuasive Artistry: Studies in New Testament Rhetoric in Honor of George A. Kennedy*. Edited by Duane F. Watson, 169-83.

Journal for the Study of the New Testament-Supplement Series 50. Sheffield: JSOT Press, 1991.

Theobald, Michael. *Die Fleischwerdung Des Logos: Studien zum Verhältnis des Johannesprologs zum Corpus des Evangeliums und zu 1 Joh.* Münster: Aschendorff, 1988.

Thibeaux, Evelyn R. "Response: Reading Readers Reading Characters." *Semeia* 63 (1993): 215-27.

Thomas, John Christopher. "'Stop Sinning Lest Something Worse Come Upon You': The Man at the Pool in John 5." *Journal for the Study of the New Testament* 59 (1995): 3-20.

Thompson, Marianne Meye. *The Humanity of Jesus in the Fourth Gospel*. Philadelphia, Fortress, 1988.

Thornecroft, John K. "The Redactor and the 'Beloved' in John." *The Expository Times* 98 (1987): 135-9.

Thyen, Hartwig. "Entwicklungen innerhalb der johannischen Theologie und Kirche im Spiegel von Joh 21 und der Lieblingsjümgertexte des Evangeliums." In *L'Evangile de Jean: Sources, rédaction, théologie*. Edited by M. de Jong, 259-99. Bibliotheca ephemeridum theologicarum lovaniensium. Louvain: University Press, 1977.

Tilborg, Sjef van. *Imaginative Love in John*. Biblical Interpretation Series 2. Leiden: E.J. Brill, 1993.

Titus, Eric L. "The Identity of the Beloved Disciple." *Journal of Biblical Literature* 69 (1950): 323-8.

Tolbert, Mary Ann. "The Gospel in Greco-Roman Culture." In *The Book and the Text: The Bible and Literary Theory*. Edited by Regina Schwartz, 258-75. Cambridge, MA: Basil Blackwell, 1990.

———. *Sowing the Gospel: Mark's World in Literary-Historical Perspective*. Minneapolis: Fortress, 1989.

Travers, Patricia. "Name and no Name." *Parabola: The Magazine of Myth and Tradition* 7.3 (1982): 42-6.

Trudinger, Paul. "'On the Third Day There Was a Wedding at Cana': Reflections on St. John 2, 1-12." *The Downside Review* 104 (1986): 41-43.

Van Aarde, A. G. "Narrative Criticism Applied to John 4:43-54. In *Text and Interpretation: New Approaches in the Criticism of the NT*. Edited by P. Hartin and J. Petzer, 101-28. New Testament Tools and Studies 15. Leiden: E. J. Brill, 1991.

Vandana, *Waters of Fire*. Park Town, Madras, India: Christian Literature Society, 1981.

von Wahlde, Urban C. "Community in Conflict: The History and Social Context of the Johannine Community." *Interpretation* 49:4 (1995):379-89.

Wallis, Bruce L. "Dickens Hard Times." *Explicator* 44.2 (1986): 26-7.

Walker, Rolf. "Jüngerwort und Herrenwort: Zur Auslegung von Joh 4:39-42." *Zeitschrift für die neutestamentliche Wissenschaft* 57 (1966): 49-54.

Warner, Martin. "The Fourth Gospel's Art of Rational Persuasion." In *The Bible as Rhetoric: Studies in Biblical Persuasion and Credibility*. Edited by Martin Warner, 153-77. Warwick Studies in Philosophy and Literature. London: Routledge, 1990.

Watson, Alan. *The Trial of Jesus*. Athens: University of Georgia Press, 1995.

Watty, William W. "The Significance of Anonymity in the Fourth Gospel." *The Expository Times* 90 (1979): 209-13.

Weaver, Dorothy Jean. "John 18:1-19:42." *Interpretation* 49:4 (1995): 404-8.

Webster, Edwin C. "Pattern in the Fourth Gospel." In *Art and Meaning*. Edited by David J. A. Clines, David M. Gunn, and Alan J. Hauser, 230-57. Journal for the

Study of the New Testament-Supplement Series 19. Sheffield: JSOT Press, 1982.

Wegner, Uwe. *Der Hauptmann von Kafarnaum (Mt 7,28a; 8,5-10.13 par Lk 7,1-10): Ein Beitrag zur Q-Forschung.* Wissenschaftliche Untersuchungen zum Neuen Testament 2. Reihe 14. Tübingen: J.C.B. Mohr [Paul Siebeck], 1985.

Wuellner, Wilhelm. "Putting Life Back into the Lazarus Story and its Reading: The Narrative Rhetoric of John 11 as the Narration of Faith." *Semeia* 53 (1991): 113-32.

Young, Brad H. "'Save the Adultress!': Ancient Jewish *Responsa* in the Gospel?" *New Testament Studies* 41 (1995): 59-70.

Ziegler, Robert E. "Identity and Anonymity in the Novels of Jerry Kosinski." *Bulletin of the Rocky Mountain Modern Language Association* 35.2 (1981): 99-109.

INDEX OF GREEK TERMS

ἀκολουθέω, 45
ἀλήθεια, 27
ἀληθής, 133, 141
ἄλλοι, 77
ἀνήρ, 74
ἄνθρωπος, 95, 96
ἄνωθεν, 48
ἄρχων, 65
βασιλεία, 27
Βασιλίκος, 27, 29, 31, 52, 53, 57, 78, 79, 80, 81, 82, 83, 84, 85, 86, 87, 88, 90, 92, 96, 137, 140, 144, 145
βλέπω, 116
γίνομαι, 38, 39
γινώσκω, 27
γραμματεῖς, 103
γύναι, 55, 56, 74, 114, 140
διδάσκαλο, 65
δόξα, 60
δύναμει, 26, 59
ἐγώ εἰμι, 91, 100, 124
εἶδεν, 116
ἡμέρᾳ, 53, 54
ἦν, 38, 39
θέλημα, 87
θέλεις, 87
θεός, 123
θεωρεῖ, 116
Ἰησοῦ, 46, 113
Ἰουδαίων, 65
κατακρίνω, 103
κόλπον, 113, 137
κυριός, 73, 123, 128
λαλιά, 77
λαὸς, 103
λέγω, 61
λόγος, 35, 36, 37, 38, 39, 40, 41, 42, 44, 60, 77, 138
μακάριοι, 123
μαρτύριαν, 42
μαρτυρούσης, 75, 77
μήτι, 75
μενώ, 47, 74
παρεγένετο, 103
πατρὸς, 113
πιστεύω, 60, 80, 81, 90, 117, 118, 132
προφητη, 73
σὰρξ, 40
σημεῖα, 26, 31, 33, 52, 59, 60, 79, 80, 82, 84, 86, 94, 96
τετέλεσται, 68
τί ἐμοὶ καὶ σοί, 55
φανέροω, 128
φιλεῖς, 97, 109
φιλέω, 97
φῶς, 37, 42
χριστός, 42
ὥρα, 56

INDEX OF NAMES

Agourides, Savas C., 110, 124, 147
Aland, Kurt, 102, 147
Alcorn, Marshall W., 13, 147
Alter, Robert, 38, 72, 147
Ashton, John, 147, 149
Aune, David, 147
Bacon, B. W., 85, 108, 147
Bal, Mieke, 6, 22, 23, 147
Barrett, C. K., 36, 59, 65, 66, 73, 75, 76, 80, 81, 83, 100, 110, 113, 115, 116, 120, 125, 147
Barrose, T., 147
Bassler, Jouette M., 64, 65, 67, 68, 69, 147
Bauckham, Richard, 111, 132, 133, 135, 147
Beardslee, William A., 147
Beck, David R., 21, 148, 156
Berlin, Adele, 7, 109, 124, 147, 148, 151
Bernard, John H., 148
Bernstein, Charles, 148
Best, E., 150
Beutler, Johannes, 94, 97, 151
Black, D. Clifton, 150, 152
Blass, Friedrich, 75, 148
Bligh, John, 148
Boers, Hendrikus, 70, 72, 73, 75, 77, 148
Boismard, M. E., 43, 148
Booth, Steve, 148
Botha, J. Eugene, 70, 72, 75, 78, 148
Bowden, John, 53, 119, 150, 154, 156
Bracher, Mark, 13, 147
Braun, Willi, 148
Brewer, William F., 14, 148, 154
Briggs, Sheila, 148
Brodie, Thomas, 35, 36, 44, 47, 49, 54, 57, 58, 60, 64, 65, 66, 71, 72, 76, 79, 83, 85, 87, 88, 97, 99, 100, 103, 110, 114, 115, 120, 122, 126, 148

Broer, Ingo, 148
Brown, Raymond, 24, 31, 35, 41, 42, 46, 52, 54, 55, 57, 63, 65, 71, 75, 76, 77, 79, 83, 89, 93, 98, 99, 100, 103, 108, 113, 115, 116, 119, 120, 122, 124, 125, 126, 136, 142, 148, 149
Brown, Schuyler, 24, 31, 35, 41, 42, 46, 52, 54, 55, 57, 63, 65, 71, 75, 76, 77, 79, 83, 89, 93, 98, 99, 100, 103, 108, 113, 115, 116, 119, 120, 122, 124, 125, 126, 136, 142, 148, 149
Bruce, F. F., 102, 130, 149, 156, 161
Bühler, P., 158
Bultmann, Rudolf, 42, 46, 57, 62, 65, 70, 71, 75, 77, 80, 81, 83, 85, 101, 115, 116, 120, 149
Busse, Ulrich, 44, 153
Byrne, Brendan, 99, 117, 134, 135, 149
Cahill, Joseph P., 72, 74, 85, 149
Carr, David, 149
Carson, D. A., 108, 113, 115, 116, 120, 130, 149
Cassidy, Richard, 149
Chapman, J. Harley, 149
Charles, J. Daryl, 42, 76, 148, 149, 152, 157, 160
Charlesworth, James H., 108, 109, 111, 113, 117, 123, 127, 128, 129, 130, 131, 149
Chatman, Seymour, 149
Colley, Ann C., 149
Collins, Matthew S., 64, 97, 112, 120, 123, 124, 126, 131, 132, 149
Collins, Raymond F., 64, 97, 112, 120, 123, 124, 126, 131, 132, 149
Cottam, Thomas, 85, 149
Cottrell, 66, 149
Countryman, William L., 118, 149

Culbertson, Diana, 43, 44, 46, 48, 150
Culpepper, R. Alan, 1, 7, 36, 40, 45, 47, 50, 56, 61, 62, 64, 66, 76, 83, 86, 87, 89, 98, 99, 101, 110, 111, 112, 113, 114, 120, 132, 133, 134, 150, 152, 153, 159
Cuvillier, Elian, 150
Darr, John, 3, 8, 150
de Jonge, Marinus, 41, 150
Debrunner, Albert, 75, 148
Deil, Paul, 150
DeJean, 150
Detwiler, Andreas, 39, 150
Dixon, John, 150
Docherty, Thomas, 10, 12, 150
Dockery, David, 96, 151
Dodd, C. H., 52, 65, 81, 83, 92, 151
Domeris, William R., 151
Donfried, Karl P., 54, 55, 148
Donnelly, Doris, 157
Droge, Arthur J., 125, 151
D'Sa, Francis X., 151
Duke, Paul D., 72, 93, 94, 141, 151
Dunn, James D. G., 151
Eckhardt, Karl A., 109, 151
Eckle, Wolfgang, 151
Eco, Umberto, 8, 151
Edwards, Michael, 58, 59, 151
Ehrman, Bart D., 102, 103, 151
Eisler, Robert, 109, 151
Eller, Vernard, 109, 151
Ellis, Peter F., 54, 83, 87, 91, 120, 126, 151
Enz, Jacob, 151
Eslinger, Lyle, 152
Evans, Craig, 152, 155
Farmer, Kathleen, 152
Fewell, Dana Nolan, 152
Filson, Floyd V., 109, 152
Fiorenza, Elizabeth Schussler, 53, 55, 99, 106, 122, 152
Fish, Stanley, 3, 15, 152
Fitzmeyer, Joseph A., 54, 148
Flanagan, Owen, 152
Flesch, William, 152
Fokkema, Aleid, 7, 8, 152

Forster, E. M., 6, 7, 152
Fortna, Robert T., 41, 94, 104, 149, 150, 151, 152, 159
Foster, Donald, 152
Fowler, Robert M., 5, 152
Freed, Edwin D., 77, 152
Funk, Robert W., 7, 8, 44, 75, 148, 152, 153
Gaventa, Beverly R., 41, 104, 149, 150, 152, 159
Gennette, Girard, 152
Getty, Mary Ann, 149
Geyser, Jane, 43, 152
Gibbons, Debbie, 64, 69, 152
Giblin, Charles H., 152
Gill, Christopher, 153
Ginsberg, Warren, 153
Girard, M., 152, 153
Grassi, Joseph A., 58, 108, 110, 153
Green, Eugene, 153
Greimas, A. J., 7, 70, 153
Gros, Louis, 92, 158
Gunn, David Miller, 152, 161
Gunther, J. J., 111, 120, 153
Guthrie, Donald, 108, 153
Habermacher, J. F., 158
Hadas, Moses, 153
Haenchen, Ernst, 44, 56, 67, 81, 83, 85, 87, 89, 101, 113, 116, 125, 153
Hägg, Thomas, 18, 21, 153
Halász, László, 9, 153
Halász, Lazlo, 9, 153
Hartin, P. J., 81, 153, 161
Hartman, Lars, 53, 153, 159
Hauser, Alan J., 161
Hawkin, David J., 110, 113, 114, 124, 133, 153
Hedrick, C. H., 159
Heil, John Paul, 103, 153
Henaut, Barry W., 153
Hengel, Martin, 119, 153
Higbie, Robert, 154
Hirsch, E. D., 3, 154
Hoare, Frederick R., 42, 154
Hochman, Baruch, 154

INDEX OF NAMES

Hodgson, R., Jr., 159
Holland, Norman, 13, 154
Holleran, J. Warren, 92, 154
Hurst, L. D., 154
Hyman, Ronald T., 154
Iser, Wolfgang, 3, 8, 154
Izevbaye, D. S., 154
Johnson, Lewis, 108, 154
Jose, Paul E., 14, 154
Jouve, Vincent, 154
Kaestli, Jen Daniel, 39, 150
Käsemann, Ernst, 154
Kaufman, Philip S., 154
Kellogg, Robert, 159
Kenneth, R. R., 92, 158
Kermode, Frank, 38, 41, 52, 61, 65, 68, 96, 111, 147, 154
Kilmartin, Edward J., 55, 154
Kitzberger, Ingrid Rosa, 154
Koester, Craig, 48, 68, 154, 160
Kopas, Jane, 53, 155
Kort, Wesley A., 155
Kotz, P. P. A., 155
Kraabel, A. Thomas, 155
Kreitler, Hans, 9, 155
Kreitler, Shulamith, 9, 155
Kügler, J., 112, 133, 155
Kurz, William S., 110, 132, 135, 155
Kysar, Robert, 85, 110, 155
Lee, Dorothy A, 155
Leonard, John, 155
Levenson, Michael, 155
Lewin, Jane, 47, 152
Lewis, Frank W., 85, 155
Lightfoot, Robert Henry, 155
Lindars, Barnabas, 60, 64, 117, 120, 125, 131, 155
Litt, Dorothy E., 155
Long, Burke O., 25, 155
Mahoney, Robert K., 155
Mangolin, Uri, 155
Manno, Bruce, 156
Marans, Nelly, 150
Martyn, J. Louis, 41, 64, 74, 86, 89, 91, 104, 150, 156, 159

Maynard, Arthur H., 56, 57, 116, 156
McConnell, F., 152
McDonald, J. Ian, 156
McGann, Diarmuid, 156
Mead, A. H., 156
Meeks, Wayne, 64, 66, 68, 156
Menken, M. J. J., 40, 156
Merkelbach, Reinhold, 21, 156
Metzger, Bruce, 101, 102, 156
Miller, Ed. L., 35, 152, 156
Minear, Paul, 116, 132, 142, 156
Miscall, Peter D., 156
Moloney, Francis J., 39, 40, 44, 47, 52, 53, 56, 60, 61, 63, 64, 66, 67, 70, 71, 72, 73, 76, 77, 80, 81, 156
Moltmann, Elizabeth, 53, 99, 156
Moo, Douglas J., 108, 149
Moore, Stephen D., 156
Moorton, Richard F., 156
Morris, Leon, 108, 118, 149, 157
Murdock, Lucy Floyd, 150
Nardocchio, Elaine F., 9, 153
Neirynck, Frans, 120, 157
Nohrnberg, James C., 157
Nugent, Dom Andrew, 104, 157
O'Beirne, Joseph, 150
O'Day, Gail R., 1, 157
O'Grady, J., 157
Ohtsuka, Keisuke, 148
Okure, Teresa, 70, 73, 75, 77, 124, 136, 142, 157
Olsson, Birger, 53, 56, 70, 72, 74, 77, 157, 159
Painter, John, 38, 87, 111, 157
Passage, Charles E., 157
Pathrapankal, Joseph, 157
Pazdan, Mary Margaret, 69, 76, 78, 157
Pearson, B., 68, 155, 160
Pelling, Christopher, 20, 153, 157, 159
Perkins, Pheme, 157
Peterson, Norman R., 38, 43, 66, 157
Pfitzner, Victor C., 157

INDEX OF NAMES

Phelan, James, 158
Poffet, Jean Michael, 39, 150
Potterie, Ignace de la, 36, 158
Pryor, John W., 65, 80, 83, 111, 158
Quast, Kevin, 45, 47, 111, 112, 113, 116, 117, 120, 124, 125, 126, 132, 134, 135, 158
Queneau, Raymond, 11, 149, 158
Radway, Janice A., 15, 158
Ramsey, George W., 158
Reardon, B. P., 18, 21, 158
Reinhartz, Adele, 22, 38, 44, 47, 50, 52, 56, 158
Rena, John, 53, 73, 76, 98, 122, 158
Rendtorf, Rolf, 159
Rensberger, David, 64, 65, 68, 158
Resseguie, James L., 92, 94, 95, 158
Reumann, John, 54, 148
Ricoeur, Paul, 158
Rissi, Matthew, 53, 54, 84, 158
Robinson, John A. T., 158
Rogers, Thomas F., 158
Roloff, Jurgen, 111, 158
Rorty, Amilie Oksenberg, 152
Ruckstuhl, Eugen, 108, 158
Russell, D. A., 20, 159
Sanders, E. P., 104, 109, 159
Sanders, J. N., 104, 109, 159
Sanders, James, 104, 109, 159
Schencke, Hans Martin, 159
Schmidt, G., 153
Schnackenburg, Rudolf, 42, 46, 52, 56, 57, 58, 59, 64, 71, 75, 77, 81, 83, 88, 92, 94, 100, 108, 115, 120, 125, 159
Schneiders, Sandra M., 64, 159
Scholes, Robert, 159
Schwartz, Regina, 21, 23, 147, 148, 161
Seeley, David, 159
Segovia, Fernando F., 4, 38, 45, 84, 110, 126, 159
Seim, Turid Karlsen, 53, 54, 72, 73, 74, 98, 99, 159

Selvidge, Marla J., 68, 73, 75, 159
Shelley, Steven M., 159
Shepherd, William H. Jr., 94, 151, 159
Sigal, P., 68, 159
Simon, Uriel, 22, 33, 47, 49, 159
Smalley, Stephen S., 160
Smelik, K. A. D., 24, 160
Smith, D. Moody, vii, 27, 86, 110, 150, 152, 160
Smith, Robert H., 46, 160
Smyth, Kevin, 159
Solages, Bruno de, 26, 160
Solotareff, Jeannnine, 150
Staley, Jeffrey Lloyd, 9, 11, 36, 37, 38, 43, 46, 53, 61, 71, 72, 84, 87, 90, 94, 160
Stewart, Claude Y., Jr., 160
Stibbe, Mark W. G., 37, 58, 61, 68, 74, 75, 83, 86, 87, 96, 98, 99, 101, 110, 111, 126, 160
Stratta, Leslie, 150
Stuhlmacher, Peter, 151
Sylva, Dennis D., 64, 160
Talbert, Charles H., 76, 83, 91, 98, 101, 103, 110, 120, 160
Tanzer, Sarah J., 68, 69, 92, 160
Theilman, Frank, 160
Theobald, Michael, 37, 160
Thibeaux, Evelyn R., 99, 139, 161
Thoma, Clemons, 65, 154
Thomas, John Christopher, 161
Thompkins, Jane P., 13, 154
Thompson, Marianne Meye, 57, 123, 161
Thornecroft, John K., 119, 161
Thyen, Hartwig, 108, 161
Tilborg, Sjef van, 42, 48, 49, 53, 54, 57, 58, 73, 74, 76, 88, 89, 111, 112, 114, 121, 133, 161
Titus, Eric L., 89, 108, 161
Tolbert, Mary Ann, 4, 18, 21, 159, 161
Travers, Patricia, 161
Trexler, Richard C., 153
Trudinger, Paul, 161
Van Aarde, A. G., 81, 161

Vandana, 161
von Wahlde, Urban C., 161
Walker, Rolf, 76, 161
Wallis, Bruce L., 161
Wansbrough, Henry, 151
Warner, Martin, 49, 59, 151, 161
Watson, Alan, 160, 161
Watson, Duane F., 160, 161
Watty, William W., 62, 110, 111, 124, 126, 135, 161

Weaver, Dorothy Jean, 161
Webster, Edwin C., 161
Wegner, Uwe, 80, 162
Whschogrod, Michael, 65, 154
Wilson, R. McL., 150
Wright, N. T., 154
Wuellner, Wilhelm, 162
Young, Brad H., 158, 162
Ziegler, Robert E., 162
Zumstein, Jean, 39, 150

INDEX OF SUBJECTS

adulterous woman, 2, 10, 31, 32, 55, 92, 101, 103, 105, 106, 137, 140

ambiguity, 5, 9, 46, 52, 55, 56, 61, 64, 65, 66, 67, 68, 69, 73, 75, 78, 79, 81, 88, 89, 92, 93, 105, 106, 110, 111, 114, 120, 121, 128, 131, 135, 136, 138, 140, 144

Andrew, 30, 33, 44, 45, 49, 104, 155

anointing, 28, 92, 98, 99, 138

anonymity, 1, 2, 3, 5, 9, 10, 11, 12, 16, 17, 19, 20, 21, 22, 24, 25, 27, 29, 33, 49, 61, 62, 76, 78, 82, 89, 96, 105, 107, 108, 110, 111, 119, 127, 135, 138, 145

appropriate response, 5, 9, 41, 43, 49, 58, 60, 69, 76, 78, 81, 82, 88, 90, 93, 95, 96, 97, 98, 99, 101, 107, 114, 123, 131, 133, 134, 135, 137, 138, 144

basilikos, 2, 10, 20, 26, 27, 29, 31, 51, 52, 53, 57, 78, 79, 80, 81, 82, 83, 84, 85, 86, 87, 88, 90, 92, 96, 137, 140, 144, 145

believing, 1, 2, 3, 4, 10, 15, 17, 32, 33, 39, 43, 46, 49, 56, 58, 59, 60, 61, 62, 64, 65, 66, 67, 68, 69, 72, 73, 75, 77, 79, 80, 81, 86, 88, 89, 90, 92, 93, 94, 95, 96, 97, 98, 99, 100, 101, 105, 106, 115, 116, 117, 118, 122, 123, 124, 125, 126, 129, 130, 131, 132, 133, 134, 136, 137, 139, 140, 141, 143, 144

betrothal type-scene, 51, 72

blind man, 2, 9, 10, 12, 28, 31, 32, 48, 61, 73, 80, 86, 88, 89, 91, 92, 93, 94, 95, 96, 131, 137, 140, 145

Book of Signs, 83

bridegroom imagery, 11, 31, 33, 42, 51

Cana, 11, 43, 48, 51, 52, 53, 59, 60, 63, 65, 67, 70, 76, 78, 79, 80, 81, 82, 83, 85, 86, 92, 95, 96, 99, 137, 147, 148, 151, 152, 155, 160

character analysis, 6, 8

characterization, 1, 2, 3, 5, 6, 7, 8, 9, 14, 16, 20, 50, 62, 63, 64, 69, 70, 71, 78, 80, 81, 89, 96, 98, 99, 106, 110, 111, 112, 121, 122, 126, 130, 131, 135, 136, 137, 138, 143, 144

confession, 24, 32, 41, 57, 66, 67, 76, 99, 100, 122, 123, 125, 130, 132, 139, 140, 141

cross, 32, 52, 62, 63, 64, 68, 84, 105, 114, 115, 124, 127, 128, 132, 141

Didascalia Apostolorum, 102

Didymus the Blind, 102

disciple Jesus loved, 2, 5, 9, 10, 15, 30, 31, 32, 33, 45, 46, 61, 62, 97, 99, 108, 109, 110, 111, 112, 113, 114, 115, 116, 117, 118, 119, 120, 121, 122, 123, 124, 125, 126, 127, 128, 129, 130, 131, 132, 133, 134, 135, 137, 138, 139, 140, 141, 142, 144, 145, 146, 147, 148, 149, 150, 151, 152, 153, 154, 155, 156, 157, 159

discipleship, 1, 2, 3, 10, 15, 16, 33, 44, 45, 46, 47, 53, 63, 67, 69, 75, 99, 118, 119, 122, 124, 131, 132, 134, 135, 136, 137, 139, 140, 144

discipleship paradigm, 2, 3, 5, 10, 15, 16, 33, 43, 63, 67, 76, 77, 78, 79, 81, 82, 88, 89, 90, 92, 93, 95, 96, 97, 98, 99, 101, 105, 106, 107, 114, 124, 131, 132, 133, 135, 136, 137, 138, 139, 144

Elijah/Elisha cycle, 17, 24, 25, 41, 147, 149
extratext, 3, 9, 15, 39, 44, 47, 48, 51, 53, 55, 56, 58, 59, 62, 64, 65, 71, 73, 75, 89, 97, 98, 104, 106, 113, 114, 115, 124, 126, 140, 141, 142
filial relationships, 24, 55, 114
following, 3, 21, 23, 25, 29, 45, 46, 47, 59, 65, 76, 91, 96, 97, 103, 106, 113, 119, 124, 126, 128, 134, 135, 137, 140, 141
Gentile Christianity, 115
Greek novels, 3, 17, 18, 21
Hebrew narrative, 3, 9, 17, 23, 24, 72
Hellenists, 49
identity disputes, 84
infirm man, 2, 57, 83, 84, 85, 86, 87, 88, 89, 90, 91, 92, 93, 95, 137, 140
interpretive communities, 3, 4, 6, 15, 51, 101, 103, 138
irony, 1, 37, 70, 78, 94, 141
Jesus' betrayal, 112, 113, 114, 121
Jesus' hour, 52, 56, 57, 84
Jesus' mother, 2, 9, 10, 31, 32, 52, 54, 55, 56, 58, 60, 61, 62, 63, 67, 69, 70, 76, 77, 78, 79, 80, 82, 95, 101, 112, 114, 115, 120, 122, 134, 137, 140, 144, 145
Jesus' origin/identity, 26, 33, 35, 36, 38, 39, 41, 42, 43, 44, 46, 47, 48, 49, 53, 54, 58, 63, 65, 69, 73, 74, 85, 86, 88, 90, 91, 92, 93, 94, 95, 100, 106, 121, 125, 140
Jesus' public ministry, 31, 83, 85, 96
Jesus' resurrection, 32, 109, 117, 118, 125, 128, 132, 134, 141
Jesus' word, 2, 5, 52, 60, 61, 66, 67, 70, 71, 72, 76, 77, 79, 80, 81, 82, 88, 89, 90, 92, 93, 95, 96, 97, 99, 101, 104, 105, 127, 131, 133, 137, 139, 140, 142
Jewish Christianity, 115
Johannine community, 99, 112, 129
John Mark, 108
Joseph of Arimathea, 30
Judas, 29, 30, 32, 113, 120, 121, 124, 141
juxtapositioning of characters, 30, 63, 69, 121, 123, 127
kerygma, 4, 56, 62
Lazarus, 29, 30, 45, 52, 64, 83, 96, 97, 100, 109, 110, 141, 142, 148, 160
literary frames, 44, 51, 52
LXX, 59
Martha, 29, 30, 31, 32, 96, 98, 99, 100, 122, 134, 138, 139, 140, 141
Mary Magdalene, 30, 32, 121, 122, 129, 131, 134, 138, 139, 154
Mary of Bethany, 29, 32, 98, 134, 138, 153
Matthias, 108
Messiah, 26, 38, 48, 59, 75, 100, 140, 156
messianic symbolism, 19, 48, 51, 55, 58, 59, 60, 61, 65, 84, 96, 97
misunderstandings, 1, 54, 68, 78
Moses, 37, 93, 103, 152
names/naming, 1, 2, 3, 9, 10, 11, 12, 16, 17, 19, 20, 22, 23, 24, 25, 29, 33, 35, 39, 44, 62, 76, 80, 94, 96, 110, 119, 127, 135
naming progression, 80, 94
narrative interpretation, 52, 57, 68, 70, 83, 98, 109, 110, 115, 116, 122, 124, 128, 129, 138
narrative staging, 74, 91
Nathanael, 30, 45, 48, 54, 127, 131, 138, 139, 140, 153
Nicodemus, 10, 29, 30, 32, 48, 51, 58, 63, 64, 65, 66, 67, 68, 69, 72, 76, 77, 79, 82, 84, 98, 103, 105, 106, 121, 134, 138, 141, 142, 146, 148, 151, 156, 158, 159
Old Testament background, 22, 48, 51, 56, 59, 76, 146, 155, 158
other disciple, 99, 114, 116, 119, 120, 124, 125, 127, 129, 130, 133
Paul, 41, 89, 104, 108, 148, 150

Peter, 27, 29, 30, 32, 33, 45, 47, 54, 83, 99, 111, 112, 113, 114, 115, 116, 117, 118, 119, 120, 123, 124, 125, 126, 127, 129, 131, 132, 133, 138, 141, 145, 147, 150, 154, 155, 156

Peter's denial, 33, 41, 71, 88, 124, 125, 141

Pharisees, 44, 48, 64, 68, 69, 91, 92, 93, 94, 95, 105, 106

Philip, 45, 46, 47, 49, 153

Pilate, 29, 30, 32, 105, 121, 141

pool of Bethzatha, 52, 57, 86, 92, 93

prologue, 35, 36, 37, 38, 39, 43, 44, 48, 49, 53, 54, 58, 60, 66, 67, 68, 84, 100, 133, 149, 156

Qumran, 111

reader identification with characters, 3, 13, 14, 15, 16, 30, 33, 40, 43, 49, 53, 62, 69, 70, 73, 78, 81, 89, 90, 98, 109, 122, 134, 136, 138, 139, 140, 143, 144

reader response, 45, 102, 130, 143

representative figures, 131

Sabbath, 57, 86, 88, 90

Samaritan woman, 2, 9, 10, 11, 31, 55, 57, 58, 61, 69, 70, 72, 73, 74, 76, 77, 79, 80, 82, 84, 87, 89, 90, 91, 95, 122, 134, 137, 140, 145

Samaritans, 31, 51, 52, 57, 69, 70, 71, 72, 73, 75, 77, 79, 137, 146

seeing, 32, 60, 61, 95, 100, 116, 117, 122, 123, 129, 130, 131, 132, 134, 139, 144

signs, 8, 26, 31, 33, 51, 52, 57, 58, 59, 60, 61, 65, 76, 79, 80, 82, 84, 86, 87, 88, 92, 94, 95, 96, 99, 105, 117, 132, 133, 134, 136, 137, 139, 144

social location, 4, 143

structuralist theory, 7, 8

symbolism, 36, 44, 45, 48, 58, 59, 65, 73, 115, 116, 127

synagogue, 27

Teacher of Righteousness, 111

temple, 20, 51, 59, 60, 65, 79, 84

textual gaps, 8, 9, 12, 78, 93, 104, 105, 106, 114, 136

third day, 43, 54, 79

Thomas, 29, 30, 32, 35, 36, 43, 44, 85, 97, 100, 109, 117, 122, 123, 127, 128, 129, 130, 131, 132, 134, 138, 139, 140, 141, 155

waterpots, 79

wedding at Cana, 52, 59, 63, 70

witness, 2, 6, 20, 26, 31, 37, 39, 40, 41, 42, 43, 44, 45, 49, 57, 58, 60, 62, 66, 67, 69, 75, 76, 77, 79, 81, 82, 84, 85, 88, 89, 90, 92, 93, 94, 95, 96, 98, 99, 101, 105, 106, 112, 115, 119, 120, 121, 122, 124, 126, 127, 129, 130, 131, 132, 133, 134, 137, 138, 139, 140, 141, 142, 144, 145

women in the Fourth Gospel, 53

BIBLICAL INTERPRETATION SERIES

ISSN 0928-0731

1. VAN DIJK-HEMMES, F. & A. BRENNER. *On Gendering Texts*. Femal and Male Voices in the Hebrew Bible. 1993. ISBN 90 04 09642 6
2. VAN TILBORG, S. *Imaginative Love in John*. 1993. ISBN 90 04 09716 3
3. DANOVE, P.L. *The End of Mark's Story*. A Methodological Study. 199? ISBN 90 04 09717 1
4. WATSON, D.F. & A.J. HAUSER. *Rhetorical Criticism of the Bible*. A Com prehensive Bibliography with Notes on History and Method. 1994. ISBN 90 04 09903 4
5. SEELEY, D. *Deconstructing the New Testament*. 1994. ISBN 90 04 09880 1
6. VAN WOLDE, E. *Words become Worlds*. Semantic Studies of Genesis 1-11 1994. ISBN 90 04 098879
7. NEUFELD, D. *Reconceiving Texts as Speech Acts*. An Analysis of 1 John. 199⋅ ISBN 90 04 09853 4
8. PORTER, S.E., P. JOYCE & D.E. ORTON (eds.). *Crossing the Boundarie* Essays in Biblical Interpretation in Honour of Michael D. Goulder. 199⋅ ISBN 90 04 10131 4
9. YEO, K.-K. *Rhetorical Interaction in 1 Corinthians 8 and 10*. A Formal Analys with Preliminary Suggestions for a Chinese, Cross-Cultural Hermeneuti⋅ 1995. ISBN 90 04 10115 2
10. LETELLIER, R.I. *Day in Mamre, Night in Sodom*. Abraham and Lot i Genesis 18 and 19. 1995. ISBN 90 04 10250 7
12. TOLMIE, D.F. *Jesus' Farewell to the Disciples*. John 13:1-17:26 in Narratolc gical Perspective. 1995. ISBN 90 04 10270 1
13. RYOU, D.H. *Zephaniah's Oracles against the Nations*. A Synchronic and Di⋅ chronic Study of Zephaniah 2:1-3:8. 1995. ISBN 90 04 10311 2
14. SONNET, J.-P. *The Book within the Book*. Writing in Deuteronomy. 1997. ISBN 90 04 10866 1
15. SELAND, T. *Establishment Violence in Philo and Luke*. A Study of Nor Conformity to the Torah and Jewish Vigilante Reactions. 1995. ISBN 90 04 10252 3
16. NOBLE, P.R *The Canonical Approach*. A Critical Reconstruction of the He: meneutics of Brevard S. Childs. 1995. ISBN 90 04 10151 9
17. SCHOTTROFF, L.R & M.-T. WACKER (Hrsg.). *Von der Wurzel getrage* Christlich-feministische Exegese in Auseinandersetzung mit Antijudaismu 1996. ISBN 90 04 10336 8
18. BECKING, B. & M. DIJKSTRA (eds.). *On Reading Prophetic Texts*. Gende Specific and Related Studies in Memory of Fokkelien van Dijk-Hemme 1996. ISBN 90 04 10274 4
19. BRETT, M.G. (ed.). *Ethnicity and the Bible*. 1996. ISBN 90 04 10317 1
20. HENDERSON, I.H. *Jesus, Rhetoric and Law*. 1996. ISBN 90 04 10377 5

21. RUTLEDGE, D. *Reading Marginally*. Feminism, Deconstruction and the Bible. 1996. ISBN 90 04 10564 6
22. CULPEPPER, R.A. (ed.). *Critical Readings of John 6*. (In preparation.)
23. PYPER, H.S. *David as Reader*. 2 Samuel 12:1-15 and the Poetics of Fatherhood. 1996. ISBN 90 04 10581 6
26. BRENNER, A. *The Intercourse of Knowledge*. On Gendering Desire and 'Sexuality' in the Hebrew Bible. 1997. ISBN 90 04 10155 1
27. BECK, D.R. *The Discipleship Paradigm*. Readers and Anonymous Characters in the Fourth Gospel. 1997. ISBN 90 04 10700 2

BS
2440
.B38
1997

DATE DUE

MY 03 '00		
JE 24 '04		

Demco, Inc. 38-293